FEMINISM AND THE NEW RIGHT

FEMINISM AND THE NEW RIGHT

Conflict over the American Family

Pamela Johnston Conover and Virginia Gray

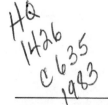

PRAEGER

PRAEGER SPECIAL STUDIES • PRAEGER SCIENTIFIC

Library of Congress Cataloging in Publication Data

Conover, Pamela Johnston.
  Feminism and the new right.

  Bibliography: p.
  Includes index.
  1. Feminism—United States.   2. Family—
United States.   3. Abortion—United States.
4. Pressure groups—United States.   5. Conservation
—United States.   6. Symbolism in politics.   I. Gray,
Virginia. II. Title.
HQ1426.C635   1983   305.4'2'0973   82-24643
ISBN 0-03-060237-8

Published in 1983 by Praeger Publishers
CBS Educational and Professional Publishing
a Division of CBS Inc.
521 Fifth Avenue, New York, New York 10175 U.S.A.

456789 052 98765432

Printed in the United States of America
on acid-free paper

To Our Sons

Terry, Kelly, and Brian

PREFACE AND
ACKNOWLEDGEMENTS

On June 30, 1982, the ratification period for the Equal Rights
Amendment ended with the ERA still three states short of adoption.
This book seeks to explain why the ERA failed. In the process we
will necessarily try to understand the emergence in the late 1970s
of various New Right groups in opposition to the ERA and to the
feminist movement generally. During the same period, the New
Right also threatened another goal feminists had once believed to be
secure: legalized abortion. Many people have expressed surprise
at the backlash against feminism and its efforts to promote women's
rights. But when these recent setbacks for women's rights are
viewed in historical perspective, it is clear that whenever women's
rights have been perceived to affect the family, conflict has erupted.
Thus, our examination of the ERA and abortion battles sheds light
on the broader and continuing struggle over the place of the family
in society.

We argue that the contemporary chapter in this conflict can
best be understood from the perspective of social movement and interest group theory. Contrary to many theorists who take a dim
view of noneconomic groups and the "irrational" individuals who
join them, we believe that the joining of social protest groups both
on the right and on the left is an instrumental act. We develop an
explanation for the origin, mobilization, and organization of both
sets of groups, an explanation that highlights the role of issues and
symbolism in attracting followers.

The abortion and ERA issues are the key to understanding
both the feminist and New Right social movements. Contrary to the
media's portrayal, however, we find that the New Right's impact is
somewhat limited. At the state level they are not as mobilized as
are feminists; their effect on public opinion or in getting state legislatures to enact their legislation is modest. Even their most potent
tactic, single-issue voting, may backfire if tried by liberals, our
data show.

Our theoretical approach, integrating social movement and interest group theories, is applicable to other status or reactive movements seeking to reassert traditional values and more generally to
non-class-based political movements of all sorts. Our findings have
implications for the strategies of New Right and feminist leaders,
especially for the reintroduction of the ERA and the Human Life
Amendment. The last chapter examines the future of the ERA and
abortion issues as we see them. Our conclusions are also relevant
to other women's rights efforts that involve change in familial roles.

Finally, our investigation into the conflict surrounding different definitions of the family reminds us of the family's prime importance in society. New Right and "pro-family" groups have been in part responsible for the new recognition accorded the American family.

In any project of this size, the authors incur a number of debts to colleagues, students, friends, and family members. In particular, the authors wish to thank those graduate students who spent long hours interviewing for little money at the White House Conference on Families: Russ Hanson, Connie Hanson, Karen Hult, Janet Hall, and Jeanne Austin. We are also grateful that at the last minute Anne Wall, Mel Gray, and Chris Conover allowed themselves to be coerced into interviewing. Access to the conference itself was facilitated by the intervention of Regent Mary Schertler and Congressman Bruce Vento. Most of all we thank the 107 delegates to the conference who let us interview them during an exciting and hectic period.

Though no large grant funded this interviewing project, at a number of critical junctures the University of Minnesota and the University of Kentucky provided financial aid through a series of small grants. We are especially indebted to Robert Holt, departmental chairman and "fixer," for arranging the Minnesota portion. Later the University of Minnesota provided a single-quarter leave and its Graduate School another grant that allowed for the timely completion of this collaboration.

Other data collection for this project depended on the help of a number of individuals and institutions. Some of the data used in this study were made available by the Inter-University Consortium for Political and Social Research. The data for the American National Election Study, 1980, were originally collected by the Center for Political Research, the University of Michigan, under a grant from the National Science Foundation. Neither the original collectors of the data nor the Consortium bear any responsibility for the analyses or interpretations presented here. The Minnesota Poll conducted by the Minneapolis Tribune under the direction of Steven Coombs furnished us with some survey data at an early stage. Lee Sigelman and the University of Kentucky poll performed a similar service at a later stage. Charles Backstrom and William Flanigan did computer runs that helped us to access these data. Archivists at the Minnesota Interchange Network and at national Interchange headquarters in Washington, D.C., were very gracious in opening their files to us. Similarly, librarians at the American Enterprise Institute in Washington, the Alan Guttmacher Institute in New York City, and Planned Parenthood in St. Paul were quite helpful on short notice. Minnesota state representative Ann Wynia passed on material that she received from interest groups. State officials from 46 states were kind enough to send reports on the political action committees and lobby groups registered in their states. Susan and Brian Job subsidized the last data foray by offering their Washington apartment; Brian Job further helped by offering his library carrel on a long-term basis.

The authors incurred even more debts during the writing stage. Initial ideas were worked through in a series of convention papers coauthored with Steven Coombs. We thank Steve as well as various paper discussants for their help. Students in our "women and politics" classes over the years also heard many of our early ideas. We are grateful to Glen Halva-Neubauer, William Berry, Stan Feldman, and Chris Conover for reading and commenting on several chapters and especially to Karen Hult for reading the entire manuscript. The seemingly endless typing job was handled cheerfully and competently by Jacalyn Plagge in Minnesota and Kim Hayden in Kentucky.

Finally, our sons Brian Gray and Terry Conover provided daily tests of the women and family conflicts we were writing about, as did the arrival of Kelly Conover about halfway through the book.

CONTENTS

LIST OF TABLES

1 / CONFLICT OVER THE AMERICAN FAMILY

The decade of the 1970s was the woman's decade. It began with thousands of women marching in the streets to protest sexism, most notably on August 26, 1970, the fiftieth anniversary of women's suffrage. Two years later, Congress overcame its 50 year opposition to the Equal Rights Amendment (ERA) and sent it to the states for ratification. The next year the Supreme Court declared a woman's decision to have an abortion to be a constitutionally protected right, thereby legalizing abortion in all 50 states. Throughout the decade the feminist movement grew in numbers and gained respectability. Women achieved a number of significant governmental accomplishments and recorded many economic gains. The United States was on the brink of becoming a nonsexist society, it appeared. The success of the women's movement seemed assured, and the future for women had never been brighter.

The 1980 election and events surrounding it mark an end to this decade and perhaps an abrupt end to this period of feminist optimism. In fact, events of the late 1970s and the early 1980s make the period described above seem quite remote. The ERA failed to be ratified within the seven-year limit; after extension of the time limit, no more states ratified. On June 30, 1982, the ERA's time ran out. In addition, publicly financed abortions were effectively curtailed by a series of congressional actions on appropriations bills and subsequent Supreme Court decisions. Meanwhile, the "pro-family" movement strives to outlaw all abortions, using a variety of statutory and constitutional amendatory tactics. The more conservative Congress and President elected in 1980 appear receptive to the New Right and much less interested in the priorities of feminism than were previous administrations.

1

Suddenly the gains of the past decade seem ephemeral. Feminists fight to hold onto their gains while their opponents seize the offensive.

How could this happen? Why has the New Right been able to threaten and begin to capture territory once held firmly by the feminist movement? Mobilization of various sectors of the New Right has received some scholarly attention very recently but by far the greatest attention has been paid by the media. The popular press terms anti-abortion and anti-ERA groups "single-issue" groups and deplores their negative impact upon representative democracy (Newsweek 1978). New Right groups such as the Moral Majority are said to have put Ronald Reagan in the White House and to have single-handedly removed six liberals from the U.S. Senate.

The scholarly treatment of these two movements is more limited. There is a decade-old literature on the Old Right and a more normative literature on the origin of the women's liberation movement but these are hardly adequate to explain the current phenomenon of the Right's ascendence and liberalism's seeming decline. The more recent scholarly work on single-issue politics tends to ignore the general dynamics underlying such issues in favor of a narrow focus on a particular issue. Finally, the substantive literature on attitudes toward feminism and toward its policy goals such as abortion and equal rights reports that a majority of the American public are in favor of the Equal Rights Amendment and a woman's right to obtain a legal abortion. We are left with little understanding of why such popular policies would stimulate such intense opposition in recent years.

We believe that a focus on abortion and the ERA—the chief collective goods sought by the feminist movement—will provide a means for understanding the change in prospects for liberal social issues in this country. The abortion and equal rights fights, however resolved in the 1980s, will not go away but will continue in some form. For these are not matters of public opinion, or fact, or individual choice; these debates are battles over the most basic unit of society—the family. An examination of the history of women's rights battles in this country will demonstrate that conflict over the family is a continuing theme.

CONTENDING CONCEPTS OF WOMEN AND THE FAMILY

Controversies centering around women and the family are bitter because rights for individual women are perceived to conflict with rights for the family unit. When the role of a woman is defined by her reproductive, sexual, and childrearing functions

within the family, then there is a "natural" division of activities
into the public extrafamilial jobs done by the male and the private
intrafamilial ones performed by the female. If women act outside
their "natural" roles, that is as individuals, that action is ipso facto
anti-family.

Degler (1980, p. 471) summarizes the import of the functional
definition of the family for women's rights:

> The central values of the modern family stand in oppo-
> sition to these that underlie women's emancipation.
> Where the women's movement has stood for equality,
> the family historically has denied or repudiated equal-
> ity. . . . Where the women's movement has called for
> a recognition of individualism, the family has insisted
> upon subordination of individual interests to those of
> the group. . . . And, finally, where the women's
> movement has asked for a person to be judged on merit,
> the family has denied merit as a basis of membership,
> approval, or love.

Not only are women's assertions of individual rights at odds
with the conventional definition of the family, they may also be at
odds with the very basis of our government and society. Susan Okin
(1979) contends that the basic societal unit within Western political
thought is the family, not the individual. Western philosophers
generally defined men as complete persons with rights and poten-
tials, but they defined women by their role within the family.
Therefore, they viewed the traditional patriarchal family as a
necessary and natural institution. These functionalist conceptions
of women's roles shaped the U.S. Constitution, current statutes
and their judicial interpretation, as well as present social thinking.
Within such a system of thought there is no room for clashes of
interest between husband and wife or between parent and child. By
definition, the interests of women and children are those of the
family; only men may exercise individual rights. Equality for
women, Okin argues, will thus require rethinking the basic assumptions of political philosophy (1979, p. 11).

When put into long-term perspective, what at first seems an
unexpected backlash against feminism and its policy goals of abortion and equal rights is no longer so surprising. The demands of
feminists raise profound doubts, doubts which the demands of blacks
and other minorities do not raise. Feminist demands are not just
demands for civil rights, control over their bodies, and equal opportunity. They are simultaneously demands for a new conception
of the family—namely that women be viewed as individuals—and a

rethinking of the basis of law, philosophy, and society. A brief examination of the history of the abortion and equal rights debates in this country will demonstrate the continuing conflict between the individual and the family.

THE ABORTION CONFLICT

Is the act of getting an abortion "a woman's right to protect her own body" or is it "the murder of an unborn child"? A review of the history of abortion conflicts in this country discloses many commonalities and some differences in how these questions have been answered over the years.

Few American women resorted to abortion before the 1820s. During the 1820s and 1830s women became more interested in controlling their own fertility but had to turn to abortion because contraception was so problematic. Until the discovery of the ovum in 1827, the destruction of the fetus before quickening (i.e., before the fourth month) was considered equivalent to contraception. Thus, in the minds of women abortion did not involve destroying a human being.

Around 1840 there was an upsurge of abortions primarily due to married women limiting the size of their families. In the past, abortions had been performed chiefly on unmarried women seeking to rectify a mistake. According to Degler's account (1980), this change in the composition of the abortion-seeking population threatened the family because it meant that married women asserted their individuality against their husbands. Abortion, more so than contraception, affirmed the woman's individual interests because abortion did not need male cooperation or even approval. Still, up to the time of the Civil War, as many as one-third of the states had no abortion laws at all. Other states prohibited abortion after quickening but not before. Most state statutes punished the doctor, not the woman, and made an exception when the life of the mother was in danger.

Directly after the Civil War, the situation changed dramatically: a physicians' campaign against abortion resulted in the adoption of 40 statutes in the period 1860-80 (Mohr 1978, p. 200). The new laws were more restrictive than the earlier ones in that they incorporated the new knowledge of procreation and stated that any interruption of gestation was a crime. Furthermore, the new laws dropped the immunities for women and also controlled doctors' advertising, demonstrating the state's new interest in the act of abortion. These laws remained essentially in force until the Roe v. Wade decision in 1973.

Mohr's research suggests several reasons for the timing of this first anti-abortion crusade. First, the sudden increase in abortions among native white Protestant women aroused fears that whites would be "outbred" by immigrants. Second, physicians seeking to form a scientific professional guild (the American Medical Association), wanted to take a professional stand against abortionist "quacks." Third, for some physicians the knowledge about ovulation meant that abortion was morally wrong. Lastly, some physicians, including the most outspoken opponent of abortion, Horatio Storer, believed that a woman's purpose was to produce children and that interference with that function threatened the family and society. Significantly, Mohr did not find that clergymen, either Protestant or Catholic, were involved in the campaign to put anti-abortion laws on the books. Also, there was little public outcry against abortion and no public protestations to legislatures to adopt the more restrictive legislation. Simply put, in the nineteenth century abortion was not a moral or religious issue involving "sanctity of life."

Most feminists refused to advocate abortion, though anti-abortion crusaders often blamed its occurrence on the women's movement. Women continued to seek and obtain illegal abortions throughout the next hundred years (1860-1970). In fact, the new laws may have had an even greater effect on public opinion than they had upon behavior. Mohr (1978, p. 263) states:

> By 1950 American public opinion considered abortion socially odious, and virtually no one in American society yet dared to call openly for its relegalization as an appropriate national practice . . . over half a century of official proscription accustomed many Americans to view the issue of abortion in absolute rather than relative terms; for substantial portions of the public, abortion was no longer a problem of practical policy but an almost uncompromisable question of right and wrong.

There was little public debate until the 1950s and 1960s when thalidomide's and rubella's deforming impact upon fetuses brought challenges to the absolute nature of state abortion statutes. In the late 1960s several states reformed their laws so as to permit exceptions in specific circumstances. In 1970, the state of New York passed a repeal law, allowing abortion for any reason during the first trimester. New York's law was endorsed as a model law by both the U.S. Commission on Population Growth and the American Future and in 1972 by the American Bar Association. Meanwhile, legal challenges were brought against other states' limitations on women seeking abortions. Significantly, by the end of the 1960s doctors were largely unopposed to abortions done early in pregnancy.

The Supreme Court's 1973 decision to void the abortion laws of 49 states surprised both opponents and proponents. Less than half the states had even liberalized their laws by this time. Invoking the constitutional right to privacy set forth in Griswold v. Connecticut (1965), the majority determined that the interests of the pregnant woman are paramount in the first trimester. During this period the decision to abort rests with the woman and her doctor. As the pregnancy progresses, the interest of the state in protecting the "potentiality of life" increases. In the second trimester, the state may intrude to protect maternal health. By the last trimester, the state may even proscribe abortion except where the life or health of the mother is at stake. The Court, after examining various legal, philosophical, and religious definitions of the beginning of life, explicitly rejected the notion that life begins at conception and that the fetus is a person in the sense of the Fourteenth Amendment. Apparently, the interests of doctors figured more heavily than the interests of women in reaching this decision. The perception that the state was interfering in the doctor-patient relationship led Justice Harry Blackmun, a former Mayo Clinic attorney, to write a pro-choice decision for the majority in the Roe case (Woodward and Armstrong 1979).

Predictably, this momentous decision was pronounced a catastrophe by the anti-abortion side and a great victory by the pro-choice side. Though nationwide organizing by supporters or by opponents of abortion had not characterized the pre-Roe period, new organizations, particularly those opposing the decision, sprang up all over the country. After Roe the rate of legal abortions approached one-third of all pregnancies, and all states adopted more uniform and liberal laws.

More recent judicial and congressional decisions have tended to blunt the impact of Roe. The 1976 Hyde Amendment, upheld by the Supreme Court in Harris v. McRae (1980), restricted federal financing of abortions under the Medicaid program. An even more restrictive version of Hyde was adopted subsequently and has reduced Medicaid abortions by 99 percent (Steiner 1980, p. 70). Though efforts to overturn Roe by passing a Human Life Amendment (HLA) have failed in every Congress since 1973, currently "pro-life" forces in Congress are pursuing several new tactics. One is a bill that declares it to be our national policy that human life begins with conception and allows the individual states to enact laws outlawing abortion (Congressional Quarterly 1981, p. 383). In contrast to the HLA, this bill needs only a simple majority to pass. Another approach is an amendment removing abortion from the Supreme Court's jurisdiction and giving Congress and the states the authority to regulate it.

This brief review reveals first that the moral and religious opposition to others obtaining abortions is of recent origin. The involvement of church leaders in the anti-abortion movement and the debates over when life begins—so characteristic of today—were notably absent in the discussions of the 1800s. The demand that all citizens adopt some churches' views on the sanctity of life is a new element in the conflict. Perhaps the claim that abortion is morally wrong is more easily accepted now because abortion was illegal for so long (1860s to 1970s).

History also shows that more restrictive laws are often passed in response to a sudden rise in the rate of abortion. In the 1840s when the abortion rate increased to nearly one-quarter of all live births, restrictive legislation followed in the 1860s. Likewise, the dramatic abortion increases following the Court's 1973 decision were followed by the curtailing of public abortion funding and may lead to an absolute ban. In both instances the increase in abortions was perceived as an attack upon the family.

Finally, the feminist assertion that women have an inalienable right to control their own bodies is relatively new. The contemporary feminist claim threatens the traditional family. As Degler (1980, p. 246) puts it, abortion

> asserts the complete sovereignty of woman over her body. It is the supreme assertion of individualism, since the claims of the woman are judged to be superior to those of the man, whose contribution to conception, at least, is precisely equal, genetically, to that of the woman.

Thus, the right to an abortion must be granted if women are to be individuals; yet, if granted, that right gives women the final authority over family size.

The intractability of the feminist and "pro-life" positions augurs for a prolonged battle. The abortion issue is irreconcilable because the functional definition of the family is "at odds" with the concept that the woman is an individual. When framed in this way the abortion issue is not likely to be resolved "because neither side is comfortable with less than total victory, each side views its cause as sacred, and both are right" (Steiner 1980, p. 71).

THE EQUAL RIGHTS CONFLICT

Now we turn to the second issue examined in this book: the struggle for equal rights embodied in the Equal Rights Amendment. Like abortion, the ERA is a concept which Americans favor. In a 1980 Gallup Poll, for example, 58 percent supported the ERA and 31 percent were opposed (Gallup Report 1981b, p. 4). Yet, the amendment failed to achieve ratification. A review of the last major struggle over equal rights, the granting of women's suffrage, helps to illuminate the difficulties faced by today's feminists.

First, there are several similarities between the suffrage and ERA struggles. An obvious commonality is their longevity. The ERA was first proposed in the early 1920s, was introduced unsuccessfully in Congress for the next 50 years, was finally approved by Congress in 1972 and sent to the states. The states failed to ratify it by the 1979 deadline but feminists won an extension to June 1982. Since no more states adopted it in that period, the ERA failed.

Similarly, the fight for the franchise extended over 70 years from Seneca Falls in 1848 to adoption in 1920. Suffrage for women thus took much longer than did the gaining of suffrage by blacks or propertyless men. The reason, according to Degler (1980), is that women's suffrage was a much more radical idea than historians have generally conceded. The vote threatened the family as functionally defined because it meant that women would move into the public (male) sphere. The women's vote was more radical than their organizing against liquor and prostitution because the latter was undertaken to protect the home or private sphere.

An underlying assumption in the argument against female suffrage was that the natures of men and women were different. Often the argument had a biological justification to it. The idea that women as a group are similar to each other but different from men (and somehow a little better than men) supported the traditional concept of the family. If similarities among women are great due to their "nature," then the individual interests of women do not need to be represented in the polity through the vote. In fact, to do so breaks down the family.

Like the vote, the ERA violates the doctrine of the two spheres because it requires government to treat each person, whether male or female, as an individual. Anti-feminist groups opposing the ERA want women to be treated as women, according to their natures which are different from the natures of men. From their perspective, the ERA invades the private sphere in which women have heretofore reigned, and forces them into the public sphere, thereby destroying their role within the family. Feminists, in contrast, demand to be treated as persons (as individuals) whose natures are the same as men.

Another similarity between the two amendment battles is that both battles were waged primarily by women against significant opposition from other women. This in itself suggests that both amendments somehow threaten an important role of women. Degler (1980, p. 343) argues that women did not support women's suffrage because it

> threatened the family as people of the 19th century understood that institution. The suffrage was the essence of feminism in that it asserted the individuality of women and assumed and asserted a woman's self-interest.

For this reason, women were the only major group to organize against their emancipation; blacks and propertyless men had not done so.

Nineteenth-century feminists ultimately recognized that the vote signified a woman's existence as a separate person apart from her family. Resistance to suffrage was overcome only after feminists dropped the individualistic argument. After the turn of the century, new feminist leadership substituted the argument that women had a special contribution to make to society, one which men could not provide, and therefore women should get the vote. The new argument supported the family, rather than threatened it. For instance, if women could get the vote, they could enact protective labor legislation for women workers. When Alice Paul and the National Woman's Party proposed the ERA in 1923, these new suffragists felt betrayed. For the next several decades, women's organizations worked against the ERA. Its individualistic implications were simply too threatening to their newly won right to vote and too threatening to the family. Thus, it is no surprise that present-day ERA opponents feel the same way as did members of the League of Women Voters and the American Association of University Women when they opposed the "Un-Equal Rights Amendment" in the 1940s (Editorial Research Reports 1978, pp. 31-32).

More recently, twentieth-century feminists have chosen the route of the early suffragists: achieving equal opportunities for individual women. As several scholars have pointed out (Adams and Winston 1980; Chafe 1977; Freeman 1975), this strategy is more difficult than its alternative, "social feminism." Social feminism, advocated by the later suffragists (those who finally won the vote) and by present-day feminists in Sweden and elsewhere, demands special benefits for women as a group, even if it means treating men and women unequally. Social feminism thus benefits women as a sex, not as individuals; consequently, it supports the family. Not only does the individualistic assumption in the ERA threaten the family unit but it is viewed as redistributive, that is it takes away opportunities from men and gives them to women. As a result, twentieth-century feminists, like the early suffragettes, may have engendered stiffer opposition than they would have using an alternative strategy.

Though the longevity, argumentation, and the woman-against-woman characteristics of the two battles are similar, the stark fact remains that women's suffrage was finally achieved whereas the ERA failed. This suggests that there must be some ways in which the two battles differ. We mentioned one above: the proponents of the suffrage shifted the basis of their argument from an individualistic argument to a "woman's nature" argument, a tactic that ERA supporters still spurn. Another distinction is the contemporary emphasis on the Biblical origin of the functional roles of men and women. The Rev. Jerry Falwell (1980, p. 151) asserts that the ERA defies the mandate that "the husband is the head of the wife, even as Christ is the head of the church." We find few instances of Biblical objection to granting women the vote, though the Catholic clergy is sometimes listed as one of the many opponents of suffrage (Flexner 1972). Thus, the injection of religion and morality into the equal rights fight appears to be new, just as it is new to the contemporary abortion debate.

ANALYSIS OF FAMILY CONFLICT

Our examination of the abortion and ERA conflicts shows the tension between the individual and the family. Yet the values for which the family stands are not only at odds with feminism but also with the values of today's world. Thus, we should expect other conflicts between modern and traditional institutions to arise and perhaps to be loosely related to the family conflict. Indeed, a number of social movements have recently sprung up whose aim is to reassert tradition: requiring the teaching of creationism in science courses, allowing prayer in the public schools, demanding an end to busing and a return to the neighborhood school, and promoting the burning of immoral rock music and the censoring of television shows. These social movements are all reactionary in that they seek to return to a time in the past when traditional values were widely shared; when people did not believe in evolution and the scientific method, when everyone prayed, when students walked to school, when music was good for the soul, when TV shows portrayed less of life's realities. Movements to regain a moral status once held necessarily depend upon the near-success of other movements expressing modern values. Thus, it is important to examine both the movement expressing the modern values and the movement advocating a return to traditional values.

In this book we will focus on the feminist and New Right social movements, though by extension the theoretical arguments in Chapter 2 apply to many of the other conflicts between traditional and modern sectors of our society. We view these social movements as the activities of rational individuals seeking to regain their status in American society. Leaders seek to do this by providing collective goods to potential followers, in this case the end to abortion and the defeat of the ERA. Chapter 3 argues that feminists have symbolized abortion and the ERA in individualistic terms. In Chapter 4 we examine the New Right and its symbolic definition of the same issues. The New Right's impact upon elite polarization, mass public opinion, and state legislatures is examined in Chapters 5, 6, and 7 respectively. The concluding chapter assesses the future of the abortion and ERA conflicts as well as the debate over women and the family.

2 / SOCIAL MOVEMENTS AND SYMBOLIC POLITICS: A THEORETICAL APPROACH

In the previous chapter we reviewed the history of the issues of abortion and the Equal Rights Amendment. Yet, certain basic questions about the current conflicts over abortion and the ERA remain unanswered. In particular, why have these concerns reemerged in the 1970s to become two of the most divisive issues facing the United States in this century? In a broader sense, why are the issues of abortion and the ERA central to <u>both</u> the feminist and the New Right movements?

In answering such questions, it is useful to step back from the specific issues of abortion and the ERA, and to focus instead on the more general processes that underlie the transformation of social conflict into social movements. In so doing, our basic goal will be to develop a fundamental understanding of the role that symbolic politics and issues play in the dynamic processes associated with social movements. More specifically, we seek to establish a sound theoretical framework with which to structure our examination of the roles that the issues of abortion and the ERA have played in the feminist and the New Right movements.

In establishing such a theoretical basis, we draw upon a vast array of literature. Until quite recently, sociologists and political scientists alike viewed the relationship between social conflict and protest from the perspective of the "collective behavior" paradigm (for a review of this perspective and recent developments see Marx and Wood 1975). Theorists following this tradition made a critical distinction between the politics of social movements and that of more institutionalized organizations such as political parties and interest groups (Gamson 1975). Social movements and the actions they engendered were seen as a type of deviant behavior symptomatic of a society in serious trouble. In contrast, established groups such as political parties and interest groups were portrayed in "pluralist" theories as "rational actors" mobilizing and allocating their resources so as to best achieve their goals (Gamson 1975).

In recent years, however, there has been a definite move away from the assumptions implicit in the collective behavior and pluralist traditions. Rather than distinguishing between the politics of social protest and that of established political groups, researchers have begun using a single theoretical framework to study both forms of behavior. In increasing numbers, theorists are treating social movement politics as a form of rational, goal directed behavior (Gamson 1975; Lipsky 1968; McCarthy and Zald 1977; Oberschall 1973; J. Wilson 1973). Clearly, this is an innovative step toward a broader understanding of the basic similarities characterizing the various forms of political behavior. Consequently, we will use this approach in our examination of the role that symbolic issues play in social movements.

With that in mind, let us examine some of the key concepts that we will be dealing with in our discussion. To begin, the notion of a social movement is central to our understanding of the issues of abortion and the ERA. In defining social movements we follow McCarthy and Zald's (1977) lead by focusing strictly on the public's preferences (rather than actions) for social change. Specifically, a "social movement" (SM) is ". . . a set of opinions and beliefs in a population which represent preferences for changing some elements of the social structure and/or reward distribution of a society" (McCarthy and Zald 1977, p. 1217; for a review of other definitions see Killian 1973). Along the same lines, then, a "countermovement" may be defined as ". . . a set of opinions and beliefs in a population opposed to a social movement" (McCarthy and Zald 1977, p. 1218). Finally, we define a "social movement organization" (SMO) as any formal organization that adopts as its goals the beliefs or preferences of some social movement or countermovement (McCarthy and Zald 1977). Conceptualized in this fashion, the differences between social movement organizations and "interest groups" are differences in degree of development rather than differences in kind. As Lowi (1971) suggests, we can think of an interest group as a highly developed form of an SMO: one that has become institutionalized.

We can turn now to a consideration of the following topics: (1) social movements; (2) the mobilization process associated with the emergence of social movement organizations; (3) the collective actions of SMOs; (4) the dynamics of SMOs; and (5) the role of issues in social movements.

SOCIAL MOVEMENTS

Where do social movements come from? Traditionally, analysts have agreed that social movements are rooted in the societal strains that accompany such things as economic crises, natural catastrophes and war (see, for example, Lipset and Raab 1970; Smelser 1963; Gurr 1970). Even the more recent treatments that emphasize the rational character of social movements acknowledge that human discontent and grievances play some role in the evolution of social movements (McCarthy and Zald 1977; Oberschall 1978).

In particular, status conflicts have, perhaps, received the most attention in explaining extremist politics in the United States. In the 1950s, for example, a group of political theorists led by Seymour Martin Lipset (1955) and Richard Hofstadter (1964) argued that people's discontent with their social status or prestige—where prestige was conceived of in terms of the individual's position in the social stratification system as typically defined in terms of occupation, education, and income—had motivated them to become involved in an extremist movement such as McCarthyism.

In recent years, our understanding of the nature of status-based social movements has undergone some change. In contrast to earlier researchers who focused on status groups narrowly defined by the traditional sociological components of status, more recent theorists have expanded the concept of "status" to include a variety of defining factors (Gusfield 1963; Lorentzen 1980; Page and Clelland 1978; Zurcher et al. 1971). From their perspective, a status group may be thought of as any group that shares a common life-style, or set of values and beliefs (Gusfield 1963). Thus, a status-based social movement represents more than simply a group's efforts to defend its prestige against others; it represents the defense and advocacy of a way of life (Page and Clelland 1978; Lorentzen 1980).

At some point during the life cycle of all social movements, there must be a transformation of unspoken grievances and discontent into more concrete goals. Beliefs and attitudes play a crucial role in this process. They are the vehicle through which grievances are translated into a more understandable form; in effect they express the discontent that people feel (Marx and Wood 1975). As Killian (1973) explains, the values or basic beliefs of a movement represent its raison d'etre; they are the collective vision of the movement's goals.

Finally, it is our belief that the issues a movement centers upon, as well as how it defines those issues, are critical to understanding not only the goals of a movement but also its strategy and potential for success. At a later point we will return to the question of how issues are used to help define a movement's goals. Let us turn now to a consideration of the process through which social movements are transformed into organizations that have the ability to take actions on behalf of the collective.

THE MOBILIZATION PROCESS

According to our earlier definitions, a social movement is simply a collective desire for change. In more concrete terms, its existence represents nothing more than an issue cleavage in society (McCarthy and Zald 1977). If there is to be any actual social change, at some point in time the supporters of a social movement must band together in pursuit of their collective goals. We refer to this process as "mobilization." As Tilly (1978, p. 69) explains, mobilization is ". . . the process by which a group goes from being a passive collection of individuals to an active participant in public life." Yet, not all supporters of a social movement are willing to become active participants in quest of a movement's goals. In fact, some social movements may never enter a mobilization phase. What accounts for the willingness of some and the unwillingness of others to become active participants?

Previous research offers basically two perspectives on the mobilization process (Useem 1980). On the one hand, theorists in the collective behavior tradition have developed both psychological (e.g., Elms 1969; Hofstadter 1965) and breakdown (e.g., Kornhauser 1959) models in which individual frustration and social disorganization play a key role in the mobilization of individuals for collective action. In contrast, more recent theorists have advocated a "resource mobilization" perspective in which self-interest, solidarity, and individual principles are major factors in the commitment of a person to collective action. Let us focus on the second perspective in some depth.

The Resource Mobilization Perspective

Mixed empirical support for the psychological and breakdown models of mobilization (for a critique, see Gusfield 1963; McEvoy 1971; Wolfinger et al. 1969), as well as theoretical concern with the assumptions implicit in these approaches, has led researchers to approach the mobilization process from an entirely different perspective (see for example: J. Wilson 1973; Tilly 1975, 1978; Gamson 1975; Oberschall 1973; Lipsky 1968; McCarthy and Zald 1977). Drawing upon the work of both economists (Breton and Breton 1969; Olson

1971; Downs 1972; Strickland and Johnston 1970) and political scientists (J. Q. Wilson 1973; Leites and Wolf 1970; Lipsky 1970; and Salisbury 1969), students of social movements have forged a resource mobilization perspective. From this viewpoint, mobilization is seen as a rational process ". . . through which individual group members' resources are surrendered, assembled, and committed for obtaining common goals and defending group interests" (Oberschall 1978, p. 306).

In more formal terms, the level of mobilization characterizing the members of a social movement may be represented as a function of two factors: (1) the value of the resources nominally under collective control; and (2) the probability of delivery when the resources are called for (Tilly 1978). Like Tilly (1978), to facilitate estimating the level of mobilization, we have narrowed our conceptualization of resources so that it pertains primarily to what economists call production factors—land, labor, and capital. Thus, our definition excludes those factors that others have labeled as intangible or normative resources: individual loyalties, obligations, and commitments (Etzioni 1968; Freeman 1979). Rather than treating such factors as resources per se, they may be described as elements influencing the likelihood that resources actually will be delivered to the group when they are called for (Tilly 1978). The greater the loyalty or commitment of an individual to a group, then the more likely he or she is to deliver resources such as money and goods when called upon.

Given this, the mobilization plan of any group should involve two key elements: (1) accumulating resources; and (2) increasing collective claims on those resources (Tilly 1978, p. 73). But, this general plan may be pursued in different ways. The mobilization of some groups is "offensive" in nature; they mobilize or pool their resources in response to existing opportunities to further their interests. In contrast, defensive mobilization occurs when a group combines its resources in direct response to an outside threat. Defined in this manner, the mobilization of many countermovements may be categorized as defensive, although what begins as defensive mobilization may eventually become offensive if the original threat dissipates (Tilly 1978).

There are several differences between offensive and defensive mobilization. First, defensive mobilization is much more likely to be "bottom-up." In effect, threats to a group are more likely to generate the emergence of a grass-roots organization than are existing or potential opportunities. Top-down organizational development is more likely in the case of offensive mobilization in the sense that leaders play a larger role in directing such efforts, because identification and articulation of the opportunities available to a group require foresight and a careful evaluation of the environment. In contrast, defensive mobilization depends on the recognition of a threat—something that may require considerably less leadership to accomplish (Tilly 1978).

Secondly, Tilly (1978, p. 75) argues that the rich and powerful often engage in offensive mobilization, while defensive mobilization tends to be the province of the poor and powerless. The rich and powerful often have surplus resources to invest; in order to maximize their interests, they can afford to take chances in what may be a risky mobilization effort. The poor, with few surplus resources if any to risk, are more likely to mobilize only if threatened. Furthermore, defensive mobilization is also less likely among the rich and powerful because they usually have the ability to forestall challenges to their interests before the threatening groups have a chance to mobilize fully.

Finally, if the level of mobilization of some population depends upon both the value of the resources committed to the group and the loyalty of group members—the probability that those resources will be delivered—then how can that level of mobilization be measured? To the extent that there exists a close relationship between organizational development and mobilization, one approach is to measure the level of organization characterizing a particular social movement (Tilly 1978). For example, it might be determined: (1) how many organizations there are that represent the goals of a particular social movement; (2) how many members those organizations have; and (3) how long the organizations have been in continuous operation. Taken together, these measures should provide an adequate picture of how organized the adherents of a social movement have become. Estimating the actual value of the resources available to such organizations, as well as the probability of their delivery, is much more problematic.

Now, let us turn our attention to those elements that are critical in assessing the degree to which the supporters of a social movement actually mobilize: (1) the interests of the supporters; (2) the existing organizational ties of the supporters; (3) the personal principles of the supporters; (4) the political entrepreneur; and (5) forces outside the movement. In our consideration of these factors we will rely heavily on the works of Fireman and Gamson (1979) and Tilly (1978).

The Role of Interests in Mobilization

In the collective behavior perspective shared grievances and interests were depicted as the key motivating factor underlying the transition from social movement to social movement organization. From the resource mobilization viewpoint, collective interests still influence mobilization, but self-interests also play a large role.

In order to understand the role of collective interests in the mobilization process, it is necessary to alter somewhat our conceptualization of such interests. In particular, it must be recognized that when collective interests are realized, or shared goals are reached, then some good has been provided for the group's consumption (Olson 1971). Such goods may be conceptualized in terms of a continuum of "publicness of consumption" bounded at one extreme by pure private goods and at the other extreme by pure public goods (Laver 1981). Although traditionally various researchers have considered several characteristics in determining the nature of any particular good, we will focus primarily on two: excludability and optionality (see, for example, Olson 1971; Laver 1981; Riker and Ordeshook 1973).[1]

Pure public goods are nonexcludable; that is, once they are provided to a single member of a group, they are available to all members of the group whether or not those members have contributed to the attainment of the good (Olson 1971, p. 14). It is important to recognize that the characteristic of excludability suggests that the nature of a particular good is defined with respect to a specific group (Olson 1971; Mitchell 1979). Some public goods are limited or available only to a particular group of people within society; other public goods, such as the provision of clean air, are available to all members of society. In effect, as Olson (1971) points out, what is a public good to one group may well be a private good to another in terms of its excludability.

Although less central to most definitions of public goods, the "optionality" of a good is also useful in determining its degree of publicness (Laver 1981). That is, in some instances people have a choice as to whether or not they will consume some good. In other cases, there is no choice in the matter; if the good is provided at all, people are required to consume certain amounts of it whether or not they so desire. In effect, for some goods, such as national defense and pollution control, there is "no exit" (Hirshman 1970; Riker and Ordeshook 1973; Laver 1981). Generally, the less the optionality of a good, the greater its publicness (Laver 1981).

With this definition in mind, we can conceptualize the goals pursued by a social movement as being public or collective goods for the members of the movement. Given this conceptualization, the mobilization process can now be examined from a cost-benefit perspective. From this viewpoint, the adherents of a social movement are rational actors in the sense that they will become "constituents" of a social movement organization—they will contribute their resources to the group—only if the personal benefits of such contributions outweigh the costs. Yet, according to Olson (1971), herein lies the critical problem confronting potential organizations: individual and collective interests often conflict with one another. Because of the nonexclusive nature of collective goods, potential constituents have no individual interests in paying any costs even though they share a common interest in obtaining the good. This creates what has been called the "free-rider" problem. Because individuals know that they will receive the public good even if they have made no contribution toward obtaining it, there is a tendency to sit back and let others put forth the collective effort necessary to obtain the good. Therefore, if groups are to mobilize they must find some way of overcoming the free-rider problem; they must, according to Olson (1971), use something in addition to the promise of collective goods to entice movement adherents into becoming contributors. [2]

The major way Olson (1971) suggests of overcoming the free-rider problem is through the use of "selective incentives": ". . . constraints or inducements that an individual actor may gain or lose contingent upon whether the actor contributes to collective action" (Fireman and Gamson 1979, p. 10). In essence, selective incentives are noncollective goods whose availability can be controlled by the group so that there is no free-rider effect involved in their administration. In particular, Olson (1971) stresses the role that material or economic incentives (such as group life insurance or a membership magazine) play in eliciting contributions.

In summary, from Olson's (1971) perspective, the shared grievances and collective goals that help to define a social movement are insufficient to produce mobilization in most instances. [3] Indeed, taken to its logical extreme, Olson's argument suggests that selective incentives are not only necessary for mobilization, but that they are sufficient as well (Fireman and Gamson 1979, p. 11). Clearly, this represents a significant departure from earlier research which argued that shared grievances and common goals were the key factor motivating mobilization. It is not surprising, then, that Olson's work has generated a considerable amount of empirical and theoretical research.

There have, for example, been several studies of large economic interest groups, the type of organization most likely to fit Olson's model. In most instances, these studies have revealed that while the Olson model is helpful it does not provide a completely adequate explanation of the mobilization process (Marsh 1976; Moe 1980, 1981). For our purposes, perhaps even more telling is the failure of the model when it has been applied to public interest groups, which fall more within the realm of social movement organizations than the economic organizations mentioned previously (Mitchell 1979; Tillock and Morrison 1979; Godwin and Mitchell 1982). Finally, experimental evidence also indicates that the free-rider effect may not impair the provision of collective goods as much as Olson implies (Marwell and Ames 1979, 1980; Smith 1980). Thus, empirical studies suggest that the provision of material selective incentives may not always be the primary explanation of why a group has been able to mobilize.

Theoretically, then, if groups do not rely exclusively on material selective incentives as a means of overcoming the free-rider problem, why do people join groups? In response to this question, several researchers have developed modifications in Olson's theory that suggest other mechanisms for overcoming the free-rider problem. Terry Moe (1980) has pointed out, for example, that if we make the more realistic assumption that individuals have imperfect information, then individuals may well overestimate the benefits of joining and underestimate both the costs and the level of supply of the good. In effect, people may come to believe that their contributions ". . . will make a difference in bringing about net personal gains" (Moe 1980, p. 32). To the degree people come to feel personally efficacious, they have a rational incentive to contribute that facilitates mobilization in pursuit of collective interests.

Similarly, Robert Mitchell (1979) argues that Olson has also ignored the costs of not belonging to a group seeking a public good. In many instances the goals of a social movement involve not only the provision of some public good, but also the prevention of some public "bad"—"entities such as polluted air and water, which have a negative value for individuals, and which once created, are potentially available to everyone in society" (Mitchell 1979, p. 99). Public goods and public bads are inextricably linked to one another; the provision of the good enables the avoidance of the bad and vice versa. Yet, they are not necessarily symmetrical to one another; often the perceived costs associated with the public bad may be considerably greater than the anticipated benefits of the related public good. Presumably, in a number of instances people will perceive the costs of not contributing to be greater than the costs of contributing, and therefore will join the group without the added inducement provided by selective incentives (Mitchell 1979).

Finally, faced with the possibility that material selective incentives do not always figure prominently in mobilization and confronted with the problem of how to explain the impact of individual motivations (i.e., loyalty, principles, guilt) on mobilization, some theorists have suggested "softening" the concept of selective incentives. That is, they have expanded the concept so that it encompasses not only material benefits but intangible benefits as well.

Based on the work of Clark and Wilson (1961), most researchers focus on two broad categories of nonmaterial incentives: solidary and purposive (Salisbury 1969; J. Q. Wilson 1973; Moe 1980). "Solidary" incentives are the rewards arising from social interaction within the group: friendship, status, the enjoyment of one another's company, for example. "Purposive" incentives concern the ideological satisfaction that accrues to people as a consequence of their supporting a group's efforts to obtain a collective good (Berry 1977, p. 21). Thus, if the benefits to the individual derived from the collective good and material selective incentives are not sufficient to justify contributing, then nonmaterial selective incentives can be used to "sweeten the pot" sufficiently to ensure mobilization.

By broadening the selective incentive concept, researchers have solved a serious theoretical dilemma. Namely, they have provided an avenue through which individual principles, group loyalties, and ideological commitments can enter into a person's membership calculus. In so doing, they have preserved a strictly utilitarian view in which mobilization is purely a function of interests; individuals join a group based solely on a calculation of their expected benefits and costs.

This may be too much to ask of the concept of interests. By broadening the notion of selective incentives so that it can encompass virtually anything, one runs the risk of reducing the argument to a useless tautology (Fireman and Gamson 1979; White 1976). Furthermore, not only is the selective incentive argument weakened by softening the concept, but the explanatory power of nonmaterial factors is also unnecessarily restricted. In particular, it is important to recognize that, in addition to serving as a source of solidary and purposive selective incentives, group loyalties and personal principles may heighten interest in the collective good itself, thus encouraging mobilization (Fireman and Gamson 1979; Tilly 1978). Finally, nonmaterial incentives are sufficiently different from material ones so that arguments that fit one category relatively well may be problematic with respect to the other. In particular, theoretical statements that seem reasonable when applied to clear-cut material incentives often become less plausible when nonmaterial incentives are considered (Fireman and Gamson 1979). In summary, then, "no useful purpose is served and something of value is lost by forcing" nonmaterial factors such as personal principles and loyalties into a utilitarian mold (Fireman and Gamson 1979, p. 21).

Consequently, we define the concept of selective incentives narrowly so that it pertains only to positive or negative material sanctions that may be added to an individual's situation in order to induce membership. In so doing, we follow the lead of Fireman and Gamson (1979) and others (Tilly 1978; Oberschall 1978) in arguing that self-interest plays a definite role in mobilization, but not an all-encompassing one. In many cases, people are motivated not only by self-interests (as narrowly defined) but also by an interest in the collective good that may be fostered by both solidarity and personal principles. With this in mind, let us turn to a discussion of how solidarity enters into the mobilization process.

The Role of Solidarity in Mobilization

As we have just seen, potentially many groups may have to rely on selective incentives to raise individual interests sufficiently to ensure mobilization. But, this may be so costly a way to mobilize that many movements may be prevented from ever doing so. Yet, there is another avenue of mobilization: existing social organizations. Typically, in a developed society social movement adherents may already belong to a number of organizations that exercise routine control over a substantial amount of their resources. Importantly, emerging social movement organizations can take advantage of these existing group structures and their already collected resources to reduce the difficulty (i.e., the marginal costs) of their own mobilization (Fireman and Gamson 1979; Freeman 1975; Oberschall 1973, 1978; Wilson and Orum 1976; Snow et al. 1980; Useem 1980).

The relationship between established organizations and the mobilization of new groups depends to a large degree on the "solidarity" characterizing the existing groups (Fireman and Gamson 1979). In this regard, Tilly (1978) has presented a particularly useful conceptualization of solidarity. Specifically, he argues that solidary organization is a function of two things: catness and netness, called "catnet" for short. Catness refs to ". . . the strength of a shared identity in a group and to the sharpness of social boundaries that comprise all those who share a common characteristic" (Oberschall 1978, p. 308). Netness, on the other hand, has to do with the density of social networks or interpersonal bonds linking the members of a group to one another (Tilly 1978, p. 62). In general, solidarity increases with catnetness.

Given that solidarity may facilitate mobilization, one tactic that group organizers might pursue is to attempt to create solidarity among the adherents of their social movement. Yet, building solidary relationships where none exist is likely to be a time consuming and costly task that has little chance for success in the short run. Consequently, a second, much more viable strategy is to make use of whatever existing solidary relationships there may be among movement adherents. In doing so, however, it is critical to recognize that the degree to which solidarity encourages loyalty to a new organization depends to a large extent on whether or not the existing group has a substantial stake in the provision of the new collective good (Fireman and Gamson 1979). If existing group loyalties are to become a major motivating factor, the interests of the solidary group must somehow be linked to the collective good being pursued by the mobilizing group.

There are several ways in which this might occur (Fireman and Gamson 1979). Sometimes existing organizations themselves are the primary catalyst underlying the emergence of social movements. The leadership of an established organization may simply coopt that organizational base to pursue the goals associated with a new social movement. Yet, not all SMO organizers are recognized leaders of some solidary group. In those cases, the organizer must draw upon the resources of other solidary groups. This can be done by tailoring the goals of the emerging social movement organization so that they are compatible with the goals of the existing group. Thus, this strategy calls for the SMO organizer to "woo" the leadership of some solidary group. Alternatively, if the leadership of the solidary group balks at such efforts, then SMO organizers may circumvent them altogether. In this alternative approach, SMO organizers use the lines of communication and social networks characterizing the solidary group to forge new solidary bonds. In essence, the SMO organizers may direct their appeals to some subgroup of the broader solidary group in hopes that they can form a new organizational base. In summary, one way to mobilize a social movement is to play upon the group loyalties that commonly characterize members of a solidary group. To the extent that the interests of that solidary group can be linked to the collective goals of some social movement, then existing group loyalties should facilitate the mobilization of the movement. Thus, solidary ties represent one avenue through which the value of a collective good is reintroduced into the membership calculus.

Finally, it is important to recognize that, as in the case of self-interest, the impact of existing group loyalties on mobilization increases with the perceived urgency of the situation. Urgency—"the difference that collective action makes to the chances of obtaining the collective good"—is a function of both necessity and opportunity (Fireman and Gamson 1979, p. 38). As Fireman and Gamson (1979, p. 28) explain, collective action is most urgent when ". . . there is no reason to believe that collective goods will be preserved without collective action" (necessity) and when there is ". . . every reason to believe that they can be preserved through collective action" (opportunity). A sense of necessity can be created in several ways. For one thing, direct threats to a group's interests can create feelings of necessity. Necessity also increases when rival possibilities for collective action are discredited. Opportunity, on the other hand, can be increased by an emerging group establishing a sense of its own credibility and effectiveness. Opportunity may also be increased by third-party support and by the appearance of possible coalition partners. Thus, by stressing the urgency of the situation, SMO organizers can enhance the impact of existing group loyalties on mobilization.

The Role of Individual Principles in Mobilization

Just as certain solidary groups may have a stake in the achievement of a particular collective good, so may individuals value the collective good for normative reasons, rather than purely out of self-interest. When people desire a collective good out of a sense of "justice, equity or right," we argue that they are acting on the basis of "principles" (Fireman and Gamson 1979, p. 26). When principles are at stake, an individual's personal interest in the provision of the collective good should be heightened; consequently, the free-rider effect becomes a less viable option. As Moe explains (1980, p. 119), if the provision of a collective good is seen as being a matter of ideological, religious, or moral principles, then an individual ". . . may feel a responsibility to 'do his part' in support of those policies, and indeed he may consider the free-rider option morally reprehensible." To some extent, then, when the provision of a collective good is desired as a matter of principle, not only is the value of the good enhanced, but the act of participating becomes rewarding in and of itself. Finally, as in the case of self-interest and solidarity, the impact of individual principles on mobilization will be greatly enhanced to the extent that the situation is perceived to be urgent (Fireman and Gamson 1979). When urgency is high, a sense of individual responsibility can become a major motivating factor in mobilizing individuals.

Furthermore, the fact that some individuals may contribute to a group out of a sense of responsibility, rather than self-interest, brings to our attention the possibility that the group targeted for mobilization is not necessarily limited to those who will benefit personally from the collective good. In particular, when a SMO does not have a pure public good as its goal, then it is possible to divide movement adherents into two classes: beneficiary and conscience adherents. "Beneficiary" adherents are those people who will benefit directly from the provision of the collective good, while "conscience" adherents are movement supporters who do not stand to benefit directly (McCarthy and Zald 1977, p. 1222). For the conscience adherents, a sense of responsibility may be the key factor underlying their motivation. Thus, in groups where the potential beneficiaries are small in number or poor in resources, it may be essential to generate a sense of responsibility among conscience adherents if mobilization is to succeed.

The Role of the Political Entrepreneur

So far we have made only implicit references to the distinctions that may characterize potential participants in social movement organizations. Yet, there are critical differences between participants—differences that play a vital role in the mobilization process. Perhaps the most important thing to recognize is that, while followers may provide the resources nominally required to fuel the collective actions of an organization, leaders are essential for the very creation of an organization.

From the resource mobilization perspective, the role of a movement leader has been described as that of a political entrepreneur: ". . . a hypothetical individual who exploits profitable opportunities by providing or promising to provide services that are designed to attract support from individuals" (Moe 1980, p. 36; also see Frohlich, Oppenheimer, and Young 1971; Salisbury 1969). As an entrepreneur the political organizer must persuade potential members to join the developing organization. In doing so, the entrepreneur may employ different strategies of mobilization that appeal to some combination of interests, solidarity, and personal principles. To some extent, the entrepreneur's choice of strategy may depend on whether the goals of the developing organization are "expressive" (focusing on satisfying individual needs) or "instrumental" (concerned with making broad changes in society), or some combination of the two. SMOs that have primarily expressive goals will emphasize group ties or solidarity, while groups with instrumental goals will appeal more to individual principles and interests in their mobilization efforts (Curtis and Zurcher 1973, 1974; Zurcher and Curtis 1973).

But what motivates the political entrepreneurs? Recent theorists have placed a heavy emphasis on the role of self-interest in encouraging individuals to assume an entrepreneurial role in the development of a SMO (Olson 1971; Frolich, Oppenheimer, and Young 1971). As in the case of rank-and-file members, the benefits that accrue to political organizers should exceed their costs if they are to continue in their role as entrepreneurs. Yet, unlike ordinary members, the free-rider option is considerably less viable for the potential entrepreneur. If an organizer chooses not to accept that role, then there may be a very real chance that the collective good will not be provided (Fireman and Gamson 1979). Consequently, potential entrepreneurs should perceive themselves as being particularly efficacious. Thus, they may take action simply because of the benefits they hope to gain from the provision of the collective good. Yet, while self-interest may be a strong motivating factor in the entrepreneur's membership calculus, the effects of group loyalties and individual responsibilities should not be discounted. As Fireman and Gamson (1979) have demonstrated, both of these factors may supplement the would-be organizer's interest in the collective good, thus raising the probability that he or she will assume an entrepreneurial role.

Finally, what triggers the entrepreneurs' initial recognition of their own interests in the collective good? In some cases, this awareness may develop gradually over time. Yet, it is as likely that some "precipitating event" acts as a catalyst in motivating the would-be political organizer to take action (Freeman 1975; Killian 1973; Snyder and Kelly 1979). To the extent that is true, the birth of a mobilization effort depends not so much on the existence of formal organizational ties, as it does on the strategic location of certain people at certain points in time.

The Role of Outside Factors on Mobilization

Social movements do not mobilize in a vacuum; the success or failure of their mobilization efforts can be greatly influenced, not only by internal factors, but also by forces outside the population being mobilized. In particular, external agents can have a "repressive," "facilitative," or "tolerant" effect on mobilization. Repressive actions raise the costs of a group's mobilization; facilitative actions lower the costs; and tolerant behavior neither raises nor lowers the costs of mobilization (Tilly 1978). Three types of external agents are important to discuss: the government, the media, and other groups.

Generally, the government has the potential power to be the most important external agent. The government controls the major agents of social control or repression in a society—the police, the military, and other information-gathering agencies. These agents of social control can have a direct and devastating repressive impact on mobilization efforts. In the United States, the government has directed considerably more of its repressive efforts toward movements of the left, rather than the right (Marx 1979). In part, this may be a function of the fact that there are more left-wing social movements; yet, the imbalance seems to persist even once this has been taken into account. Though apparently less likely in the United States, the government can also take actions that facilitate the mobilization efforts of a social movement (Marx 1979).

The government is not the only actor in society that has the potential to repress or facilitate an emerging social movement organization. The mass media can play a critical role in mobilization attempts, particularly when adherents of a social movement are widely dispersed geographically. To some extent, the mass media may act as a conduit for the facilitative or repressive efforts of the government as well as other groups. Or, the media itself may take one side or the other in a social conflict. The media's treatment of a social movement can have an important impact on both recruiting movement adherents into active participation, and converting members of neutral bystander publics into movement supporters. The media can facilitate mobilization by promoting a positive public image of the movement and its leader, or it can hinder the development of a group through negative publicity (Marx 1979; Molotch 1979).

Outside groups as well can facilitate or repress mobilization attempts. Through the contribution of their resources, they may actually subsidize the growth of an SMO (Moe 1980; Freeman 1979; McCarthy and Zald 1977). This type of aid may be especially important for a social movement whose potential beneficiaries have relatively few resources of their own. Outside groups may also encourage mobilization by providing lines of communication, possible contacts, and sources of information (Marx 1979). Alternatively, established groups outside the population being mobilized may prevent mobilization by reversing tactics. Finally, probably the most effective repressive tactic is the withholding of resources.

Summary

In summary, we have seen that a number of factors influence the typical process through which a social movement is transformed into a social movement organization(s). To some extent, people may join a group out of self-interest. But, at the same time, existing group loyalties and individual principles raise the likelihood that people will join because they value the movement's goals. In addition, political entrepreneurs play a pivotal role in the mobilization process; without their leadership mobilization becomes difficult, if not impossible. Finally, external actors such as the government, the mass media, and other groups can have a substantial influence on mobilization that may be either repressive or facilitative.

COLLECTIVE ACTION

To this point, our focus on the mobilization process has concentrated on how a group develops the capacity to act collectively.
Yet, whether that potential will be converted into concrete collective
actions depends to a large extent on the group's power: its ability
to make ". . . its interests prevail over others with which (it) is in
conflict" (Tilly 1978, p. 125). The "contenders" for political power
include: (1) "members of the polity" who are recognized or accepted
actors in the political arena; and (2) "challengers" who "contend
without routine or recognition" (Tilly 1978, p. 125). Because they
both encounter less repression and occupy a more privileged position vis-à-vis the government, members of the polity usually wield
more political power. Thus, groups with a high level of mobilization and significant amounts of power—such as members of the polity—should be better able to respond to opportunities and threats
that arise in the environment. Given this, let us consider, first,
what determines a group's strategy, and secondly, how to measure
its success.

Strategies of Action

One role of the political entrepreneur is to help formulate
strategies, or plans of attack, that will govern the social movement
organization's behavior. We have already discussed the "mobilization" strategies that guide the accumulation of resources. Now, we
focus on the strategies of "advocacy" that underlie the collective
actions taken in pursuit of group goals (Berry 1977).
Where a group is in contention for political power, the government is typically the primary target of influence (Tilly 1978).
Groups attempting to alter national policy may focus on Congress.
Alternatively, a group may determine that the most viable strategy
is to concentrate on state or local government units. Even when
changing governmental policy is the major goal of an SMO, the targets of influence need not be limited to governmental actors. Specifically, where there is a large "bystander public" a group may
attempt to win over some of these individuals in an effort to bring
public opinion to bear on governmental actors (Freeman 1979).
In formulating a general strategy of influence, SMO leaders
are constrained by factors both internal and external to the organization. Internally, the goals of the organization and movement may
dictate the general strategy of influence that is adopted. Secondly,
not only is the level of mobilization important to determining advocacy strategies, but it is also essential to consider the type of

resources that have been mobilized. As Freeman (1979) has pointed out, some organizations are rich in material resources such as money and land. Such resources are essential for the development of the professional staff that would be necessary were direct lobbying chosen as a major strategy. In contrast, other SMOs are money "poor" and people "rich"; while they may lack capital, they have an abundant amount of intangible resources such as human labor and time. Such organizations are more likely to resort to constituency lobbying or protest as a general strategy of influence. Thirdly, the choice of an advocacy strategy is also constrained by the structure of the organization. A centralized, hierarchical organization may be best suited for pursuing institutional changes through traditional channels of influence. In contrast, a decentralized, segmented organization must focus its strategy on those activities that can be executed adequately by a small group without much division of labor. Thus, internally, the goals, level of mobilization, type of resources mobilized, and structure of the SMO all interact to limit the range of available strategies.

External factors also play a role in reducing the strategic options open to an SMO. First, whether or not the group is a member of the polity will be an important factor in determining the range of viable options. Challengers, for example, may have their access to institutionalized channels blocked, thus eliminating various strategies from their options (Gamson 1975). Secondly, as Freeman (1979, p. 176) points out, ". . . all resources . . . have constraints on their uses" that mold the strategic options available to a group. Thirdly, in choosing a strategy, SMO leaders must take into account their expectations about the tactics of potential targets (Mottl 1980). Finally, the strategy of a group is also affected by the existing group environment. If, for example, there are opportunities for coalition formation, the strategy of a group may be fundamentally altered (Berry 1977; Costain 1981b).

Once the targets of influence have been identified and the various internal and external constraints on strategy taken into account, then SMO organizers may map out a general plan of attack. Where the government is a target of influence, direct lobbying of governmental decision-makers is one obvious strategy that may be adopted. Some of the specific tactics involved in direct lobbying include the use of legal channels, such as litigation and administrative intervention, and the presentation of information through testifying before congressional committees and releasing research results.

A second general strategy is to lobby decision-makers through movement constituents. For example, groups that have some measure of acceptance in the polity can employ their own constituents to pressure decision-makers through specific tactics like letter-writing campaigns (Berry 1977). Alternatively, groups outside the established avenues of influence may organize their constituents into some form of protest as a means of bringing pressure to bear on law-makers (Tilly 1978).

A third strategy of influence is indirect lobbying: using the public to place pressure on decision-makers. In this regard, electoral activities figure prominently. For example, groups can make campaign contributions, endorse candidates, publicize the voting records of incumbent office-holders, and even align themselves with a political party. In recent years the encouragement of single-issue voting—picking a candidate based only on his or her stand on a particular issue—has become a popular way of lobbying through the voting booth.

The Success of Collective Action

Over the long run, what determines the success of the collective actions taken by a group? How may success be measured? Generally, researchers have tended to ignore questions concerning the impact that a group may have once it has mobilized (for exceptions to this see: Gamson 1975; Tilly 1978; and Snyder and Kelly 1979). William Gamson (1975) represents perhaps the major exception to this generalization. Gamson (1975) argues that the overall success of a group can be conceptualized in terms of the fate of the organization and the distribution of advantages. For groups that are challengers, one measure of success is whether or not they achieve some degree of acceptance from their targets of influence. In addition, Gamson (1975) argues that gaining new advantages is also an important measure of success, particularly in the case of members of the polity. While on the face of it, "gaining new advantages" may seem like a rather simple notion, one quickly recognizes that it is not always easy to define when this occurs. This is especially likely to be the case when the collective goods sought by a group are intangible and deal with things such as value changes. Let us briefly explore how these concepts might be operationalized.

"Acceptance," as Gamson (1975) defines it, refers to the relationship between a group and its antagonists—those actors that it is in conflict with. A more positive relationship between the challenging group and its antagonists is taken as evidence of some degree of acceptance. Of particular relevance to our own concerns is the question of how to measure acceptance when one target of change is the public itself. In such instances, Gamson suggests that it is important to distinguish between acceptance of the group itself by the public and support of the group's proposed program or policies.

Acceptance would refer to the attitudes of the public toward the group itself, while acceptance of the group's policies is more properly thought of as gaining new advantages.

Let us elaborate on the conceptualization and measurement of this second dimension of success. "Gaining new advantages" may be more formally defined as occurring whenever an SMO obtains new benefits; that is, it is successful in securing the enactment of some aspect of its program (Gamson 1975). Implicit in this conceptualization is the assumption that new advantages are defined by the group itself; new advantages, in effect, reflect the attainment of group goals. This suggests that gains may include concrete policy changes as well as more elusive shifts in the public's values and attitudes. Furthermore, as Gamson (1975) points out, no assumptions are made about whether or not the SMO actually caused the benefits to occur.

Based on such a conceptualization, actually measuring the attainment of new advantages first requires the identification of the group's goals. Once this has been accomplished, some measure of goal achievement is needed. Where group goals are embodied in a concrete set of policy proposals, the analyst can determine the success those proposals have received in various legislative arenas. On the other hand, where group goals are less concrete, such as when a group desires to alter public opinion, then the focus must shift to perceptions of success. In this regard, Gamson (1975, p. 36) suggests that perceptions of the group itself, the group's antagonists, and more neutral bystanders such as historians and journalists may all be useful sources in determining the success of a group.

THE DYNAMICS OF SOCIAL MOVEMENTS

Internal Dynamics

Internally, there is a reciprocal relationship between the goals and the structure of a social movement organization. Initially, the structure of an SMO may be dictated by the nature of the movement's goals. For example, movements that seek to change individual or member behavior (i.e., movements with expressive goals) tend to develop decentralized structures, while movements that have instrumental goals or those that focus on societal changes are more likely to develop highly centralized structures (Curtis and Zurcher 1973, 1974).

Social movements with widely dispersed adherents are often faced with a critical organizational dilemma: do they develop a federated structure in which supporters are enlisted in local chapters that are then loosely linked to one another through some national organization, or do they develop a single national organization? A federated structure allows for a mobilization strategy based on solidary relations, and once developed, the organization can use those solidary relations as a basis for pursuing expressive goals. At the same time, a federated structure may result in the SMO having a disproportionate amount of intangible resources (human labor and time) that places limits on the sorts of strategies that may be pursued (McCarthy and Zald 1977).

In contrast, purely national organizations must rely on individual self-interest and personal principles in their mobilization efforts. Because their constituents are isolated (i.e., not bound together by solidary relations), the flow of their resources to the organization may be less stable. Consequently, unfederated organizations are likely to devote a greater proportion of their resources to advertising and media appeals in order to maintain a given level of resource mobilization (McCarthy and Zald 1977). In either case, once established, the structure of the organization will continue to influence the types of collective actions that may be taken, and subsequently goal attainment and change.

External Dynamics

Not only does an SMO continually undergo changes in its internal structure, but it also experiences changes in its external organizational environment: the context of SMOs in which it exists. In this regard, McCarthy and Zald (1977) have suggested a particularly useful way of conceptualizing an SMO's organizational environment. "All SMOs that have as their goals the attainment of the broadest preferences of a social movement constitute a social movement industry (SMI)" (McCarthy and Zald 1977, p. 1219). Thus, more than one SMO might pursue the goals of a particular social movement. Furthermore, different SMIs may be combined into categories of broader inclusiveness which are labeled "sectors." Thus, conservationist groups and anti-nuclear organizations represent two SMIs that fall within the same environmentalist sector. Ultimately, with respect to social movements, the broadest sector would be the "social movement sector" which would encompass all of the SMIs in a society, regardless of which social movement they were attached to.

Within their own SMI and the broader social movement sector, individual organizations are forced to relate to one another. To some extent, these relationships may be competitive. Competition arises, quite simply, because individuals have limited resources to

invest in SMOs. As a consequence, they are forced to choose between social movement industries, and within industries among
particular organizations. Furthermore, when the amount of individual resources available to the social movement sector increases,
it is likely that new SMOs and SMIs will develop to compete for those
resources (McCarthy and Zald 1977). But, because they lack an established constituency, new organizations are at a disadvantage in
this competitive environment. Nonetheless, organizations can im-
prove the likelihood that they will continue to exist by differentiating
themselves from their competition. Thus, in a particularly competitive SMI, new organizations are likely to begin with very narrow
goals and limited strategies (McCarthy and Zald 1977).

Yet, just as competition might be one response to an environment of limited resources, so might cooperation. The degree of
cooperation among organizations within an SMI and across SMIs may
be thought of as varying along a continuum. On one end of the continuum is simple cooperation among organizations that does not require any sort of structural or goal transformation on the part of
the organizations. As Zald and Ash (1965-66) explain, this sort of
limited cooperation is most likely when there is a need for some
sort of special expertise or competency in order to pursue a particular strategy of influence. For example, an organization that
wished to engage in lobbying through the courts might cooperate
with an organization that had greater legal expertise than itself.

Coalition formation represents a second, more intense, form
of cooperation among organizations. A coalition involves two or
more organizations pooling some of their resources to pursue an
outcome in a situation involving a mixture of conflict and coordination (Hinckley 1981). Although there is a pooling of resources and
a coordination of strategies, in most coalitions the individual organizations maintain their separate identities (Zald and Ash 1965-66).

Finally, perhaps the most extreme form of cooperation among
SMOs is the merger (Zald and Ash 1965-66). In a true merger, the
individual group identities are suppressed, and in their place a new,
all-encompassing organization develops. Mergers are expected to
have a drastic influence on the support base of an organization, as
well as the obvious influences on its structure. Zald and Ash (1965-
66) suggest that mergers are most likely to occur when there is a
single, overriding goal that all of the participant organizations can
agree on. Furthermore, they argue that mergers are more likely
to occur in the course of "losing battles"; when organizational leaders perceive that their cause is lost and that they are losing members, they may resort to a merger in order to save face and restore some of their former vitality.

Thus, the external organizational environment is critical to understanding the structural dynamics of SMOs. As a consequence of competition, SMOs may alter their goals and their structure in order to ensure their survival. Alternatively, SMOs may seek some form of cooperation with their competition. In the course of such cooperative efforts, the SMO may undergo both structural changes and goal transformation.

Goal Transformations

The goals of a social movement and its respective SMOs are not fixed; rather, they evolve and change in response to internal as well as external forces. In general, such changes in the goals of an organization will be guided by the leadership. Internally, the very establishment of a movement organization may cause the leadership to shift the goals away from the pursuit of the collective good and toward the maintenance of the organization. Preserving the organization becomes a goal in and of itself which demands and merits some expenditures of resources (Zald and Ash 1965-66). In addition, the political entrepreneur may initiate a change in goals in response to the demands of the group's members (Moe 1980). Finally, a change in the leadership of an SMO may bring with it a change in goals.

Externally, the organizational environment may create pressures that force political entrepreneurs to adjust the goals of their organizations. To survive in a particularly competitive environment, the goals of an organization may be altered so as to differentiate it from other organizations. Such shifts represent a major source of goal transformation (Zald and Ash 1965-66). Not only may organizations alter their goals in order to compete with other groups, they may also change their goals so as to facilitate interorganizational cooperation. Such transformation may result in an organization assuming a more diffuse, general set of goals.

Goal transformation may also be brought about as a consequence of collective actions taken. Both success and failure may produce adjustments in goals. Furthermore, different patterns of conflict may encourage different forms of goal transformation. Specifically, an escalation in conflict is typically accompanied by a broadening of the issues and goals involved. Thus, what begins as a specific, relatively narrow demand for change may evolve into a much broader set of goals.

THE ROLE OF ISSUES

To this point, we have not discussed the actual language through which leaders converse with the supporters of a movement. We posit that issues are critical to understanding how elites and masses communicate with one another; they represent the major means for translating grievances and conflicts into more readily identifiable demands. In essence, we assume that the desire for a certain collective good can be represented to the public by a specific issue. Thus, the public's reaction to a social movement depends upon the meaning they attach to the issues championed by that movement.

If we follow the logic of the resource mobilization perspective, the public's reaction to an issue should be determined primarily by the issue's substance, the content of the demands that it embodies. From this viewpoint, then, people respond "rationally" to the issues associated with a social movement. In effect, the emotionality so evident in the collective behavior paradigm has been minimized by those adhering to a resource mobilization framework. Yet, recent research (Kinder and Sears 1981; Sears, Hensler, and Speer 1979; Sears et al. 1980; Sears and Citrin 1982) on symbolic politics suggests that individual reactions to an issue depend, not only on the intrinsic content of the demands it represents, but also a great deal on how those demands are symbolized or "packaged" for the public (Bennett 1980). Certain symbolic issues evoke extraordinarily strong emotions that play a major role in determining individual behavior.

We argue that both symbolism and substance are important to understanding how the public responds to an issue; it is the interaction of these two elements that determines the public's reaction to issues and therefore to social movements. The implications of such an argument are twofold. First, it interjects an element of emotionality into the "cold" and "sterile" view of people implicit in the resource mobilization perspective. Second, with respect to symbolic politics, such an argument forces one to recognize that the symbolization of an issue is simply a way of interpreting the issue's substance. Ignoring either an issue's symbolism (as the resource mobilization theorists are likely to do) or its substance (as symbolic politics theorists tend to do) will result in an incomplete view of an issue's meaning. Accordingly, let us begin our discussion by considering the dynamics that underlie the process of issue symbolization.

Issue Symbolization

The origination of an issue may be thought of as a process through which individual concerns become public ones. This process of issue emergence is shaped by the dynamic interaction of two factors: the circumstances that "trigger" or spur the recognition of some problem, and the "initiators" or political actors who convert the problem into an issue that is capable of capturing the public's attention (Cobb and Elder 1972b; Bennett 1980). The "triggering mechanisms" or circumstances surrounding an issue's emergence may assume a variety of forms. Some issues are "structural" in the sense that they are rooted in basic life experiences; others are "agenda" issues intentionally placed before the public by the government or the media; and still others are "crisis" issues born out of specific social and economic traumas. Similarly, the actors who help to convert individual concerns into public issues may be political elites or members of interest groups; less frequently an issue may emerge as a consequence of grassroots or diffused, broad-based public concern (Bennett 1980, pp. 112-13).

Once an issue has been introduced to the public, its substance must be defined. This process of issue definition is best described as one of symbolization, where a "symbol" is simply ". . . any communication device that represents or stands for some other thing" (Bennett 1980, p. 250). We can think of any issue, no matter how dry, concrete, or seemingly emotionless, as constituting a "symbolic representation" of certain demands (Bennett 1980, p. 249). Furthermore, the specific symbolization given an issue depends not so much on the content of the demands themselves as it does on the actors defining the issue and the communications concerning it. Thus, the same issue substance may be defined or symbolized in very different ways. Finally, it is important to recognize that the process of issue definition is simultaneously a group-level and individual-level phenomenon in the sense that the symbols used to define an issue act as a bridge between the public and the private by linking the "issue and the individual's experience in meaningful ways" (Bennett 1980, p. 248). In summary, then, symbols are used to interpret or represent the substance of an issue; thus the meaning of the symbols defines the meaning of the issue.

At the aggregate level, two aspects of the symbolization process, the type and the mode, are important. With respect to the type of symbolization, Cobb and Elder (1973) have suggested a typology of political symbols that may be loosely adapted for our purposes. The symbols used in the definition of issues may pertain to four types of hierarchically ordered objects: the community, societal norms, formal roles and organizations, and situational settings. The first category contains higher-order symbols of the community and the basic values underlying its organization (e. g. , "democracy," "The American Way of Life, " and "the family"), while the second deals with symbols representing the general rules of society as well as the norms of the political system (e. g. , "majority rule," and "marital fidelity"). The third category encompasses those symbols associated with formal roles and organizations (e. g. , "the presidency," and "the church"). The final category deals with the lower-order symbols associated with specific nongovernmental actors and issues (e. g. , "the women's movement" and "busing").

Also important to understanding how an issue is defined is the mode of symbolization. Issues may be defined in terms of either "referential" or "condensational" symbols (Edelman 1964; Cobb and Elder 1972a, 1973; Bennett 1980). Referential symbols reduce the scope of meaning associated with an issue by defining it in specific, concrete, neutral terms. In contrast, condensational symbols expand the scope of meaning, defining an issue in abstract, ambiguous, emotionally charged terms. Finally, while it is theoretically easiest to think of symbols as falling into one of two distinct categories—referential or condensational—it is probably more accurate to describe the mode of symbolization as a continuum.

Yet, although we can talk about symbols falling somewhere along a referential-condensational continuum, it must be recognized that symbols have no intrinsic meaning; they are not naturally referential or condensational. Rather, individuals bestow meaning upon symbols and their referents. Specifically, people may associate two types of meaning with symbols. The first type is cognitive—"the objective meaning or substantive content associated with the symbol. " The second is evaluative—the affect elicited by the symbol (Cobb and Elder 1973, p. 313). The cognitive meaning or informational content of a symbol may range from high to low; a symbol with a high amount of cognitive meaning is well grounded in substantive information. Similarly, the affective meaning of a symbol may range from being highly positive to being highly negative. The source of such affective meaning may be the cognitive content, however little, that is associated with the symbol. Alternatively, when cognitive sources of meaning are lacking, the source of a symbol's affective meaning may lie in other related symbols or past socialization experiences.

Taken together, the cognitive and affective meaning of a symbol define an individual's basic orientation toward the symbol. Cobb and Elder (1973) have identified four basic orientations toward a symbol. First, where cognitive content is well-developed and affect is high, the individual is said to have an "ideological" orientation toward the symbol. People with this type of symbolic orientation are likely to be the initiators of actions taken in defense of the symbol. Furthermore, their actions are likely to be both instrumental and expressive in nature. Next, individuals with well-developed cognitive content and low affect may be described as having a "pragmatic" symbolic orientation. The symbol will motivate them to take action only when it is in their self-interest to do so. Third, people who lack information about a symbol but, nonetheless, have a strong affective attachment to it may be described as "reactive" or "manipulable." In essence, such individuals are "followers" whose emotional reaction to a symbol spurs them into action. As Cobb and Elder (1973, p. 314) explain, such people are "vulnerable to manipulation and available for activation by elites who initiate action in the name of the symbol." Finally, persons for whom a symbol has both low cognitive and affective content can be said to be "apathetic."

Several expectations about individual and group behavior flow from this typology. For example, the meaning of symbols should vary across groups within society. Within groups there should be greater consensus on the cognitive or substantive meaning of a symbol. Similarly, one would anticipate more agreement on the affective meaning or valence of a symbol within groups than across groups. The masses and political elites should also differ in the meaning they associate with various symbols. One would expect elites to attribute a greater and more organized amount of information to political symbols. Consequently, elites (such as the political entrepreneurs essential to mobilization) should have a predominantly ideological or in some cases pragmatic orientation toward political symbols. In contrast, the masses are less likely to associate much cognitive meaning with symbols and therefore should be more apt to have either a reactive or apathetic orientation toward political symbols, depending upon the affective meaning of the particular symbol (Cobb and Elder 1973).

The fact that individuals lend their own meaning to various political symbols also has several implications for the process of issue definition. Since an issue defined in referential terms would be one involving relatively few symbols with which most individuals associate minimal evaluative meaning and a limited, specific cognitive meaning, referential symbols should evoke primarily apathetic reactions from the masses, and perhaps pragmatic reactions from political activists. Consequently, in defining an issue the use of referential symbols should serve to reduce the scope of conflict (Bennett 1980). In contrast, an issue defined in a condensational fashion would be one evoking symbols that, in most people, trigger strong emotions and relatively broad, ambiguous cognitive meanings. Thus, condensational symbols ought to stimulate reactive and ideological responses among individuals. Therefore, in defining an issue the use of condensational symbols should help to expand the scope of conflict, thus encouraging escalation (Bennett 1980).

Similarly, the type of symbols used in defining an issue helps to shape individual reactions. It is expected that individuals will associate more diffuse and heterogenous cognitive meanings with higher-order than with lower-order symbols. With respect to affective meaning, people are expected to acquire their feelings toward higher-order symbols relatively early in life, and this affect should be stronger and more stable than that attached to lower-order symbols (Cobb and Elder 1973). Therefore, these symbols are likely to be quite central to individual belief systems. Consequently, within society there should be greater significance and common affective sentiment attached to the higher-order symbols. Taken together, these arguments suggest that when conflicts erupt around higher-order symbols they are likely to attract a larger number of people and to be more intense and emotional than those conflicts centered around lower-order symbols. Thus, in defining an issue the use of higher-order symbols should promote the escalation of conflict, while lower-order symbols help to reduce the scope of conflict.

Issue Substance

To this point, we have seen that the symbolic language used to define an issue's content in and of itself greatly influences individual reactions to the issue. How political activists define an issue—how they symbolically represent the demands of a social movement to the public—will have a significant effect on how people respond to that movement. Yet, this is not to suggest that the actual substance of the issue is unimportant. On the contrary, the content of the demands embodied in an issue is a significant factor in explaining the public's reactions to the issue and their perceptions of the goals of the related social movement. With this in mind, let us consider how variations in substance may influence public reactions to an issue.

Recall that from our perspective the goals of a social movement, and consequently the substance of related issues, may be conceptualized as the desire for certain public or collective goods. Thus, the nature and utility of the good involved essentially determine the substance of the issue. We argued earlier that, for our purposes, two characteristics are especially useful in establishing the nature or "publicness" of a good: excludability and optionality. Similarly, the substance of an issue is affected not only by the nature of the good involved, but also by the good's perceived utility:

whether it is positively or negatively valued; and whether the utility is easily calculated and thus known, or whether it is hard to estimate and consequently relatively unknown.

Differences in the nature and utility of goods are quite important, since they may influence the scope and intensity of conflict surrounding an issue, and thus the ease with which the issue may be resolved. Specifically, the greater the "social significance" of an issue, the greater the number of people who will be affected by the provision of the good (i.e., the more public the good), the broader the (potential) scope of conflict and the more difficult the resolution of the issue (Cobb and Elder 1973). As discussed earlier, what represents a public good for some may well be perceived as a public bad by others. Such conflicts over whether utility is increased or decreased by a good will be reflected in the two competing sides of the issue. Consequently, the greater the disagreement over a good's utility, the more intense the conflict engendered by the issue. Finally, issues and conflicts involving goods with easily calculated and known values should be easier to resolve than those concerning goods whose values and consequences are hard to estimate (McGlen 1981; Morrison 1979; Oberschall 1973).

In addition to the nature of the good and its utility, other related characteristics of the demands embodied in an issue influence the scope and intensity of conflict surrounding the issue. The complexity of the demands has an impact on the conflict surrounding it. In general, issues dealing with highly complex, technical matters will be limited to a very narrow range of conflict, while those concerning nontechnical demands are more easily expanded to reach a broader public (Cobb and Elder 1972b). Next is the question of whether or not the resolution of the issue is reversible. For example, the decision to make a nuclear attack is irreversible; once a nuclear war has been initiated, one cannot return to a prewar state if things do not work out as planned. Issues involving irreversible outcomes should be more difficult to resolve and the conflicts surrounding such issues should be more easily expanded (Oberschall 1973; Morrison 1979).[4]

The Interaction of Issue Symbolization
and Substance

Thus, as we have seen, various characteristics of an issue's substance have a considerable impact on how intense and widespread the conflict will be over that issue. Yet, it is critical to recognize that individuals have imperfect information about the substantive demands represented by any one issue; people are often unsure about what an issue entails. This uncertainty is reflected in the variation characterizing the public's perceptions of an issue. Furthermore, perceptions may differ systematically as a consequence of rival political entrepreneurs defining an issue in different ways. For example, some political activists might employ condensational, higher-order symbols in an effort to intensify and widen the scope of conflict surrounding an issue. At the same time, in an attempt to contain the controversy, opposing leaders might use referential, lower-order symbols in defining the identical issue. Consequently, the public is expected to disagree over the nature and expected utility of the good involved as well as other aspects of the issue's substance (McGlen 1981; Laver 1981). With this in mind, let us consider how different ways of symbolizing an issue's substance are related to variations in the public's perception of it.

First, there may be considerable disagreement over the nature of the good itself, particularly who will be affected by its provision. To some extent, such perceptions depend upon how one defines the group within which excludability is not feasible. By using condensational and higher-order symbols, political leaders can create ambiguity about who will be affected by a good, and thus expand the lines of conflict. For example, if the issue of gun control is depicted as directly affecting all members of society, including the law-abiding ones, then substantially more people will be drawn into the conflict than when the issue is defined as only affecting criminals. By either broadening or reducing the group of people who see themselves as being nonexcludable from the consumption of a good, political entrepreneurs can shape the scope of a conflict.

Perceptions of who will be affected by a good are also influenced by judgments about the good's optionality. Because the personal relevance of a good should be higher when consumption is not optional, individuals should react more strongly to issues involving "no exit" goods. This should be especially true in the case of public bads. Although political activists actually may not be able to alter the optionality of a good, they can certainly define an issue so as to either attract attention to or downplay that aspect of it. In summary, then, the manner in which an issue is defined can affect the public's perception of the good involved and thus influence the pattern of conflict over the issue.

Secondly, the way in which an issue is symbolized can shape the public's perception of the utility of the good involved. Political activists can encourage conflict, and therefore issue polarization, by stressing the public bads that may accompany some public good. In fact, the very essence of a countermovement depends upon some entrepreneur fostering perceptions of the public bads that may be associated with some good. The impact of these bads can be exaggerated by defining them in terms of condensational, higher-order symbols. Thus, for example, the conflict over busing was broadened when opponents of the issue "upped the ante" by defining the potential bads associated with busing not simply in terms of integration, but also in terms of higher-order symbols: e.g., busing destroys the "neighborhood school" which in turn has a deleterious impact on "family life." In the same fashion, the symbolization of an issue can affect the individual's ability to estimate the utility of the good involved. Referential symbols will make it easier to calculate the utility of the good, while condensational symbols will tend to make the value of the good more ambiguous and less easily calculated.

Finally, the way in which an issue is symbolized also influences perceptions of the complexity and reversibility of the demands embodied in an issue. The use of condensational and higher-order symbols can help to reduce the complexity of an issue, thus making it easier to broaden the conflict over the issue. For example, a seemingly technical issue like water fluoridation was simplified by using emotionally charged, higher-order symbols (Cobb and Elder 1972b). Similarly, while the symbolization of an issue may not actually alter the reversibility of the outcomes associated with the issue, it can be used to heighten the importance of that characteristic. Irreversibility, in particular, becomes especially crucial when it is associated with higher-order, condensational symbols. For instance, environmentalists often evoke the higher-order symbol of "future generations" when discussing the potentially irreversible consequences of failing to protect wilderness areas from the encroachment of commercial developers.

In summary, issues are the language of social movements. They are the means through which collective desires for change are translated into more readily understandable goals. Yet, perceptions of the substance of an issue can vary depending on the symbols used to define it. In particular, the mode and type of symbolization greatly influence the public's perception of the nature of the good involved, its utility, and its other characteristics as well. Furthermore, once it has been defined, an issue is still subject to different meanings because the same symbols evoke varying reactions across individuals. Political activists and others who define issues for the public's consumption are aware of this, and consequently make deliberate use of those symbols best suited for their purposes. With this in mind, let us consider how different strategies for defining an issue's substance relate to various strategies of mobilization.

Issues and Mobilization

Based on our earlier discussion, it can be argued that the success of all three major strategies of mobilization—appeals to self-interest, solidarity, and personal principles—is affected by the public's response to those issues championed by the social movement. In particular, the success of each strategy is influenced by perceptions of the substance of the issue (the nature of the good and its utility) and the urgency of the situation, both of which are affected by the symbolization of the issue. We need to explore, then, exactly how variations in issue symbolization and substance influence mobilization efforts.

Perceptions of the Nature of the Good

With respect to the nature of the good, a common element runs through all three mobilization strategies. Regardless of which strategy is adopted, mobilization should be more effective and more widespread when the good has greater relevance to the actors subject to mobilization. In the case of appeals to self-interest, the good must be relevant to the individual's personal (self-) interest; mobilization based on solidarity depends on the perceived relevance of the good to the solidary group; and in an appeal to principles, the good must be relevant to the individual's personal principles (as opposed to self-interests).

Generally, as discussed earlier, individual perceptions of the relevance of a good are shaped by the good's excludability and optionality. Where the strategy is centered upon individual self-interests, the goal is to make people feel as though they are part of the group which cannot be excluded from consumption of the good, and that they have little choice in the matter. Similarly, successful appeals to solidarity depend upon the individual perceiving that some solidary group that is important to him/her will be affected by the good. Finally, in the case of mobilization through individual principles, the personal relevance of the good to an individual is relatively unimportant. What does matter is establishing some link between the individual's principles and those groups for whom the good is personally relevant. In effect, appeals to personal principles are a key way of mobilizing conscience adherents—people who lack a personal stake in the collective good. Thus, for example, during the 1960s Northern civil rights activists supported Southern integration efforts, not because they would be directly affected by it personally, but because Southern blacks, a group whose well-being was

integral to their sense of justice and equality, would be deeply affected by it.

Furthermore, as explained earlier, the relevance of a good
can be enhanced by defining it in terms of higher-order, condensational symbols. Where appeals are being made to self-interest,
they should be those higher-order, condensational symbols most
central to the individual's relevant personal interests. If, for instance, economic well-being is paramount to the people being mobilized, then the use of code words or symbols such as "full employment" and "national economic security" may be useful in defining an
issue. Similarly, where solidary relationships form the basis for
mobilization, higher-order symbols relevant to the solidary group
should be employed so as to enhance identification of the group with
the issue at hand (Kowalewski 1980). If, for example, existing
church groups are being used as a "springboard" for mobilization,
then symbols such as "God," the "Bible," and "sin" may be especially effective tools. Finally, where mobilization efforts are based
on personal principles, evoking the principles themselves is probably the most successful way of defining the issue. This may be a
relatively easy strategy to pursue since people often think of ideological principles more as symbolic slogans than as abstract principles to be applied to specific situations (Zellman and Sears 1971).
Thus, symbols such as "equality," "freedom," and "justice" are
often used in the definition of an issue when an attempt is being made
to gain the active support of a large number of conscience adherents.
In summary, appeals to self-interest, solidarity, and personal principles can each be made more successful by tailoring the definition
of the nature of the good to suit the strategy.

Perceptions of the Utility of the Good

The utility of the good is also critical to mobilization. It is
especially important to determine whether it is perceived as a public bad or a public good since that will greatly influence the type of
mobilization—defensive or offensive. Of particular relevance in
distinguishing between the concepts of a public bad and a public good
is Morrison's (1979) threefold classification of public goods:

1. "Threatened" goods: "Public goods we have and
   which we do not want to lose, but which are perceived by some as threatened . . . goods which
   may become bads."
2. "Lost" goods: "Public goods which we have lost
   and which we want to recover . . . goods that
   have become bads."

3. "New" goods: "Public goods which we never had, but which some now want" (Morrison 1979, p. 130).

In terms of this typology, offensive mobilization generally would involve the pursuit of new goods, while defensive mobilization typically would concern the protection of threatened goods. From our perspective, mobilization in pursuit of lost goods may be either offensive or defensive in nature depending upon how long the good has been lost. When the good has only recently been lost, it will tend to resemble a threatened good and consequently mobilization is more likely to be defensive. On the other hand, the longer a good has been lost the more it will come to look like a new good subject to offensive mobilization. [5]

For several reasons, defensive mobilization should be easier than offensive mobilization. Regardless of the specific strategy, mobilization will tend to be easier if the utility of the good is known and multifaceted. In effect, people are more likely to take action in pursuit of known goals that are valued for a number of reasons. Defensive mobilization should be easier because the threatened good has a known and multifaceted value while the potential bad that must be prevented has an ambiguous value. The natural ambiguity of the potential bad allows people to infer greater negative consequences than might actually come to pass, thus making the expansion of the conflict more likely (Morrison 1979; McGlen 1981). Furthermore, the ambiguity of potential bads can be heightened through the use of higher-order, condensational symbols. For example, with regard to the issue of busing, people know the value of neighborhood schools; it is a good whose utility can be strongly linked to higher-order symbols such as the "family" and the "community." In contrast, who is to say whether busing to achieve integrated schools will have positive or negative consequences; nor is it possible to say how serious those consequences might be. Following the same logic leads us to expect that offensive mobilization should be more difficult, because generally new goods are more likely to have unknown values and consequences.

With respect to specific strategies of mobilization, appeals to self-interest are more likely to yield results if mobilization is defensive rather than offensive. In the case of offensive mobilization, appeals must be made to the individual's personal interest in some new good. But, in defining an issue so as to make such an appeal, there is an inherent trade-off between establishing the utility of the new good and broadening the range of people who perceive the good to be personally relevant. In order to establish the good's utility it needs to be defined in terms of referential symbols that reduce ambiguity about the good and evoke pragmatic reactions from individuals.

Yet, at the same time, if widespread mobilization is necessary for success, the issue ought to be defined in terms of condensational, higher-order symbols which more people are likely to react to. Thus, offensive mobilization through appeals to self-interests may often entail contradictory strategies for defining the issue.

In contrast, defensive mobilization through self-interest should be considerably easier. Generally, this is true because there is an asymmetry in the interests associated with threatened goods that can be exploited by employing higher-order, condensational symbols in the definition of an issue. To begin with, the value of the threatened good is usually well-established and may be linked to basic values, while the potential bad is shrouded in ambiguity, thus making it easier to expand the conflict (Morrison 1979). Secondly, the nature of the good itself may have an asymmetrical effect on mobilization to the extent that people react more strongly to certain characteristics when they concern a public bad. In particular, the possibility of "no exit" from a potential bad should spur more people into action than the thought of having no choice about some public good. A third reason why defensive appeals to self-interest should be more successful is that threats generalize easier than opportunities, and this tendency is exacerbated through the use of condensational, higher-order symbols (Tilly 1978). A threat to a particular interest may be easily generalized to a threat for a number of other related interests, raising the individual's personal stake in taking collective action. In contrast, opportunities to gain a new good are less likely to be taken as a sign that a number of other opportunities exist. For all these reasons, defensive appeals are likely to arouse greater feelings of self-interest, and consequently encounter greater success than offensive ones.

Mobilization through solidary ties may also be easier in the case of threatened goods. The same asymmetry of interests that characterizes appeals to self-interests is also likely to occur in the case of group interests. People are more likely to react strongly to threats made against the interests of some important solidary group than they are to react strongly to new opportunities for the group. In addition, mobilization in pursuit of new goods is more likely to require substantial alterations in existing organizational structures and patterns of mobilization (Tilly 1978). In some instances, entirely new organizational structures may have to be developed in order for successful collective actions to be taken. Thus, existing solidary ties, while useful to an offensive mobilization effort, may have to be supplemented substantially by new individual relationships. In contrast, solidary relationships may be more readily adapted to defensive mobilization efforts because responses to threats may be handled more easily through existing organizational structures. This will be especially likely when the threatened good has been defined so that it is closely linked to those goods integral to the organization's existence.

Mobilization based on appeals to principles may also be more successful in the case of defensive mobilization, again because of an asymmetry of interests. Simply put, goods associated with personal principles are expected to be valued more highly than opportunities in the face of threats (Tilly 1978). This should be especially likely in the case of isolated conscience adherents who, due to a lack of personal or solidary-based interest in the good at stake, are being mobilized entirely on the basis of personal principles.

In summary, with respect to the utility of goods, it is expected that defensive mobilization in protection of threatened goods will tend to be easier than offensive mobilization in pursuit of new goods. The known value of threatened goods, their generalizability, and the possibility of "no exit" all conspire to raise the stakes, so that people often feel that they have more to lose in the case of threatened goods than they might have to gain from some new good. Furthermore, through the process of issue symbolization, all three strategies of mobilization can play upon this asymmetry of interests to facilitate defensive mobilization. By using higher-order, condensational symbols, political entrepreneurs can heighten the ambiguity surrounding some potential bad and thus exaggerate the interests perceived as threatened. Thus, the natural advantages characterizing defensive mobilization efforts can be increased even further.

Perceptions of Urgency

Finally, all three strategies of mobilization are influenced by the urgency associated with taking collective action. As noted earlier, urgency is a function of necessity and opportunity (Fireman and Gamson 1979). Yet, while both necessity and opportunity affect urgency, it is expected that necessity will be more important in the case of threatened goods and opportunity more relevant to determining the urgency associated with new goods. Even more important, although various characteristics of an issue may not alter the true urgency associated with taking collective action, they are expected to influence perceptions of both necessity and opportunity. Furthermore, it is posited that it will be somewhat easier to exaggerate the necessity of taking collective action. Commonly, there is an acute sense of urgency about acting now to save a threatened good that is often missing from efforts to gain a new good. Thus, once again, defensive mobilization should be easier than offensive mobilization.

With this in mind, let us briefly explore how certain elements of an issue's substance and symbolization may affect perceptions of necessity. In the case of threatened goods, a sense of necessity may be heightened because of the irreversible nature of decisions concerning many public bads, an irreversibility that often does not characterize the related public good. For example, we cannot replace the redwoods once they have been cut down; if, however, we don't cut the redwoods today we can always do so at some point in the future if our preferences and needs change (Morrison 1979, p. 131). A sense of necessity may also be heightened by the no-exit quality of many public bads. In essence, people may tend to overestimate the necessity of taking action when consumption of the bad is unavoidable. Thus, perceptions of necessity may be accentuated in the case of irreversible issues that have a no-exit quality. In addition, because the perception of these characteristics can be enhanced through the use of condensational, and/or higher-order symbols, the necessity of taking collective action may be even further exaggerated.

Summary

We argue that the successful use of an issue to aid mobilization depends upon establishing for the public three things: (1) the nature of the good being sought and its relevance to those groups subject to mobilization; (2) the utility of the good; and (3) the urgency of taking action. With respect to all these things, the manner in which an issue is symbolized can have a significant effect on the public's perceptions. By using condensational, higher-order symbols that evoke strong emotional reactions an issue can be defined so as to increase its relevance to certain groups, raise its perceived utility, and heighten its perceived urgency. Furthermore, it is often easier to do this in the case of threatened as opposed to new goods, thus making defensive mobilization easier than offensive mobilization. This may help to explain why countermovements are often quickly mounted to combat what is perceived to be a threatening social movement. It also accounts for the emotional fervor that typically accompanies a countermovement.

CONCLUSIONS

In this chapter, we have outlined an approach for studying the emergence of social movements and the subsequent development of social movement organizations. From our perspective, social movements appear when substantial portions of some public have significant political, economic, or social grievances. Various members of this disenchanted public may rationally decide to become political activists in some social movement organization. We have argued that such people are motivated by self-interests, solidary ties, and/or personal principles. Once formed, such organizations may take a variety of actions aimed at furthering the goals of the social movement. Over time, the fate of these actions determines the degree of success that the social movement enjoys.

Critical to our approach is the notion that issues are the language through which social movements organize and take action. As such, an understanding of the substance of issues and the symbols used to define that substance is crucial. In particular, we have argued that the meaning of an issue is a function of the symbolic representation of substantial demands. Some issues are defined so as to evoke extraordinarily strong emotional reactions while others are defined so as to minimize emotional reactions. Thus, how an issue is defined will have an important effect on mobilization efforts. With this in mind, in the next two chapters we examine the role that the specific issues of abortion and the Equal Rights Amendment have played in the feminist and New Right movements.

NOTES

1. In addition to excludability, most definitions of a "public good" also focus on "jointness of supply" (Laver 1981; Riker and Ordeshook 1973). Pure public goods are jointly supplied; that is, one member's consumption does not in any way diminish the supply available to others. However, jointness of supply is not especially relevant to the sort of goods we will be considering.

2. Olson (1971) argues that only in very small groups is it possible for the collective good to represent sufficient reward in and of itself to produce mobilization.

3. As mentioned, one exception would be in very small groups. Another exception would be when a few members of a group can expect to benefit disproportionately from the provision of the good, in which case, it may "pay" them to contribute without being induced by selective incentives.

4. The "categorical precedence" and "temporal relevance" of demands are also useful in understanding the substance of an issue (Cobb and Elder 1972b). But, these characteristics are not as relevant to the issues we will be considering and thus are not discussed.

5. "Lost" goods resemble "threatened" goods the most when they have only recently been lost in the sense that the value of the

lost good is more apparent and the urgency to reclaim the good may be greater. With the passage of time, however, the lost good will come to resemble more and more a new good in the sense that its value will become ambiguous and the urgency associated with recovering the good will dissipate.

3 / THE FEMINIST MOVEMENT

The proposition that issues are central to the growth of movements can be demonstrated by an analysis of the role of the abortion and ERA issues in the feminist movement and in the New Right countermovement. We have argued that these two issues, in turn, are part of a longer-term debate over the place of women within the family. In the next two chapters we describe the growth of each movement and the role played by family issues. We begin with the feminist movement.

THE ORIGINS OF FEMINISM

The decade of the 1960s, in contrast to the 1950s or even the 1970s, was a period of rapid cultural, social, and political change which set the stage for both the feminist movement and its counter-movement. Several important trends have been linked to feminism's emergence: blacks' success in the civil rights movement; an acceleration of the trend, begun in the 1950s, for more married women and mothers of young children to work outside the home; the expansion of opportunities for higher education and subsequently for student organizing on campus; traumatic national events such as the assassinations of national leaders, urban and campus riots, and the Vietnam War and the protest against it. These societal strains, particularly those accompanying the war and race questions, proved to be fertile ground for a variety of social movements: the counterculture or "hippie" movement, the New Liberals, the New Left, the civil rights movement, the ecology movement, the peace movement, and the women's liberation or feminist movement.

51

Feminist Discontents and Grievances

Women's perception of sexism in ideology and in practice spread slowly as more of them left universities to enter the work place in the 1960s. There they found low wages, occupational segregation by sex, and sexist hiring and promotion practices. While their objective status was the same as before (or perhaps even a bit better), their subjective status was different: now women began to perceive their status as inferior. Some, veterans of civil rights and New Left organizing, heard Stokely Carmichael say that "the only position for women in the movement is prone" (quoted in Freeman 1975, p. 57). Encouraged by the recent successes of other movements, women no longer held themselves responsible for existing conditions. Instead, they blamed their problems upon sexism in a variety of settings: home, school, job, politics, church, government, and society. This process of liberating oneself from blame was called "politicizing the personal." That is, the discontents in personal relationships were no longer unique to the individuals involved but their sexist aspects were linked to the unequal power balance between men and women.

Women interpreted their discontents and grievances in different ways, depending upon their basic political beliefs and philosophies. Radical and socialist feminists argued that a revolution was necessary to bring about equality between the sexes. For socialist feminists the revolution involved overthrowing capitalism as a first step. Reform-minded feminists, in contrast, sought to bring women into the mainstream of existing society and to put them on an equal footing with men. Though these feminists (e.g., Betty Friedan) sometimes used the term "revolution," they did not envision the overthrow of capitalism or the state. Both ends of the feminist spectrum, it should be emphasized, did have systemic change as a goal because both groups thought sexism pervaded every societal institution.

The radical and reform elements of the feminist movement also tended to adopt different styles and structures for action, usually related to their leaders' political beliefs and experience. The radical women tended to have a history of organizing in the civil rights and New Left movements and often adopted the technique of consciousness-raising practiced in small groups. Their structure was ideal for motivating women to recognize the political bases of their personal problems. The structure helped to achieve expressive goals but was not so functional, however, for facilitating sustained political activity. This loose alliance of small groups was called the women's liberation branch of the feminist movement.

Reformist women, with backgrounds in labor unions, political parties, and women's volunteer organizations, usually started organizations with more traditional features: a federal structure, dues, elected officers, etc. Their political actions included the more traditional lobbying and electoral activities aimed at bringing about long-term changes in the system. These more structured groups composed the women's rights branch of the feminist movement.

Feminist Goals

Feminism, whether radical or reform, has two broad goals: to change women's self-perceptions so that each individual woman is free to grow and achieve self-actualization whatever her circumstances and to change the institutional and societal conditions that create inequalities between the sexes. In short, women should be autonomous as individuals and equal to men.

Given these goals, the first target of most feminists was the family. Reform feminists such as Friedan reacted against the "momism" of the 1950s family and argued that roles other than housewife-mother must be allowed for women to be fulfilled. The existing structure of the nuclear family must be modified through equal division of household labor, communal and extended family living arrangements, part-time employment, and a variety of other policies that now seem rather mild. The family should be reformed, not abolished; after all, most of these women had husbands and children and lived in fairly traditional households.

Other feminists, however, took more serious issue with the family. In particular, radical feminists such as Firestone (1970) and Atkinson (1974) saw the major source of women's oppression to be their role in reproduction. Biological differences between the sexes give rise to male domination of women; men therefore are the enemy, not capitalism nor the state. It was said that "all married women are prostitutes" and that women would never be free until the patriarchal family was abolished. There was even a Society for Cutting Up Men (SCUM). These arguments were widely circulated by a media hungry for "good copy." In fact, Friedan (1981, p. 52) argues in her latest book that it was radical feminism that provoked Phyllis Schlafly and others:

> For the reactive rhetoric of sexual politics, distorting
> or denying certain painful or taken-for-granted real-
> ities of women's life, hardened into a ritual feminist

mystique that triggered an even more distorted and
virulent anti-feminist reaction.

It is clear, however, from our analysis in Chapter 1 that even
Friedan's milder version of reform feminism would be perceived
as a threat to the family because she was demanding autonomy and
freedom for the individual woman, not for women as a sex. To
politicize the personal is inevitably to politicize the family as traditionally defined. Given feminism's broad goals and the anti-male,
anti-family sentiments expressed by the more radical feminists in
the late 1960s, it is not surprising that the policy objectives of all
feminist groups would be perceived in the same anti-family light.

Feminist Issues

Feminism's goals are far reaching and forward looking,
proposing many changes for society. Specifically, feminists have
worked toward changes in the areas of child care, rape law,
spousal abuse, wage discrimination, sex role stereotyping in textbooks and in the media, property laws, divorce and child custody
laws, the advertising of employment positions, and occupational
segregation by sex. These issues are illustrative of the many role
equity issues pursued by feminists. As Gelb and Palley (1982)
explain, such policies extend rights enjoyed by other groups and
are narrow in scope. Feminists have had to fight much harder for
abortion rights and the ERA. These are examples of role change
issues, policies that are broader in scope and that produce change
in female roles.
The broad goals of equality and individual autonomy provide
the basic rationale for feminists' arguments in support of the ERA
and abortion rights (see Petchesky 1980, p. 662). With regard to
the ERA, feminists contend that equality is not present as long as
social and economic conditions differ between men and women.
Only a constitutional amendment of equal rights can guarantee
equality in law and lay a basis for the actual achievement of equality. Autonomy stresses the rights of individuals such as the freedom to pursue a career, to have or not to have children and so forth.
These are private decisions that would be ensured by a constitutional amendment of equal rights. For example, housewives supporting the ERA maintain that its adoption would lend dignity to
their role because it would become a position of choice.
Feminism's goals are also expressed in arguments on behalf
of abortion rights. They view reproductive freedom as basic to
the achievement of equality insofar as being tied down to large

numbers of children may reduce a woman's ability to take advantage of job choices. If men can pursue careers without worrying about childbearing and childrearing, then women are not equal unless they too can choose to have children. Further, the right to choose an abortion is a right to bodily self-determination (Petchesky 1980, p. 663). The right to have control over one's body evolves out of the concept of property rights, and particularly the concept of "property in one's person." Therefore, the woman, acting as an autonomous individual, must be allowed to choose abortion because it is her body and because she is the primary childrearer. The feminist contention is simply that the woman must make the choice about abortion; it does not say what the woman should decide, or on what basis (moral, religious, or otherwise) she should decide.

Besides the relation of the ERA and abortion rights to feminism's goals for a nonsexist society, a more strategic consideration impelled contemporary feminists toward these two issues. They were already on the societal agenda in the late 1960s. They could not be ignored though some moderate feminists preferred to stay out of the abortion controversy. There was already interest group support for both issues and it appeared that feminists were joining potentially winning causes. In the case of the ERA, older feminists, principally the National Woman's Party, had kept the amendment alive from the 1920s to the 1970s. Experienced congressional allies such as Representative Martha Griffiths were able in 1972 to force the proposed amendment to a floor vote where feminist and liberal lobbying could be effective. In the case of abortion rights, a number of medical, liberal, and population groups were meeting success in reforming states' abortion laws in the late 1960s. Before that effort had gotten very far, the Supreme Court granted what amounted to a repeal of all states' abortion laws in 1973. So the goal of reproductive freedom was seemingly achieved without a great deal of effort by feminists.

Thus feminists were involved in the ERA's passage and the securing of abortion rights, but their support was not decisive, particularly in the latter instance since it was decided in the judicial arena, not the legislative arena. Still, in the minds of the general public and particularly in the minds of the people who later joined in a countermovement, feminism was irretrievably linked to abortion, and abortion to the ERA. We will argue that this linkage occurred not because feminists were singlehandedly responsible for these policies. They were not strong enough as a movement by early 1973 to have accomplished so much alone.

Rather, we think that feminists' arguments in support of ERA and abortion were more threatening than were other groups' because feminists appealed to condensational symbols such as equality and autonomy for individual women. Individual rights for women are perceived as antithetical to the family, as explained in Chapter 1. Hence, such feminist arguments were more threatening, and more memorable, than were the arguments of other groups for the same policies. Feminists of the late 1960s and the early 1970s defined the issues of abortion and ERA in the terms they did because they were trying to transform a nascent social movement into a set of organizations that could act collectively. In the next section we examine the beginnings of this transformation.

THE MOBILIZATION OF FEMINISTS

Entrepreneurs

The mobilization process depends most crucially upon its leaders, political entrepreneurs who design organizations so as to attract followers to social movements. In the instance of the feminist social movement, the awareness of sexist practices had been spreading slowly since the early 1960s, yet it took specific events to precipitate the leaders' recognition of the need and opportunity for mobilization. For Betty Friedan, that event was the failure of a conference's leaders to treat sex discrimination as seriously as race discrimination. At the conference's end, Friedan and others formed an action organization because they felt that the time for conferences was over (Freeman 1975, p. 55). Thus began in June 1966 the National Organization for Women, the first and the largest organization among the women's rights branch. By 1980 NOW had 120,000 members and over 800 local chapters (Akey 1981).

The next year Shulamith Firestone had a similar negative experience which led her to establish the first women's liberation caucus. A New Left Conference leader refused to allow Firestone to present a resolution on female representation because the problems of the American Indian were more pressing (Evans 1979). She left the conference and began the women's liberation branch of the feminist movement. This sudden recognition of the need for a feminist movement separate from the other movements of the 1960s was repeated so often that the experience came to be known as a "click": the moment when one suddenly becomes radicalized.

For both Friedan and Firestone their previous experiences in organizing other movements provided a further impetus to start a new social movement. Firestone and the other women at the New Left Conference had years of organizing experience. Now Firestone realized that women needed to organize against their own oppression just as much as they had needed to help Southern blacks

previously. Similarly, the 28 others joining Friedan in starting
the National Organization for Women (NOW) saw that by using their
experience in civil rights and labor movements they could make a
difference for women.

Both the women's rights and the women's liberation sectors
of the feminist movement engaged in offensive mobilization, that is,
their leaders tried to attract members to attain their new goals of
equality and autonomy. The women's rights sector's mobilization
proceeded just as we would expect on the basis of the arguments
laid out in Chapter 2. A top-down structure was created: Friedan
and her cohorts started a national organization and encouraged
local chapters to join them. Soon a federal structure emerged
with local chapters collecting dues and sending a certain portion
on to the national organization. Officers were elected at each
level. As befits a core of skilled organizers, NOW got off to a
fast start: in one year the membership grew to 1,200; by 1974,
the membership was 40,000 with 700 local chapters (Spokeswoman
1975, p. 2). NOW members fit the profile of those who typically
engage in offensive mobilization. A survey of NOW members in
1974 showed that most were employed full-time, a plurality were
in professional jobs, and most were highly educated (Freeman
1975, p. 92; Carden 1974).

In 1968 Betty Boyer and others departed from NOW to start
another national feminist group, Women's Equity Action League
(WEAL). These more conservative women wanted to focus on employment, taxes, and education issues and to ignore abortion rights.
They adopted a federated structure but remained a small national
organization with only 3,500 members. Later they joined in the
support of abortion rights (Gelb and Palley 1982, p. 28). The
other major women's rights organization is the National Women's
Political Caucus, founded in 1971 by Bella Abzug, Gloria Steinem,
Betty Friedan, and Shirley Chisholm. Their aim is to get more
women elected and appointed to public office and to lobby for
women's issues. Like NOW, the Caucus is organized in all the
states, has 300 local chapters, and 45,000 members nationally
(Akey 1981).

The women's liberation sector of the feminist movement, in
contrast, was mass-based and had no national top-down organization. This is the structure we would expect, given their expressive
goals, experience, and ideology. Radical women created thousands
of small groups with few or no ties with one another, no hierarchical structure, and no elected leaders. As Freeman (1975) and
Evans (1979) have so ably pointed out, these structural characteristics are suited to personal change and growth but not to instrumental action. The outcome was a lack of internal coherence,

fragmentation, divisiveness, and an inability to channel energy into sustained political action.

After 1972, the women's liberation sector of the movement began to lose ground to the women's rights sector. For one thing, many radical women began to join NOW and other women's rights groups. Also NOW started its own consciousness-raising groups to provide its members with some personal politicization; at the same time NOW became more accepting of lesbian and radical members. NOW's slogan became "out of the mainstream, into the revolution." The women's rights sector, in contrast to the women's liberation branch, generated a number of social movement organizations (SMOs) that functioned as interest groups lobbying for feminist issues.

Strategies of Mobilization

Early feminist leaders professed forward-looking goals for a nonsexist society and consequently took an offensive mobilization posture. Their goals, like those of many other social movements, fit the definition of collective goods: these goods are jointly supplied and available to all women whether or not they are members of a feminist group. For example, the Equal Rights Amendment was a collective good whose ratification would have affected everyone regardless of group membership. Similarly, the securing of abortion rights maintains them for everyone who chooses that option. Given the familiar "free-rider" problem, we must inquire into the motivation for joining NOW or any other feminist SMO. Since feminist accomplishments would be available to all, why join a feminist group in the late 1960s?

Self-Interest and Selective Incentives

From our discussion of women's shared grievances and feminism's collective goals, it appears that these discontents would be ameliorated by adopting the set of policies feminist leaders proposed. Yet, these collective benefits would accrue regardless of any individual's actions. Therefore, according to Olson (1971), material benefits must have been offered selectively to entice potential members to join. Yet, none of the accounts (e.g., Freeman 1975 or Evans 1979) of early mobilization mentions the existence of such material benefits. Thus, we look for other avenues for mobilization.

Solidarity

Early feminist leaders such as Friedan and Firestone instead relied upon solidarity with existing organizations to attract members. Initially, Friedan took advantage of her cohort's solidary ties with political parties, labor unions, civil rights groups, and women's volunteer organizations. In its first year NOW benefited from the help of the United Auto Workers in staffing its national headquarters. The use of the communication network established by the Commissions on the Status of Women in the states was also crucial. Such preexisting networks were avenues for attracting women who felt like second-class citizens. Next Friedan attempted to create new solidary relationships by organizing mass demonstrations and protests around the country. For instance, the strike of August 26, 1970 expanded NOW's membership tremendously, by 50 to 70 percent in some cities (Freeman 1975, p. 85). Shortly thereafter, NOW instituted consciousness-raising (C-R) groups for its members to provide even stronger solidary bonds. Finally, NOW and other women's rights' groups have a greater claim upon latent feminist loyalties when the situation is desperate. For example, in the final months of the ERA ratification drive, money and memberships poured into NOW headquarters.

In like manner, Firestone appealed to the sense of common identity shared by women active in the civil rights and student left movements. Their communication network, consisting of journals, newsletters, and homes to stay in, has been repeatedly identified as important for the emergence of women's liberation groups around the country (Evans 1979; Freeman 1975). What Tilly (1978) calls "catnetness," i.e., the strength of shared identity and the density of networks, was particularly strong among the left. When the link was made between women's oppression and blacks' oppression, feminist leaders could build upon the strong solidary attachments accruing from years of organizing together. The C-R group was an important vehicle for forging solidary bonds among potential recruits new to leftish movements. Since such groups fulfilled expressive goals, they tended to be attractive when members' personal situations were urgent, i.e., in a time of life crisis rather than in a time of political crisis. Later, when these more radical women began to join reformist groups like NOW, they in turn strengthened its solidary basis.

Personal Principles

Finally, the role of individual principles appears to have been great for both sectors of the feminist movement. Evans (1979) and

Freeman (1975) both identify ideological principles as an important motivation for joining feminist groups and seem to give them equal weight with solidarity. For the women's rights branch, the analogy to blacks was often made. It was only just that the sexes be treated equally under the law, they argued. The success of the National Association for the Advancement of Colored People (NAACP) in bringing legal challenges implied that the time was ripe for women to mount similar assaults upon institutional sexism. Furthermore, the necessity for collective action was underscored by the negative experiences many professional women had in the working world. Unless women started their own movement like blacks had, inequalities would continue. Early feminist leaders were able to attract male followers as well because these conscience adherents believed that equality was a basic right.

For the women's liberation sector (WLM), the principle that women should be free and autonomous individuals was an extension of their views about other oppressed groups' rights to freedom. It was only just, therefore, that women's problems be treated as seriously as other groups'. The necessity for collective action by women was made clear when New Left men failed to treat their fellow female radicals as equals. The opportunity for success seemed high to these women with years of organizing experience. Moreover, the costs of not belonging to a WLM group appeared great because no one else was going to take care of women. If their goals of equality and autonomy were to be achieved, they believed that women had to start their own movement. Thus, a sense of urgency heightened the individuals' responsibility for collective action.

The Role of Outsiders in Mobilization

Although the women's rights branch of the feminist movement was formed in an era of governmental inaction, within a few years governmental actions were much more helpful. By 1972 congressional allies of feminists, many of them congresswomen themselves, had managed to pass the ERA. Congressional supporters of the women's movement helped to direct and organize the women's lobby. In fact, one scholar (Costain 1981a) at least implies that Congress's impact upon early feminist mobilization was equal to the women's lobby's impact upon Congress. Overall, by the early 1970s Congress was having a facilitative effect upon the movement.

The role of the media also evolved, but over a longer period of time, from being quite negative to being helpful. Initially, the establishment media ignored women's liberation groups and the formation of NOW. In the first few months of 1970, however, there was a press blitz in which virtually every major newspaper, magazine, and network did a story on feminism (Freeman 1975). These stories tended to play up the more sensational aspects of women's liberation activities: bra-burning, witch hexes on Wall Street, and the presence of lesbians (Robinson 1978, pp. 99-100). By 1973, the media's attention had turned to more moderate feminist organizations such as NOW. More serious examinations of women's status were regularly presented by major news organizations. Eventually, the media came to have a facilitative effect by legitimating the women's rights groups and their activities. In fact, New Right groups now complain about the liberal feminist bias of the news.

Finally, the outside groups already mentioned—unions, civil rights groups, and New Left groups—helped to lower the initial cost of organizing. Other established organizations such as religious groups, civil libertarian groups, and traditional women's volunteer groups lent an air of respectability to the feminist movement when they cooperated in lobbying efforts. The relationship with traditional women's groups like the League of Women Voters (LWV), the Business and Professional Women (BPW), and the American Association of University Women (AAUW) was particularly interesting. Their help was by no means assured. They had stressed volunteerism and nonpartisan political activity and, except for the BPW, they were still opposed to the ERA by the late 1960s.

Several reasons have been offered for the help traditional women's groups gave to feminists. First, the membership base of traditional and women's rights organizations is quite similar so it is plausible that members of traditional groups were undergoing their own consciousness-raising at the same time (Boles 1979, p. 50). Second, leaders of traditional women's groups feared they would lose potential members to feminist groups unless they changed their posture to encouragement (Boles 1979; Costain 1981a, p. 109). Thus, there were internal and external pressures on the traditional voluntary sector to cooperate with feminists on certain issues.

The Role of Issues in Feminist Mobilization

There was a plethora of issues for feminist leaders to tackle in the late 1960s, among them employment, child care, ERA, rape, and abortion. All of these related to feminism's goals of changing individual women and society. Of these, abortion and the ERA were issues already placed on the governmental agenda by other groups. In 1968 NOW adopted a Bill of Rights, whose first demand was that the ERA be passed by Congress and ratified by the states. Its last demand called for "the right of women to control their own reproductive lives," thus putting the abortion issue squarely in feminist terms.

Since the ERA was being considered in Congress (though not very seriously) and abortion reform was proceeding in the states (though slowly), it would have been difficult for the fledgling feminist organizations to have ignored these issues. Initially the pro-ERA and pro-choice positions did disrupt NOW. Union support ceased because the United Auto Workers were still in opposition to the ERA though two years later they reversed their stand. Furthermore, some feminists thought the movement should avoid the controversial issue of abortion and left to form WEAL. At the same time, a group of radical women accused NOW of having a reformist, not repeal, stand on abortion and left to form "The Feminists." Thus, NOW was unable to retain for very long its status as an umbrella feminist organization.

Feminist leaders sought to use the ERA and abortion issues to mobilize their followers. With regard to the ERA, leaders first tried to demonstrate the relevance of the amendment to its potential adherents. The ERA would solve some of women's discontents about the workplace; it was a rallying point for marches and demonstrations that conferred solidarity; it was directly linked to the principle of equality for all. For example, ERAmerica mentions "for full and permanent equality" and "a matter of simple justice" in its literature. The ERA's relevance was enhanced by defining it in terms of the symbol equality (Boles 1979). Equality is a high-order, condensational symbol particularly useful for attracting conscience adherents.

The ERA, of course, was a new good and feminists were engaged in an offensive mobilization effort, an inherently difficult task. As explained above, feminists needed to gain followers by stressing the far-reaching effects of the amendment and its potential to solve all the grievances of women. Yet, the short sentence "equality of rights under the law shall not be denied or abridged by the United States or any state on account of sex" is subject to a variety of interpretations. Once in the Constitution, the statement is nearly irreversible. Moreover, the stress on the symbol equality tends to expand conflict. These qualities set the stage for a reaction against the amendment.

Likewise, the feminists' symbolization of the abortion issue both transformed abortion politics in the late 1960s and allowed for a later escalation of the conflict by defensive mobilizers. In the mid-1960s abortion was defined primarily as a narrow and technical medical issue rather than a moral one. Except for the Catholic

Church, very few people could see dangers arising from incremental reforms in state abortion laws (Tatalovich and Daynes 1981,
p. 37). However, the demand for repeal phrased in terms of "a
woman's right to control her own body," voiced by NOW in 1968,
by radical women's liberation groups, and in 1969 by the newly
formed National Association for Repeal of Abortion Laws (NARAL),
was a different story. Lawrence Lader, the founder of NARAL,
contended that equality is meaningless unless a woman controls her
own procreation; birth control is the most basic of women's free-
doms (Lader 1973, p. 18).

Once again feminists' language was calculated to demonstrate
the relevance of the collective good to the individuals targeted for
mobilization. The absolutist stance was especially designed to
appeal to the self-interest of the younger and more radical feminists
concerned about reproductive control. Furthermore, solidary ties
were reinforced since all women share the possibility of pregnancy.
Finally, the repeal language used responded to individual principles.
Such condensational symbols were interpreted by others to mean
"abortion on demand." Thus, the same language that attracted
many feminists repelled others and led to conflict.

FEMINIST COLLECTIVE ACTION

Beginning in 1968, the number of women's rights organizations
began to multiply as did the number of women's liberation small
groups. All women's rights organizations tended to have similar
structures but focused on somewhat different issues, though eventually all were pro-ERA and pro-choice. As we would expect of
offensive mobilization, women's rights groups usually had federated
structures operated from the top down. All of these groups adopted
a strategy of advocacy and selected their targets of influence. They
concentrated on Congress to pass the ERA; they focused on certain
state legislatures for abortion law repeal; they brought suit in several federal courts. Since the groups were stronger at the national
level than at the grass roots level, they tended to select targets in
Washington, New York City, or elsewhere that could be swayed by
the national media.

Forms of Collective Action

Their activities in support of the ERA provide a good example
of feminists' methods for advocacy. NOW undertook direct lobbying
of congressmen and congresswomen to pass the ERA. Once the

amendment was sent to the states for ratification, major proponent groups formed a coalition, ERAmerica. Begun in 1976, this coalition represents 250 organizations, including feminist groups, traditional women's groups, liberal organizations, and churches. Its members supply lobbying expertise, expert testimony, and money. Feminist organizations also initiated a limited amount of litigation during the ratification period. For example, NOW intervened to protect its own boycott of nonratified states.

Feminists and their allies also engaged in grassroots lobbying. To get the ERA out of Congress the BPW generated 100,000 letters to members of Congress (Freeman 1975, p. 218). Feminists also participated in protest activities. Some of these were directed at the Congress. Others, such as the strike of August 26, 1970, were designed to impress the bystander public as well. Toward the end of the ratification drive a few feminists even fasted in an effort to pressure the Illinois legislature.

Electoral activities have become an increasingly important weapon. For the last several years, the National Women's Political Caucus (NWPC) has been identifying pro-ERA candidates and helping to elect them in the unratified states. For example, in 1980 the Caucus had political action committees (PACs) in eight unratified states, spending around $60,000 (Congressional Quarterly 1980e, p. 1814). Finally, in recent years feminists have begun to advocate a single-issue voting strategy based on legislators' ERA votes.

Feminist activities on the abortion issue are another example of advocacy strategies. Initially, the targets of influence were those state legislatures considering abortion reform or repeal in the late 1960s. Members of women's liberation groups disrupted legislative hearings, arguing that women were the only real experts on abortion (Hole and Levine 1971, p. 296). Later one group, the Redstockings, held their own counterhearings on abortion. Radical feminists were also active in providing abortion referrals before abortion was legalized. In contrast, moderate feminists and traditional women's groups testified in state legislative hearings, lobbied, organized phone banks, and gathered signatures for petitions.

During the pre-Roe period feminist organizations were new entrants to an already active group environment. It was definitely in their interest to pursue a strategy of cooperation with the more entrenched activists. One important ally was the 200,000 member American Civil Liberties Union (ACLU) which entered the abortion controversy in 1968 by denouncing all abortion laws on the grounds that "every woman, as a matter of her right to the enjoyment of life, liberty and privacy, should be free to determine whether and when to bear children" (quoted in Epstein 1981, p. 8). Subsequently the ACLU pursued a series of test cases. Population groups such as the Population Law Center and Zero Population Growth were also important allies in the pre-Roe period. Finally, feminists worked with physicians' groups. The change in the attitude of physicians was perhaps the most instrumental factor in the initial reform of state abortion laws and in the Supreme Court's decision to repeal abortion laws.

Once the Roe decision was announced in January 1973, the composition of the organizational environment changed somewhat. Many leaders, especially in the medical establishment, felt that the abortion battle was won and turned their attention to other more pressing issues (Jaffe et al. 1981, p. 46). A handful of groups, primarily feminists and single-issue abortion groups, tried to cope with the implementation of the Court's decision. Feminist lobbying activities expanded to include litigation; NOW entered amicus curiae briefs in several cases (O'Connor 1980, pp. 96-98). NARAL, changing its name to the National Abortion Rights Action League, continued its leadership as the largest single-issue abortion group. Since its membership is predominantly female, urban, liberal, professional, and feminist (Gelb and Palley 1981, p. 5) and most of its leadership is feminist, a substantial amount of feminist abortion rights activity is routed through NARAL. It presently has 100,000 members and chapters in all states (National Abortion Rights Action League, personal communication, undated b). Other important feminist allies in the abortion fight were the Religious Coalition for Abortion Rights (RCAR) and Planned Parenthood (PP). The latter currently is mounting a $3.6 million education and organizing campaign (Planned Parenthood, personal communication, undated).

In the mid-1970s feminist organizations like NOW began to engage in electoral actions to defeat pro-life congressmen. By 1980 feminist groups and their pro-choice allies were using the targeting strategy favored by pro-lifers in 1978. For example, the Friends of Family Planning formed a PAC in 1979 to support pro-choice incumbents and challengers in the 1980 congressional elections. Voters for Choice and NARAL used similar targeting tactics.

Success of Collective Action

The success of the feminist movement, like that of any other movement, can be evaluated in terms of two criteria: gaining acceptance and gaining new advantages. Feminist social movement organizations have clearly gained acceptance as members of the polity. Their diverse targets of influence, be they Congress or state legislatures or other public officials, accept feminist groups as valid spokespersons for women. In terms of new advantages, a number of early feminist goals—equal credit legislation, equal access to educational opportunities, changes in state laws on rape, divorce, and child custody—have been attained. Yet, the successes tend to be those policies perceived as role equity issues. When the policies involve significant role change, feminists have experienced difficulty. The attempt to secure constitutionally the collective good of equal rights has failed. Furthermore, the goal of abortion rights was achieved, only to be chipped away by federal funding reductions and now is threatened by the passage of a constitutional amendment or statute overturning Roe.

While we will examine reasons for feminism's lack of concrete success throughout the book, certain elements of an explanation are clear from our survey of its mobilization and organizational phases. First, feminists, especially the radical women's liberation movement, framed their appeals to potential members in condensational symbols: equality and justice would be brought about by the ERA; freedom and control over one's own body would be gained from abortion choice. Such appeals were necessary, it appeared, to attract members on the basis of self-interest, individual principles, and solidarity. However, such broad symbols, especially when linked to other sweeping changes in the late 1960s, kindled the opposition.

By the end of 1972, according to Boles (1979) and Hacker (1980), the ERA conflict had escalated. It moved from being what Boles describes as a relatively closed technical debate among interest groups in Congress to being a broad-based, emotional debate among ad hoc groups in the community. The number of states ratifying decreased after 1972 and the rescissions or second-thoughts began. The pro-ERA forces did not even organize an effective coalition until 1976 when ERAmerica was formed. Its efforts resulted in one more state ratifying (Indiana in 1977) and in Congress's extending the deadline in 1978. But even an all-out effort, well-publicized and well-financed, from 1980 to 1982 did not result in any more adoptions.

The abortion conflict has been described by Tatlovich and Daynes (1981) as having undergone a similar transformation from an interest group conflict in the 1960s to a community conflict in the 1970s. In the 1960s, debates on abortion law reform were technical, not moral, debates among interested parties such as medical doctors. In contrast, the Roe repeal decision was an abrupt departure from past incremental decisions and opened the door for an escalation of conflict among ad hoc community groups on both the pro-choice and pro-life sides. Feminist symbols were especially notable in this debate for their absolutism. Given the coincidence of the timing of the two issues, it was easy for abortion, ERA, and women's liberation to become intertwined in the minds of the mass public.

Since the Roe decision in 1973 the momentum has shifted to the antiabortion side at the state and national levels in both the judicial and the legislative branches. As we have discussed already, there was a crucial organizational failure immediately after the Roe decision when pro-choice groups temporarily rested, though feminist groups were among those still active in this phase. This illustrates the difficulty of keeping a sense of urgency alive once the new good has been attained.

The rise of pro-family and other New Right groups in the mid-1970s played an important part in deterring feminists from meeting their goals, particularly in defeating the ERA and in turning the tide on the abortion issue. In the next chapter we explore the role of these groups in expanding the scope of these conflicts.

4 / THE NEW RIGHT

Just as feminism began as a reaction to the traditionalism of the 1950s, the very success of the feminist movement spawned another movement: the pro-family sector of the New Right. This sector initially mobilized against abortion rights and the ERA but by the late 1970s it had expanded to other women's issues and had appropriated the "pro-family" label. At the same time, other sectors of the New Right, as well as some parts of the Old Right, began to coopt the pro-family movement. The secular New Right grew from a focus on economic issues to encompass social and family issues, and the Religious Right openly joined in the fight against feminism. By 1982 this loose coalition of organizations had managed to defeat the ERA, to limit severely abortion rights, and to curtail enforcement of anti-discrimination laws. Thus, it is appropriate for us to consider all sectors of the New Right in our analysis.

THE ORIGIN OF THE NEW RIGHT

The emergence of feminism as a serious force sometime between 1970 and 1972 coincided with a number of other movements that together transformed the traditional lines of class conflict in this country. The expansion of higher education enlarged the intelligentsia; it, in turn, was inclined to reject traditional norms and life styles (Ladd 1978, p. 51). Economic advances moved many blue-collar workers into the same middle-income category previously occupied by the New Intellectuals, thus forming a New Bourgeoisie. However, this new middle class of blue-collar workers, often dubbed the Silent Majority, was supportive of traditional con-

68

servative values and the "old morality." Meanwhile, the war in Vietnam affected moral and social norms (Phillips 1982, p. 21). Finally, rioting by college students and urban blacks disturbed many people.

Grievances and Discontents

Many members of this New Bourgeoisie came to feel that their morals, their standards, their religion, indeed all those things they held dear, were under attack from the counterculture and the New Intellectuals. The very structure of society was seriously threatened by a number of "isms" such as humanism, liberalism, and feminism. Because of its visibility and its link with the New Intellectuals, we argue that the feminist movement came to represent in concrete terms the larger status conflict in society. From the Silent Majority's perspective, women's liberation symbolized all that was wrong with America. While the old class conflict between the working and middle classes was lessened by the rising economy, the status conflict was exacerbated as rapid changes denigrated the Silent Majority's life-style, family structure, and morality. Improved economic circumstances allowed time to focus on the radical nature of the changes advocated by feminist and other social movements of the late 1960s and early 1970s.

Like the temperance and the anti-evolution movements earlier in the century, the Silent Majority sought to restore the moral status quo. It rejected the values of feminists and the New Intellectuals and demanded symbolic recognition of traditional values and life-styles. Thus, there was fertile ground for leaders who would organize against specific threats like legalized abortion, gay rights, busing, textbooks selected by professionals, airwaves regulated by the government, pornography, sex education in the schools, and later on against the Education Department and the Trilateral Commission. Similarly, the time was ripe to organize against the perceived sources of those threats: modernism, relativism, humanism, individualism, intellectualism, professionalism, and feminism.

The Role of Beliefs and Attitudes

Certain beliefs and attitudes aided the Silent Majority's interpretation of these specific events and their possible causes. We have mentioned that members of the New Bourgeoisie tend to be conservative. A basic principle of conservatism is order. Reichley (1981, p. 7) describes this core value as

the prerequisite for enjoyment of all other human values (security, community, affectional relationships,
social justice, even freedom). But unfortunately . . .
order is also fragile, thinly stretched over the mouth
of chaos, maintainable only through unremitting efforts
at social discipline and self-restraint.

The belief in order leads conservatives to fear the unknown,
to magnify the consequences of change, and to see rapid change in
one area of life as threatening other values. According to this perspective, the key institutions that maintain order are the family and
religion. The strength and stability of families determine the vitality and moral life of society; thus, as the family goes, so goes the
nation. In addition to the family, the church cherishes and trans-
mits the values of the state, i.e., Western cultural values of Christian churches. Hence, the stability of society depends upon Christians.

A second belief of conservatives is in limited government:
the state should perform certain housekeeping functions and not in-
terfere with private property, the family, and the church. The
changes brought about by the welfare state thus can be opposed on
purely secular grounds as intrusions of "big government" into private life and property. In fact, such interference is often viewed
as just another step toward communism.

The changes of the late 1960s and early 1970s then were interpreted by the Silent Majority as threatening order and as hurting
capitalism. Particularly threatening were changes in the family
and the evident demeaning of Christian values. Gradually, a social
movement emerged that sought to restore the values it saw as lost:
order, stability, religion, home, morality, freedom. The movement calls itself the New Right, partially to distinguish itself from
the Old Right who allowed these changes to happen.

Movement Goals and Issues

Though the movement's goals are quite broad and vary somewhat by sector (as will be seen), all parts of the New Right are in
agreement about the goals of restoring family, religion, and morality to their place, creating order, and maintaining freedom from
big government.

A number of issues could be linked to these broad goals. The
issues the New Right has chosen to emphasize are those which best
reestablish the Right as the group that defines public morality, in
short issues that put humanists and feminists in their place (Fair-

banks 1981, p. 9). If the evils advocated by secular elites are defeated, then official recognition is gained for the cultural values and
life-style of the New Right. In other words we contend that an issue
like the ERA is chosen more for its symbolic value than because it
would really hurt housewives if the ERA were passed. Thus, a con-
gressperson's support of the Education Department or opposition to
the defense budget becomes immoral. From the perspective of symbolic politics (and from the perspective of the New Right), these are
not contradictory positions held by irrational individuals. Rather,
these are stances which defend their culture and morality against
pro-education people and anti-defense people. Being against education and for defense are rationally related to New Right goals.

The defensive goals of the New Right translated rather easily
into opposition to the ERA and abortion issues espoused by feminists.
First of all, order is threatened by feminism in general and by the
ERA in particular. Fitzgerald (1981b, p. 25) casts Phyllis Schlafly's
argument against the ERA in these very terms:

> Sexual freedom has dissolved the bonds of the society,
> leaving nothing but a quasi-criminal anarchy in the
> home, the workplace, and the school. She claims that
> "women's lib" bears large responsibility for this an-
> archy, and she calls for the strengthening of the laws
> against it.
>   . . . if women behave themselves sexually, then
> men will have to marry them, stay married, and sup-
> port them. That there exists a trade-off between
> sexual propriety and financial security for women is in
> fact the underlying theme of all the "pro-family" groups
> from the Right-to-Lifers to the fundamentalists.

Similarly, legalized abortion is a threat to order, and hence
to civilization as we know it. Legalizing abortion tears up the social
contract. It is alleged that anyone who would kill fetuses would also
murder the aged and the handicapped, and in general be willing to
carry out a Nazi-like extermination of undesirables.

Second, the ERA as advocated by feminists threatens the
church and family. It is argued that the Bible sets up a hierarchy
of God-man-woman, that will be violated by the ERA. Furthermore,
the granting of equality to individual men and women threatens the
family and its functionally defined roles:

> Man and woman have never been equal, aren't equal
> and can never be equal as long as they exist. Each
> was given a different role, a role that complimented

(sic) the other, roles that blend into a harmonious unit.
This unit is called the family and the family is the core
of society. Now society can be good or depraved, civi-
lized or uncivilized. It either possesses order or chaos
depending on the degree in which the male and female
sex roles are accepted or rejected. Thus, it is, that
moral degeneration replaces moral virtues, and
SOCIETY RETRACTS BACK, back, back INTO BAR-
BARISM!! (Parents of Minnesota, no date).

Likewise, abortion is viewed as a threat to the family and to
the church because it violates the commandment "thou shalt not kill."
All Christians should oppose abortion, "because it is a violation of
God's fundamental laws for human society and will surely draw down
His judgment on the whole nation, not only on those who have and
perform abortions, but also on those who tolerate and pay for them"
(Christian Action Council, no date). Those who root their opposition to abortion in the Bible believe that any allowance for reproductive choice is government intrusion into their religion.

Third, the ERA can be viewed as an expansion of federal
power into areas heretofore reserved either to the states or to the
family: marriage, property, child custody, and abortion regulation (Schlafly 1977, p. 130). Senator Sam Ervin writes in the
Phyllis Schlafly Report (1977, p. 5) that: "The Equal Rights Amendment will convert the States from sovereign authorities in the constitutional field now assigned to them into rather meaningless zeroes
on the nation's map."

If ERA is a federal power grab, then it follows that abortion
is too because ERA and abortion are seen as intertwined. The nation's Court told states to deregulate abortions, further intruding
upon the right of a male to control his wife and his wife's body. The
Right seeks to "reprivatize" relations within the family by repealing
laws against spousal and child abuse that assert the rights of individuals within the family. Rather, the Right wants to protect the
family as a corporate entity against government. Further, from
the perspective of conservatives, it is not surprising that the first
attack upon abortion rights should be to limit federal funding of
Medicaid abortions. The welfare state is an intrusion upon private
property; abortion is also; therefore, welfare funding of abortions
is a double insult.

Finally, there is the suggestion that the long-term result of a
weakened society is socialism. Welfare destroys the work ethic
and abortion destroys the family ethic (Sobran 1981, p. 15). Once
private property, the family, and religion have been destroyed (i.e.,
brought under control of the state), then some form of socialism

takes over. Moreover, some conservatives see the ERA as a step toward socialism and ultimately communism. The argument is that the Soviet Union has an ERA and therefore people who want communism in this country will support the ERA. Some feminists, they contend, are unwitting dupes of this cause; others are Marxists and hence naturally would be for the ERA.

In summary, the New Right regarded feminists' advocacy of the ERA and of abortion repeal as an attack upon church and family, and ultimately as an attack upon the very basis for an orderly society. Because of the centrality of these issues to core beliefs of conservatism, the ERA and abortion conflicts provided a motivation for a countermovement. As Petchesky (1981, p. 235) points out, the backlash against feminism is in fact a measure of the _effectiveness_ of the women's movement in changing women's roles. In the next section we describe the process by which the Silent Majority was mobilized into the New Right.

THE MOBILIZATION OF THE NEW RIGHT

Though conservatives were obviously deeply troubled by the changes they observed in American society in the late 1960s and the early 1970s, initially there was surprisingly little reaction. The most plausible explanation for the long incubation period is that many conservatives, especially those who were fundamentalists or evangelicals, believed in the separation of church and state and valued personal piety rather than social involvement. At some critical point, the threat from secular elites became so great that fundamentalists jettisoned their belief in the wall of separation. The Right came to see itself as an embattled minority whose job it was to restore morality through politics. Hence, morality became politicized for them just as the "personal" had become political a few years earlier for the feminists. This mobilization occurred at different times for different sectors of the Right and greatly depended upon when entrepreneurs became politicized.

The Entrepreneurs of the Right

Several political entrepreneurs played a major role in initiating the mobilization process. Many of them can recall their "click" points. For Richard Viguerie, publisher of Conservative Digest and direct mail expert, the "click" came when President Jerry Ford chose Nelson Rockefeller as his Vice-President in 1974 (Viguerie 1981, p. 50). For Jerry Falwell, founder of Moral Majority and prime-time preacher, the "click" was either the Supreme Court's 1973 abortion decision, or the pornography explosion, or the FCC's applying the fairness doctrine to remarks about homosexuals, or the regulation of Christian schools (Fitzgerald 1981a, pp. 121-122). For Phyllis Schlafly it was in 1971 when a friend persuaded her to read and debate the ERA rather than national defense (Felsenthal 1981, p. 240).

Schlafly is a particularly interesting example. She literally was the anti-ERA movement for many years and is the major figure in the pro-family sector of the New Right. As is often true of social movement leaders, she was an experienced entrepreneur. In fact, she did not find time from her other organizing activity to found STOP ERA until October of 1972. In this effort she used her own communication network, primarily the 3000 recipients of the Phyllis Schlafly Report, and money from her Eagle Trust Fund. An early ERA supplement to the Report became the STOP ERA newsletter which now has about 30,000 subscribers (Felsenthal 1981, p. 195).

Schlafly immediately made a difference in the ERA ratification process. By February 1973, only a few months after she entered the ERA fray, nearly every ERA news story mentioned Schlafly (Felsenthal 1981, p. 242). That year she convinced legislators in Nebraska to rescind their earlier vote and was instrumental in Alabama's defeat of the amendment. By the late 1970s Schlafly was leading all the anti-ERA campaigns in the 15 unratified states.

In 1975 Schlafly attempted to broaden her constituency beyond the ERA to other pro-family issues. She started the Eagle Forum which now claims 50,000 members nationwide (Akey 1981). It is self-described as "a national organization of women and men who believe in God, Home, and Country, and are determined to defend the values that have made America the greatest nation in the world" (Eagle Forum, no date a).

For leaders of smaller local organizations, some of the precipitating events were the school textbook controversy in 1974 in Kanawha County, West Virginia; state ERA ratification battles; the Supreme Court's 1973 abortion decision; battles over gay rights such as Anita Bryant's crusade in Dade County, Florida, or the 1978 referendum in St. Paul, Minnesota; eliminating prayer in the public schools; busing problems in Boston and Los Angeles; or attending the International Women's Year (IWY) Conference in Houston in 1977. IWY was the equivalent of "boot camp" for many conservative women, according to pro-family leader Rosemary Thomson (1981, p. 22). In Houston they discovered that Judeo-Christian values, the nuclear family, and other institutions had been replaced by humanism and feminism, all funded by the federal government. Thomson says:

The unfair bias of this $5 million taxpayer financed
fiasco and the disgusting display of open lesbian affec-
tion and homosexual didos (sic) literally traumatized
those of us who believed in traditional moral values
(Thomson 1981, p. ii).

The Structure of the New Right

While the feminists used a top-down organization in an uphill
struggle on behalf of a new public good, the Right often uses the
mirror image. First, "pro-family" organizations on the Right thus
far are mass-based, "bottom-up" organizations, as we would predict for a defensive mobilization effort. There are hundreds, if not
thousands, of grassroots groups that form on an ad hoc basis. Often
an organizer like Schlafly will be in touch with the local organization
but the ad hoc group will not be started by her nor will it join her
organization. These groups exist until the threat is defeated, then
disband. Second, the counter organizations are typically engaged
in trying to veto rather than initiate change. For example, they try
to stop busing at a crucial point, to defeat a gay rights referendum,
or to defeat the ERA in 15 states. The latter is much easier than is
trying to pass the ERA in 38 states. Because the New Right is mobilizing on behalf of public goods that are threatened or lost, their
struggles are typically easier than are those working for new goods.

The divisions among various New Right groups roughly parallel
the goods they see threatened. The oldest sector is the secular New
Right. The secular New Right sees capitalism, economic stability,
and ultimately freedom as threatened by big government, bureau-
cratic regulation and intervention, the retreat from the gold standard, and the American worker's lack of productivity. New Right
leaders blame both liberal policies pursued by administrations since
1945 and the ineffectual opposition of the Old Right for this economic
decline. The secular New Right champions its own solutions to economic decline, such as the supply side theory of Arthur Laffer, and
rejects traditional Republican "balance the budget" economics.

However, within the secular New Right itself, there are important social theorists such as George Gilder (1981) who blame
our economic problems on a loss of faith, morals, and family structure. Most of the New Right's leaders—such as Paul Weyrich,
Richard Viguerie, Terry Dolan, and Howard Phillips—are social as
well as economic conservatives who are far more upset with the
moral and cultural tone of 1970s liberalism than with its economics.
Weyrich himself says their conservativism is based in religion, not
economics (Phillips 1982, p. 48). The major organizations in this

sector are Weyrich's Committee for the Survival of a Free Congress, Dolan's National Conservative Political Action Committee (NCPAC), and Phillips' Conservative Caucus. Disaffected with the Old Right, in the mid-1970s these three men split off and formed their own organizations, taking fortunes such as the Coors beer money with them. Aided by the new federal laws on political action committees (PACs), they and Viguerie raised further money through direct mail contacts.

A second sector of the New Right is the Religious Right. The Religious Right sees religion, the family, and morality as threatened by various social movements such as humanism, liberalism, and feminism. Developments like no prayer in public schools, reproductive freedom, IRS regulation of the tax status of Christian schools, pornography, and explicit television shows are perceived as direct assaults upon religious freedom and the traditional values fostered by church and home. Leaders of the Religious Right tend to agree with the New Right's economic conservatism as well. In fact, secular New Right leaders in late 1978 recognized the electoral potential of born-again Christians and the organizing potential of the "Electronic Church." The next year Viguerie, Robert Billings, and Ed McAteer lent their expertise in mass mailing and organizing to the Christian Right, helping to start several major organizations, most notably the Moral Majority.

The principal groups in this sector are: Jerry Falwell's Moral Majority, James Robinson's Religious Roundtable, and Pat Robertson's Christian Voice. These groups claim huge national memberships and large budgets: Moral Majority has a 400,000 person mailing list and a budget of $1.2 million; Roundtable, a budget of $750,000; Christian Voice, 190,000 members and a budget of $1.5 million (Congressional Quarterly 1980b, p. 2).

The third sector of the New Right is the "pro-family" movement. This sector views the family as a primary target of attack by humanists, feminists, liberals, and bureaucrats. While they tend to be economic conservatives like the secular New Right, religious conservatives like the Religious Right, and anti-communists like the Old Right, they accord the protection of the family highest priority. Some observers, such as conservative Alan Crawford, assert that the pro-family movement just occupies the women while the men worry about the more important things:

> While the men of the New Right symbolically guard the
> frontier from external threats, exercising their ener-
> gies on macho issues like gun ownership, national de-
> fense, law and order, and "free-market" economics,
> the women—with some help from sympathetic male
> politicians and preachers—protect hearth and home
> from threats to their way of life (1980, p. 144).

Initially, this sector was composed of single-issue groups such as anti-abortion and anti-ERA groups. In the late 1970s this countermovement started calling itself "pro-family." Such a label is a shorthand way of summarizing opposition to feminism and coopts the family as the movement's symbol. The pro-family newsletter The Right Woman portrays itself in this way:

> The media have attempted to erroneously paint the Pro-Family Movement as being only anti-abortion and anti-ERA. The Pro-Family Movement is a broad-based coalition of social conservatives who recognize the value of the person, the importance of the family, the rights and responsibilities of parents, and the importance of restricting government so that there can be personal freedom (Gasper 1981, p. 64).

We can find no one taking credit for the term pro-family, but it might have been invented by secular New Right leaders. Weyrich of the Committee for the Survival of a Free Congress was the first to recognize the mobilizing potential of family issues, according to Viguerie (1981, pp. 152-154). Weyrich has sought to add pro-life and pro-family groups to the New Right's coalition because he views the battle over family values as "the most significant battle of the age-old conflict between good and evil, between the forces of God and forces against God, that we have seen in our country" (Conservative Digest, 1980b, p. 15).

The three sectors of the New Right (the secular New Right, Religious Right, pro-family Right) have interconnected philosophies, bases of support, leadership, and tactics. Unlike the women's liberation sector of the feminist movement, all three sectors of the New Right have made the transition from social movement to social movement organizations and are organized for political action. Given this integration, we think it is appropriate to analyze the entire New Right countermovement, not just the pro-family sector.[1]

Strategies of Mobilization

Thus far we have concentrated upon the leadership and structure of the New Right. But why do people join? What kinds of appeals are effective to the constituencies described above? In this section we examine the three motivations for joining, as well as the effect of urgency.

Self-Interest and Selective Incentives

New Right leaders identified a number of policies whose defeat would help to restore the moral status quo. The achievement of these goals was in the interest of conservative individuals. Yet why incur the cost of joining a group for collective benefits? None of the literature we examined from New Right groups mentioned any selective material benefits beyond receiving a newsletter or mailings. The answer lies in the fact that defensive mobilization through self-interest is easier than is mobilizing for a new good. The individual's personal stake in taking collective action is high, rendering selective incentives less crucial.

Solidarity

New Right leaders have relied heavily upon existing solidarity networks such as fundamentalist churches, the Catholic Church, and the Old Right's organizations. Leaders of the New Religious Right quote Scripture asserting that it is a Christian's duty to get involved in politics. Christian Voice and other groups publish morality ratings of congressmen to aid Christians in performing their duties. Because of their religiosity, fundamentalist Christians ought to be high in what Tilly (1978) calls "catnetness." Several writers (Fitzgerald 1981a; Guth 1981, p. 23) have stated that the most fertile ground for the Moral Majority is among the "first modernizing generation," those who move off the farm into the smaller cities and experience culture shock. They find that their fundamentalist values are not shared by everyone, and their economic status is not high. Therefore, they retreat into the shelter of the church.

Similarly, many pro-life and pro-family groups have relied upon solidarity with the Catholic Church in their appeals. The church's opposition to abortion was enunciated in 1968 in Humanae Vitae, providing a moral absolute to be followed by millions of Catholics. In 1975 the National Conference of Catholic Bishops approved a Pastoral Plan for Pro-Life Activities that was the political implementation of the church's position. Though the Catholic hierarchy and the national Right to Life (RTL) organizations are circumspect in their connections, some allege that the church is frequently directly involved in local political activities. Jaffe et al. (1981, p. 78) write: "Local RTL organizations have from the earliest days been dominated by anti-abortion Catholic supporters, Catholic symbolism and imagery, and—most important—Catholic resources."

The Mormon church appears to function in much the same way as many of the leaders and some of the organizations (e.g., United Families of America) of the pro-family movement are Mormon.

In addition, New Right organizers have successfully appealed
to the economic conservativism and patriotism of the Old Right.
The organizers of the New Right took the Old Right's money and
mailing lists and expanded them, thus significantly lowering initial
mobilization costs. They were able to link causes like defeating the
ERA to Old Right goals such as capitalism and small government.
Schlafly, for example, argues (Eagle Forum, no date b) that the
ERA is just a blank check for federal judges, bureaucrats, and politicians.

Normative Appeals

It also seems likely that many people join New Right groups
out of normative motivations. These individuals desire collective
goods like the defeat of the ERA, reimposition of the gold standard,
or a ban on abortions, because they see these goods as involving
important moral and philosophical principles. They value the preservation of the traditional family, the protection of religion against
secular humanism, and the preservation of economic freedom from
"big brother" in Washington.

The genius of New Right organizers lay in their ability to identify changes in society that conservatives find threatening, to locate
a cause for these changes, and to link particular liberal and feminist policies to these changes and their causes. At a highly symbolic level, then, New Right leaders appeal to individual principles.
They tend to advocate constitutional amendments (e. g., balanced
budget, no ERA, the HLA) rather than statutes because the constitution embodies the principles of our society. They are particularly
effective in calling upon constituents' religious principles and their
sense of order. Their effectiveness is enhanced by the fact that
threatened goods are valued more highly than new goods; hence, defensive mobilization based on ideological incentives is relatively
easy.

Urgency

The urgency of the conservative position by the mid to late
1970s also helped its leaders' defensive mobilization efforts. Recall that in the case of threatened goods, urgency is primarily a
function of necessity. Certainly a continuing theme of New Right
entrepreneurs is the need to act now. For example, evangelists'
appeals include phrases like "the hour is at hand; we are on a fast
slide to national suicide unless Christians take a stand and save
freedom." The writings of pro-family and secular New Right leaders are similarly apocalyptic. It was urgent that the ERA be stopped
before the 1979 (later the 1982) deadline. Moreover, it is urgent

that recently lost goods like abortion bans be recovered since from
the New Right's perspective, babies are being legally murdered
every day.

A related point that lowers the cost of mobilization on behalf
of familiar goods is their relative certainty compared to new goods.
It is easier to create a sense of urgency about familiar goods than
about unknown goods. The traditional nuclear family and all male
combat troops, for example, are known quantities. People who fear
the ERA will bring changes within their own family or within the
army are attracted by Schlafly's assertion that the ERA's defeat will
remove such changes. Furthermore, fears about these unknown new
goods are easily generalizable. Witness how easily Schlafly has tied
the ERA into a variety of distressing situations: homosexual marriages, abortion on demand, and the weakening of our nation's defense. In like manner, pro-life groups have been able to move from
simply being against abortion to linking abortion advocacy to a number of other distasteful things: euthanasia and lack of concern for
the handicapped and the aged. New Right entrepreneurs like Schlafly
or Falwell often use condensational symbols to heighten the ambiguity
about new goods and the threat to old goods.

In a situation of urgency it is easy to portray the costs of not
belonging to a group as high. The costs of "goods" like ERA, abortion, or governmental regulation seem more known and certain than
do the anticipated benefits of passing a new amendment. Thus, if a
leader could make potential converts feel efficacious—feel that their
joining would make a difference in preventing the world from declining—then relatively few selective incentives would be called for.
Schlafly is said to be particularly effective in making previously
apolitical women feel that they can make a difference. She puts them
through training schools where she gives detailed directives on lobbying, press conferences, and so forth. In return, her followers adore
her.

For all these reasons, the New Right's defensive mobilization
was easier than feminism's offensive mobilization and could be accomplished rather quickly. Schlafly's quick successes in a few states
considering the ERA as well as the passage of several Hyde Amendments restricting abortions further created a sense of opportunity
among potential followers. There was suddenly a good chance of
stopping the ERA and of doing something about abortion.

The Role of Outsiders

Finally, outsiders, particularly the government, churches,
and the media, have facilitated the growth of the New Right, sometimes unwittingly. Journalists have not generally been fans of the

New Right; in fact, they tend to deplore the single-issue tactics of
New Right fundraisers and of anti-ERA and anti-abortion groups as
factionalism that threatens to destroy representative government
(see Newsweek 1978; Crawford 1980). Yet their focus on the size
and impact of these groups may have been misplaced. Rosenberg
(1982, pp. 27-28), for example, criticizes the press for its reporting on the Moral Majority:

> What should have been portrayed as a relatively new
> social and political development of modest size and
> power was transformed into a nearly invincible jugger-
> naut that seemed to be on the verge of overwhelming
> American life. It doesn't matter if one considers Fal-
> well a prophet or a hypocrite; he and his movement
> have been the beneficiaries of one of the biggest hype
> jobs in recent memory.

Whereas the media tended at feminism's inception either to
ignore the phenomenon or to sensationalize it, they took the rise of
the New Right seriously and helped to convince the American people
of its import.

Government also played a facilitative role in several interesting ways. Government-sponsored conferences invigorated the pro-
family movement. We have already mentioned that the 1977 IWY
conference in Houston first awoke many conservative women to the
evils of feminism. The 1980 White House Conference on Families
(WHCF) reinforced that perception. Pro-family leader Connaught
Marshner (1980) said it really "lit the fuse." Social conservatives
reacted by forming the National Pro-Family Coalition to present
their own agenda to the conference and urged members to get involved in delegate selection in their home states. They were successful in electing delegates in several states, particularly those
composing the Minneapolis conference site. Yet, their primary
complaint was that the selection process, incorporating appointments
to achieve balance in viewpoints, had been rigged against elected
delegates. The effect of the WHCF was to provoke the Silent Majority into action, according to Rosemary Thomson's account (1981) in
Withstanding Humanism's Challenge to Families: Anatomy of a
White House Conference. Newly formed Christian groups met with
politically experienced anti-ERA and Right to Life groups and
cemented an alliance against President Carter. Many disaffected
WHCF delegates went directly to work for Reagan in their states'
primaries and later in the November general election.

An example of what pro-family conservatives had learned in
four years comes from the state of Arkansas. In 1977, 26 women

from the newly created Arkansas Federation for Responsible Legislation attended their state IWY convention where they were disturbed by "the feminist domination" of the proceedings (McGuigan 1981, p. 36). Afterwards, the group changed its name to FLAG (Family, Life, America under God), altered some of its tactics, and concentrated on lobbying legislators against ERA. By the time the Arkansas election of delegates to the 1980 WHCF conference came around, FLAG was strong enough to elect an entire slate committed to pro-family goals. Thus, governmentally funded conferences facilitated networking among conservatives at the state level as well as at the national level and lent a sense of urgency to their opposition to feminism. [2]

Particularly since the 1980 elections congressional allies have also facilitated the growth of all three sectors of the New Right. They have popularized new theories such as supply-side economics, new policies like the Family Protection Act (one of the first offensive moves of the pro-family movement), and new strategies such as banning abortions by statute rather than by constitutional amendment. Similarly, the election of Ronald Reagan to the presidency provided a significant stimulus to the growth of all three sectors of the movement, even though in his first two years Reagan tended to concentrate on the secular New Right's economic agenda rather than the social agenda. Still, Reagan has appointed a number of pro-family leaders to important posts: for example, Jo Ann Gasper, editor of The Right Woman; Marjorie Mecklenberg, president of Minnesota Citizens Concerned for Life; and Onalee McGraw, another pro-family leader. With the experience gained from service in Washington, we can expect that the New Right will be able to advance its causes more effectively. At the same time, based on Costain (1981a) the presence of governmental allies should facilitate the development of even more New Right groups.

Lastly, churches as institutions have aided the mobilization efforts of the New Right in important ways. The impact of TV evangelists upon the Religious Right is fairly obvious and direct. Prime-time preachers seek members and raise funds for their political groups. From those on their mailing lists, they again raise money and advise them how to vote. For example, Christian Voice is featured on Pat Robertson's Christian Broadcasting Network. The Voice claims membership from 37 denominations and a mailing list of 150,000 laymen and 37,000 ministers (Guth 1981, p. 10). In 1980 it contributed $200,000 to candidates (Guth 1981, p. 15) and published "morality ratings" for its members' guidance in voting. This entry into politics was functional for the evangelical churches as well. Between 1960 and 1975 evangelical churches had experienced both a membership surge and a "rise to respectability" as their members for the first time approached the status and income levels of mainline Protestants. Ministers needed something newer than personal piety to hold onto their upwardly mobile congregations. As Guth (1981, p. 4) argues:

> The new visibility of evangelicals, then, may be due in large part to the increased wealth, growing community concern and involvement and greater organizational skills which come with education and occupational advancement.

Likewise, the Mormon church has been very active in the pro-family movement, especially in their anti-ERA efforts. For example, in the state of Florida Mormon Church leaders divided the state along church boundaries and made assessments from their congregations (Miami Herald 1980, p. 1). In the last two weeks before the 1978 elections their contributions totaled $26,000 to an anti-ERA PAC and $15,000 to four anti-ERA candidates.

The Catholic Church has played an equally important role in facilitating the growth of the pro-family movement, primarily its anti-abortion efforts. The church followed up on its 1975 Pastoral Plan by providing money, promoting anti-abortion groups from the pulpit, engaging in joint lobbying efforts, and leafletting on Sundays immediately before elections. In fact, the director of the National Right to Life Committee says flatly: "The only reason we have a pro-life movement in this country is because of the Catholic people and the Catholic Church" (Jaffe et al. 1981, p. 73).

At the national level the Bishops' Committee for Pro-Life Activities has its own PAC, the National Committee for a Human Life Amendment. Half of its funds appear to come from individual contributions from Catholic dioceses (Jaffe et al. 1981, p. 74). Its Washington lobby was particularly influential in 1977 on the passage of the Hyde Amendment. Further, two states in which the anti-abortion movement is unusually active, Missouri and Minnesota, are states in which local Citizens Concerned for Life groups are closely allied with the Catholic Church. For example, in Minnesota the church is the largest single contributor to the MCCL, and the two have a colobby in the legislature (Minneapolis Tribune 1978, p. 8A). By the time of the 1980 election Minnesota Citizens Concerned for Life (MCCL) campaign strategies were used as a model around the country by anti-abortion groups.

For the Catholic Church the decision to enter the abortion fray may have had a political as well as a moral motive. According to Jaffe et al. (1981, p. 76), in 1975 liberal bishops agreed to support a singleminded position on abortion in exchange for conservatives' support on progressive domestic and foreign policy positions.

In summary, there is no doubt that fundamentalist, Mormon, and Catholic churches and their ministers have been effective in adding members to the pro-family and Religious Right sectors of the New Right movement. Their facilitative role extends to fund-raising, promotional activities for demonstrations and picketing, and directives to voters. The media and government, sometimes unintentionally, have also facilitated the movement's growth.

The Role of Issues in Mobilization

New Right entrepreneurs in the mid-1970s needed an issue or issues to capture the attention of their potential constituents, one that would distinguish them from the Old Right but symbolize all those liberal changes conservatives resented. The ERA and abortion were two issues that readily fit their needs for emotional issues uniting conservatives against liberals. First of all, both issues were on the societal agenda, and had received a good deal of attention. They could be developed faster than new issues. Second, they could be linked to basic tenets of conservatism as described earlier in this chapter. Third, since feminists had been advocating the ERA and abortion rights in condensational terms (see Chapter 3), it would be easy to shock potential followers into joining conservative groups just by playing up feminist rhetoric. For example, Concerned Women for America prepared a brochure entitled "To Manipulate a Housewife" that simply consists of feminist quotes about the family, marriage, and the ERA. Fourth, both the ERA and abortion causes were quite urgent. The ERA had sailed through 22 state legislatures in its first year and appeared to be on the brink of ratification. Similarly, the abortion rate rose sharply after 1973. Banning abortions was an urgent cause if one wanted to save lives. Fifth, there is ample evidence that the secular New Right sector saw these two issues as the kind of family issues that would arouse the quiescent conservative masses. Secular New Right leaders like Weyrich felt that the Old Right had made a mistake by focusing on economic issues and excluding social and family issues. Thus, the focus on family issues was part of a calculated strategy for mobilization.

The ERA

The transformation of the ERA conflict from a narrow technical debate to an emotional community conflict is primarily the story of one woman, Phyllis Schlafly. Without her talents at defining the issue and mobilizing followers, the ERA probably would be in the

Constitution today. Though Schlafly was initially provoked into action by the suspicion that the ERA was another "federal power grab," she did not exclusively emphasize that aspect in her state campaigns. Rather she emphasized the ERA's threat to the traditional nuclear family, specifically the housewife's function within the family. The ERA, she maintained, would have allowed homosexual marriages, mandated unisex toilets, invalidated the requirement that men support their wives, permitted abortions, and required that women go into combat along with men. Schlafly stressed the "no exit" quality of the amendment, capturing those who say they are for the "E" and the "R" but not the "A." She asserted that the amendment allowed for no compromises or exceptions on the basis of sex:

> It will mandate the gender-free, rigid, absolute equality of treatment of men and women under every federal and state law, bureaucratic regulation and court decision, and in every aspect of our lives that is touched directly or indirectly by public funding. . . . The Positive Woman opposes ERA because she knows it would be hurtful to women, to men, to children, to the family, to local self-government, and to society as a whole (Schlafly 1977, p. 68).

Schlafly also maintained that nothing good could come from the ERA because it added nothing to equal pay laws already on the books.

Schlafly's success in getting her followers to believe in these claims can be seen in one of Tedin's studies (1980). He found that among anti-feminist activists, 85 percent believed that the ERA was very likely to result in unisex toilets while more than 90 percent believed that the amendment would lead to homosexual marriages, alter basic family structure, change relationships between the sexes, and result in women being drafted (1980, p. 14). In contrast to the mass public which distinguished among the more and less plausible consequences of the amendment, anti-feminist activists' beliefs were part of a ritualistic response. They were initially opposed to the ERA and then came to believe the worst about it, Tedin argues.

Other pro-family organizations besides Schlafly's STOP ERA tend to emphasize the same family aspects. For example, her Eagle Forum organization supports the right of society to designate different roles for men and women; textbooks that teach the "truth about the family, monogamous marriage, and motherhood"; the right of a woman to be a full-time wife and mother; and the right of employers to give job preference to a wage-earner supporting dependents (Eagle Forum, no date a). The organization's motto is "for God, Home, and Country," again showing the linkage with those symbols most central to the Religious Right.

Appendix A lists the national and state organizations on record against the ERA. The pro-family category is the largest category. Note the high-level symbolism of their names, combining the cause of women, country, and family: Citizens for God, Family, and Country; Concerned Women for America; Intercessors for America; Pro America; Pro Family United. Further in the state list note the defensive tone of many of the titles: Committee for Retention and Protection of Women's Rights; Protect Our Women; Restore Our American Republic; Women United to Defend Existing Rights. Moreover, the literature of these groups stresses their opposition to feminism. For example, a leader of the United Families of America lists the enemies of the family as feminist ideologues, family regulators, professional educationists, and government manipulators (Marshner 1982).

We argue that leaders of the pro-family movement are using high-order symbols such as America and the family to enlist followers on the basis of their ideological principles. Furthermore, such symbols are central to conservatives' self-interests and enhance identification with solidary groups. Their language tends to be condensational and expansive: a number of horrible consequences will follow from the ERA's adoption. Therefore, followers must unite together against ERA proponents and destroyers of the family.

A number of groups (listed in Appendix A) from the Religious Right have also opposed the amendment. Jerry Falwell, for example, is credited (Viguerie 1981, p. 126) with having done more than any other person to defeat the ERA in Virginia. Literature of the Religious Right tends to depict the ERA and other feminist policies as a "parade of horribles" designed to hurt the church and religion. For example, Moral Majority's literature says:

> For too long now we have witnessed the concerted at-
> tack waged by ultra-liberals and so called "feminists"
> against the family structure in America—the very foun-
> dation on which our society rest. As a result, America—
> our beloved country—is sick. And when a country be-
> comes sick morally, it becomes sick in every other way
> (Moral Majority, no date).

Such language is designed to appeal to the solidarity among fundamentalists as well as to stress the high-order symbol of the church, thereby expanding the conflict with feminists.

The Old Right also furnished early opposition to the amendment. In late 1972 (Boles 1979, p. 67) the John Birch Society's newsletter began to warn members about this "subversive proposal." Young Americans for Freedom asserted that the ERA gains nothing but loses much because it gives unlimited power to the federal government. As one would expect, the literature of the Old Right generally tends to focus on the "creeping socialism" and "federal power grab" aspects of the ERA. However, groups from the Old Right have not been particularly active in the conflict and many of them rely on Schlafly for their material.

In discussions of the ERA, secular New Right leaders generally depict feminism as anti-family. As already mentioned, the secular New Right's chief contribution to the ERA conflict has been to recognize its potential as a family issue and to coopt the pro-family and Religious Right sectors.

Abortion

The anti-abortion effort does not have a single leader of Phyllis Schlafly's stature. Rather, the battle is led by a number of single-issue abortion groups, the largest of which is the National Right to Life Committee (NRLC) which claims 11 million members (Akey 1981). Note the positive tone of the names of the groups listed in Appendix B, in contrast to the defensive tone of the anti-ERA groups: Concerned for Life, For Life, Right to Life, Life and Equality. These groups are united in their pro-life emphasis; they are trying to regain a lost good, not just protect a threatened good.

Their literature uses symbols designed to emphasize solidarity with religious groups and ideological principles. For example, the president of American Life Lobby writes in an anti-Planned Parenthood brochure:

> Pray that God will not unleash His wrath on this nation before we as His soldiers have the opportunity to turn this immoral and unthinkable evil away from His eyes. Pray that God will sustain our families as we work (American Life Lobby 1980).

Their motto is "for God, for Life, for the Family, for the Nation," thus combining a number of very high-order symbols.

Another group, the Minnesota Citizens Concerned for Life (no date), argues that the right to life is the basic right upon which all other issues of human rights and justice depend. Theirs is an appeal to individual principles. They believe that the pro-life issue is as important as was slavery and as deserving of being treated as a single issue.

A second important category of groups listed in Appendix B includes the pro-family groups, i.e., multi-issue groups focusing on more than abortion. For example, Schlafly's Eagle Forum supports "The right to life of all innocent persons from conception to natural death" (Eagle Forum, no date a). This condensational language stresses relevance to self-interests since any individual could be subsumed into the category from "conception to natural death." Schlafly herself sees a direct link between the ERA and abortion. She reasons that if the ERA were passed any restriction on abortion would be construed as impacting only on one sex (Schlafly 1977, p. 89). Other pro-family groups classify abortion as a form of child abuse that the state should protect against.

A third large category is the religious organizations listed in Appendix B. The literature of these groups tends to depict abortion as a "national sin," thus appealing to religious solidarity. For example, the Moral Majority's literature says:

> For six long years Americans have been forced to stand
> by helplessly while 3 to 6 million babies were legally
> murdered through abortion on demand—each baby is a
> precious living soul in the eyes of the Lord (Moral
> Majority, no date).

In their literature the act of abortion is morally wrong because it is proscribed by the Bible. Abortion leads to a series of horrible consequences for those involved as well as for society. Catholic literature, in particular, uses condensational symbols linking the life and well-being of the unborn with that of the elderly, the mentally and physically handicapped, the sick and the dying. Their Respect Life program seeks to heighten respect for all human life around the world—from conception to natural death—in all physical and social conditions.

Finally, the secular New Right sector as represented by Conservative Digest depicts abortion as destroying the family ethic, just as welfare destroys the work ethic (Sobran 1981, p. 15). Their language is particularly appealing to those lower-middle-class and working-class people whose identities are found in their families. Such people feel tension between the family and society rather than between the individual and society (Skerry 1978, p. 82). Abortion then is easily construed as another governmental interference with the family structure and feminism as the force behind this intrusion. The secular New Right then appeals to the self-interests of people adversely affected by government and to the principles of freedom and limited government.

Summary

As the above discussion implies, the role of the ERA and the abortion issues in the mobilization process is highly symbolic. It is an attempt to reestablish the Right as the group that defines public morality. Fairbanks cites several pieces of evidence for this symbolic politics argument (1981, p. 9). First, the New Right focuses its attention on constitutional amendments (e.g., defeating the ERA or passing the HLA) because the Constitution is a higher symbol than is a statute. Second, the New Right has few positive programs for combatting the evils it is against. For example, chastity centers have been their major proposal to prevent teenage pregnancy. Third, the Right chooses the major institutions of society as its battlegrounds—the media, the churches, the schools—because they shape the culture and define morality. Finally, the New Right supports politicians who employ its symbolic gestures in preference to supporting those who live by its moral code. For example, they have campaigned against ministers, for convicted homosexuals, and for divorcé Ronald Reagan.

Nowhere does the symbolic meaning of family take on more significance than in Ronald Reagan's 1980 acceptance speech at the Republican National Convention. He talked about a return to the American values of family, work, neighborhood, and peace. Columnist Richard Cohen (1980) subsequently wrote that family was a code word for Reagan. Family functioned much as a flag does: to represent something bigger.

> Family, of course, does not, strictly speaking, mean family. It means no Equal Rights Amendment and no abortion. It means no gays and no living together and no smooching and worse before marriage and no married ladies with hyphenated names and the prefix Ms. before it (Cohen 1980, p. 16A).

In symbolic terms, the Right has captured the family turf: to be pro-family is to be against the ERA, abortion, and everything feminists advocate. To be feminist is, by the same token, to be anti-family. To be against the family is to be the enemy of one of the highest symbols in our society.

As a defensive mobilization effort, the New Right was able to develop rather quickly its opposition to the ERA and to abortion as well as other issues. We would expect this type of opposition to be easier to mount than would be the feminists' uphill battle to establish the issues. A large portion of the New Right's symbolic campaign against these two issues was conducted as a reaction to femi-

nist condensational symbols of a decade earlier. As Friedan (1982)
charged, the sexual politics and anti-male rhetoric of radical feminists in the late 1960s seemingly have engendered a violent reaction.

COLLECTIVE ACTIONS BY THE NEW RIGHT

Once the New Right had been mobilized, in part through the
symbolic meaning of the abortion and ERA issues, then various New
Right groups began to engage in collective action designed to bring
about their goals of restoring order, morality, and freedom. Primarily they used strategies of advocacy as did the feminists earlier.
Their targets of influence were varied: Congress is a target presently on abortion legislation; the state legislatures have been targets
on ERA; the courts have generally been perceived as having been
captured by liberal elements. Thus, several efforts have concentrated on stripping the courts of jurisdiction over sensitive matters.
As we would expect from the early stage of a countermovement,
much energy has been devoted to winning over the bystander public.

The grassroots structure of the New Right movement also constrained its choice of advocacy strategies. The New Right thus far
uses some labor-intensive strategies but also rather capital-intensive
strategies such as targeted direct mail. Further, its structure of
ad hoc groups is useful for short-term efforts to defeat changes in
one state such as the ERA, but has not yet proven useful for longer-
term passage of new legislation. Until the 1980 election, New Right
leaders were also constrained by the fact that they were out of power.
Their strategies were necessarily anti-incumbent. With the election
of Ronald Reagan in 1980, it became possible for the first time to
entertain the possibility of enacting their own social agenda. Hence,
we already see their strategies shifting from primarily defensive to
offensive.

Forms of Collective Action

Particularly in the early stages of its mobilization, the New
Right pursued a strategy of grassroots lobbying, especially protest—
picketing, demonstrations, and sit-ins. Anti-abortion groups in
particular have been prone to use this strategy up to and including
violence. Abortion clinics and birth control counseling centers have
been subjected to arson, shootings, firebombing, vandalism, assaults on the staff, and disruption of clinic operations by sit-ins and
pickets. Many of these acts are still unsolved crimes but a series
of coordinated actions in January 1978 have been traced to the group

"People Expressing a Concern for Everyone" (PEACE), according to NARAL (NARAL, no date a). The largest peaceful demonstration is the March for Life that has taken place in Washington each January since 1973.

Given the New Right's investment into computerized, direct mail, they rely on that network to stimulate large volumes of constituent mail to legislators. This is the second type of grassroots lobbying. New Right groups can direct appeals to prior contributors asking them to send an enclosed postcard to several public officials. For example, a recent Conservative Caucus mailing asked fellow conservatives to help in its campaign to "defund the Left," specifically to abolish the National Endowment for the Humanities because it gives money to support pro-communist propaganda, anti-family feminist movements, and anti-defense organizations. Viguerie maintains that direct mail is primarily a form of communication with constituents and advertising to potential followers, made necessary by the fact that liberals control the media. He asserts that his company has 4.5 million names and has produced as many as 720,000 letters to a single official on a single subject (Viguerie 1981, pp. 91, 96). Without direct mail, he says, there would be no New Right.

The direct lobbying efforts of New Right groups have been primarily directed at legislators, not the courts. Anti-abortion groups attempt to influence legislators through demonstrations and testimony at congressional hearings. In the early 1970s pro-life groups tended to use testimony designed to provoke disgust toward abortion procedures—glossy pictures of fetuses, linking the pro-choice position to Hitler or to forced death for old people. But over time their tactics have become less emotional, partially due to the influence of the rest of the New Right.

A particularly notable example of lobbying is that of Phyllis Schlafly. She has led rallies and demonstrations, lobbied, and testified at nearly every legislature in the unratified states. Dressed in pink, her Eagles come armed with loaves of homemade bread, jars of jam, and apple pies. In her testimony and press conferences, Schlafly usually relies on information already presented in her Phyllis Schlafly Report.

The New Right's greatest strategic innovations, however, have been their indirect lobbying, specifically their efforts to influence the outcome of elections. The New Right pioneered in creating PACs as the electoral arms of its major organizations. Relying on the direct mail fundraising technique, conservatives have been able to raise considerable sums of money. They then target liberal incumbent legislators and pour money into the opponent's campaign. Their first successes were in 1978 when New Right groups defeated Iowa's Senator Dick Clark and New Hampshire's Senator Tom

McIntyre. Among the more visible PACs are LAPAC (Life Amendment Political Action Committee), NCHLA (the National Committee
for a Human Life Amendment), NPLPAC (National Pro-Life Political Action Committee), Life-pac, and NCPAC (National Conservative Political Action Committee). The latter is the largest and most
successful of these groups, having raised $5.8 million in 1981–82
alone (Washington Post 1982, p. A4).

Encouraged by its success in 1978, in 1980 NCPAC targeted
six liberal senators for defeat. LAPAC targeted 12 incumbents,
"the deadly dozen." In addition, New Right organizations attempt to
register their constituents to vote; for example, the Moral Majority
claims (Viguerie 1981, p. 8) to have registered 2.5 million new voters in 1980. Then they conduct voter identification drives to isolate
their voters. Several groups (for example, Christian Voice and the
Christian Voters' Victory Fund) record congresspersons' votes on
key issues and release morality ratings as guides to voting.

All of these electoral tactics are used in conjunction with a
single-issue strategy; that is, certain issues such as abortion or the
ERA are "litmus test" issues. If incumbents differ from the PAC
on this one issue, then they are marked for defeat, even if they have
supported the general aims of the group. For example, LAPAC
targeted Senator Frank Church for defeat because he did not support
a constitutional amendment even though he had voted against abortion several times. The intent of their strategy is to make an example out of a few liberal incumbents so that others will rethink
their positions on abortion. To quote Father Charles Fiore, chairman of NPLPAC on their purpose, "It's not so much that they will
have seen the light, but that they'll have felt the heat" (Conservative
Digest 1980a, p. 13).

The defeats of Senators George McGovern, Birch Bayh, Frank
Church, and John Culver in 1980 did send fear into other liberal
congressmen. An allied tactic first used in the 1980 congressional
elections was the negative smear campaign. Months before the election and even before a conservative opponent had been selected,
newspaper and TV ads were run that attacked the incumbent's record.
This advertising campaign continued throughout the election and was
not always welcomed by the challenger.

The logical extension of the single-issue strategy is the single-
issue party, represented by New York State's Right to Life Party.
RTL was started in 1970 by women disturbed by the impending passage of New York's abortion repeal law; by 1980 it had grown to the
state's fourth largest party. In 1976 its leader Ellen McCormak ran
for president on the RTL ticket.

A final tactic used by the New Right is prayer. For example,
Intercessors for America "is an organization which encourages

Christians to pray for our nation and those in positions of authority" (Intercessors for America, no date). They send members a month-ly newsletter providing detailed prayer priorities, articles on na-tional issues, instructions on the principles of intercessory prayer, and reports of answered prayer.

Success of the New Right

The New Right's collective actions since the mid-1970s have achieved some degree of success. First, the various sectors of the New Right have achieved at least partial acceptance by members of the polity. They are recognized as valid spokesmen for conserva-tives. The Reagan administration consults regularly with all three sectors, and many leaders of New Right groups have been appointed to office, though not a satisfactory number from their perspective. Further, the New Right has been accepted by the media: their views are regularly solicited by TV talk show hosts, newspapers, and magazines. The mass public, however, appears somewhat less ac-cepting of some elements of the New Right, especially the Religious Right and some of its activities. In 1980 the Gallup Poll found that 60 percent believe it is wrong for religious groups to campaign against candidates they don't agree with; 59 percent (including 55 percent of the Catholic respondents) believe it is wrong for a Catho-lic cardinal to label voting for pro-choice candidates as sinful (Gallup 1980, p. 1C).

A second measure of success is whether the social movement has gained new advantages. The secular New Right has injected supply-side economics into public policymaking and has won a tax cut, though the latter might be attributable to other forces as well. The Religious Right has achieved its goal of electing Ronald Reagan, has stopped federal funding of school busing and most abortions, and is close to victory seemingly on the school prayer issue. The pro-family Right also tries to claim victory on ending most federal funding of abortions, is apparently making progress on banning abor-tions altogether, and has defeated the ERA. Though ERA proponents blame its demise on big business, no one denies that Phyllis Schlafly, STOP ERA, and other pro-family groups were instrumental in the defeat. As we described in the last chapter, the emergence of the anti-ERA movement dramatically slowed the progress of the amend-ment through the states and escalated the conflict greatly. Similar-ly, it appears correct to attribute the cessation of abortion funding and the growing tenuousness of abortion rights to anti-abortion groups operating out of the New Right movement. They escalated the conflict after 1973 and have been working quite assiduously since then.

In a larger sense the New Right victories listed above also mark a stemming of the tide of liberalism and feminism as social movements. The New Right is not just winning on particular issues like the ERA but it is beginning to win its larger, more symbolic goal of restoring morality to America, and to regain its place as the definer of the culture. The "Over the Rainbow" celebration Phyllis Schlafly held in Washington, D.C., on the night of ERA's demise (June 30, 1982) was the symbolic putting of feminism in its place, complete with a telegram of congratulations from the President of the United States.

DYNAMICS OF THE NEW RIGHT

In addition to its strategies of advocacy pursued through protest, lobbying, and electoral activities, the New Right has sought alliances with other social movement organizations. Though the New Right arose in reaction to the Old Right and the Republican establishment, in recent years it has been cooperating with those old enemies. The 1980 election was a notable example in that Ronald Reagan was a part of the Old Right but was embraced by the Republican mainstream and championed by the New Right to such an extent that it claims credit for his victory. The New Right has sought to enforce their interpretation of Reagan's mandate by urging him to enact their social agenda.

Within the New Right movement itself we have stressed the unusual degree of cooperation among its three sectors: the secular New Right, the Religious Right, and the pro-family Right. The older secular New Right has aided and abetted the evangelical and pro-family branches. Its leaders serve on boards of directors of the leading pro-life PACs. Its journal, Conservative Digest, regularly has articles praising the pro-family movement. The Religious Right and the pro-family movement often overlap on social issues, supporters, and concern with morality and family. In fact, this high degree of cooperation has been formalized in the Library Court group. This Washington-based organization was formed in 1979 to coordinate family issues. Its chairman is Connaught Marshner, also director of the Family Policy Division of the Free Congress Foundation headed by Paul Weyrich. The Library Court coalition represents more than 20 organizations ranging from the National Christian Action Coalition, to American Life Lobby, the Religious Roundtable, Family America, the American Legislative Exchange Council, and the Conservative Caucus (Viguerie 1981; Conservative Digest 1980c, pp. 26-27).

In spite of this high degree of cooperation, some areas of competition remain. One notable example is Phyllis Schlafly's degree of aloofness from her Old Right colleagues, from the secular New Right, and from the rest of the pro-family movement. Schlafly, for example, does not sell her Eagle Forum or STOP ERA mailing lists to other organizations. Given the Right's dependence on direct mail advertising and fundraising, mass mail experts would clearly like to have access to her followers. It is plausible that Schlafly, founder of her own pro-family Eagle Forum, wants to lead the pro-family movement by herself rather than merge her organization with the rest of the movement.

A second public example of competition occurred in the first two years of the Reagan presidency when the secular New Right squabbled with the pro-family and the Religious Rights over whether the economic or social agenda should take precedence. There is obviously still a gulf between those who trace America's decline as a world power to economic difficulties and those who attribute it to moral decay. If the American economy worsens, the New Right's success may be threatened because current economic policies are identified with the supply-siders and because public attention will probably turn away from social issues to economic issues.

A third area of competition within the New Right is the uneasy alliance of the evangelical Right with the Catholic pro-life movement. Liberal social justice Catholics view the Christian Right as a threat to the broad penumbra of social issues encompassed by the pro-life position (poverty, housing, employment, civil rights, capital punishment, peace, etc.) and ultimately as a threat to Catholicism itself (Higgins 1980, pp. 108-110).

CONCLUSION

This chapter has examined the discontents experienced by members of the Silent Majority in the late 1960s and early 1970s. The basic beliefs of conservatism allowed one of these major trends—feminism—to be perceived as threatening to American society. A number of entrepreneurs employed three basic types of incentives to mobilize people into the New Right social movement. Furthermore, they skillfully used the abortion and ERA issues to facilitate the mobilization process. The next three chapters assess the impact of the New Right upon elites, masses, and state legislators.

NOTES

1. This label does not include the Old Right represented by
Barry Goldwater or William F. Buckley, Jr., the Republican establishment of Gerald Ford, or the neoconservative Right represented by Irving Kristol. The New Right, in fact, is united against
these conservatives because the latter failed to stop the tide of the
welfare state when in power under Nixon and Ford. The New Right
is anti-intellectual, anti-Eastern, and populist; some say it is an
extension of the Wallace movement (Phillips 1982, p. 49). At least
some of the Old Right return the antipathy. Goldwater, for example,
has said that social conservatives are giving conservatism a bad
name and that every Christian should "give Jerry Falwell a kick in
the ass." Nevertheless, there are still significant areas of agreement between the Old and the New Right: both are anti-communist,
patriotic, and pro-free enterprise.

2. Feminists, for their part, displayed much less interest
in the conference and did not work as hard to get elected as delegates.
According to Friedan (1981, p. 103) they simply assumed that the
right wing would take over. The White House itself soon regretted
Carter's 1976 campaign pledge to have such a conference, made to
appease his Catholic constituents. The conference took four years
to plan, involved disputes over the family qualifications of its first
director (a divorced woman), lengthy fights over delegate selection,
and confrontation over the substance of the recommendations.

5 / POLITICAL ACTIVISTS AND THE NEW RIGHT CONFLICT

In the past two chapters we have examined from an historical perspective the role of the abortion and the ERA issues in the feminist and New Right movements. Both issues appear to be major focal points for the symbolic conflict being waged over the American family. But, while our analysis seems consistent with the pattern of events outlined earlier, we have not yet explored empirically our explanation for the conflict. In this chapter, we undertake to remedy that situation by considering the following questions: how do involved members of the public symbolize these issues; why have people become activists with respect to these issues; and finally, what sorts of tactics do they use.

In our analysis we focus on political activists—individuals who are known both to have a definite interest in the issues currently confronting the American family and to have assumed an active role in resolving those issues. We do so because it is among activists that we would expect to find the clearest support for our ideas about the symbolism of abortion and the ERA. If, indeed, these issues are symbolic of basic life-style and value conflicts concerning the family then this ought to be apparent in the perceptions of activists.

Yet, while the decision to begin our empirical analysis by focusing on political activists was a relatively easy one, determining which activists to study was not. Given that we are interested in the conflict over these issues, it was essential to consider activists from both camps. Yet, at the same time, the relative dearth of information about New Right activists, as compared to that about the feminists, led us to put an emphasis on obtaining data concerning the former. Unfortunately, as with previous right-wing movements, obtaining empirical information about the New Right posed something of a problem given the wariness of its members toward representatives of academia. This problem was exacerbated by the fact that a number of different organizations compose the New Right coalition (Crawford 1980; Falwell 1980). Thus, simply focusing on the membership of any one New Right organization would have produced an overly narrow view of the movement's membership as a whole. Instead, what was needed was an opportunity to interview members of a number of different New Right organizations, and at the same time, a chance to obtain information about opponents of the New Right.

The White House Conference on Families described in the previous chapter provided just such an opportunity. As mentioned earlier, in a number of states the delegate selection procedures had produced heated controversy among several clusters of groups: "liberal" organizations such as the National Organization for Women, the American Civil Liberties Union, and the National Abortion Rights Action League; New Right organizations such as STOP ERA, the Moral Majority, and the Eagle Forum; and various professional organizations concerned with the family. Because many of the delegations represented a mixture of these groups, it was felt that the conference afforded an excellent opportunity to study not only members of the New Right but also political activists who opposed the movement.

DATA

Having made the decision to use the White House Conference on Families as a research theater, it was further decided to focus on the conference being held in Minneapolis, Minnesota, in June 1980. As one of the three federally sponsored conferences, this one was composed of delegations from 13 Midwestern and Southern states—a composition which made it perhaps the most conservative of the three conferences.[1] Furthermore, the delegate selection process was particularly conflictual for this conference.

In contrast to many previous examinations of right-wing activists (e.g., Brady and Tedin 1976; Chesler and Schmuck 1969; Elms 1969; Wolfinger et al. 1969), we exercised considerable control over the nature of the sample. In our interviewing, we were able to draw a random sample of delegates from certain select states, rather than having to rely on haphazard sampling methods that might have biased our sample in favor of cooperative and perhaps less extreme individuals. In order to maximize the number of potential New Right activists, we randomly selected half of the delegates from the five states in attendance that had not yet ratified the Equal Rights

Amendment: Arkansas, Illinois, Louisiana, Missouri, and Mississippi. In addition, because of the availability of comparable data at the mass level in Kentucky and Minnesota, we sought to interview all of the members of those two delegations. Overall, we completed personal interviews with approximately 71 percent (107) of the delegates originally targeted for interviewing (about 20 percent of the delegates attending the conference).[2] In almost every case, our failure to obtain an interview was a consequence of the extreme time constraints the delegates were operating under rather than their lack of cooperation.

From the perspective of some researchers, the sample resulting from this procedure may be disturbingly small and representative of a relatively unspecifiable population. While acknowledging that there may be some grounds for concern, we would argue that the problems are not serious ones. Although the size of our sample is small, it does compare favorably with that of other studies of political extremists (e.g., Brady and Tedin 1976, n=154; and Elms 1969, n=40). Similarly, although we cannot pinpoint precisely the populations represented by the delegations at the conference, evidence from the delegate selection process does suggest that the delegates were drawn from organizations representing a variety of causes central to the controversies we are studying. Furthermore, given that the states made some effort to select "balanced" delegations, our sampling procedure guaranteed that there would be a number of conservatives as well as a substantial number of nonconservatives to use as a comparison group—a critical element that is often missing from examinations of political extremists. In addition, the timing of the interviewing was very favorable since it preceded the rash of attention that the media accorded the New Right during the 1980 presidential election, thus allowing us to interview some of its members before they became extremely suspicious of such endeavors. In short, though this data base and our sampling procedure by no means ensured that our results would reflect a broad cross-section of the New Right and its opponents, we believe that they did produce a sample that is more than adequate for an initial exploration of the controversy between the New Right and the feminist movements.

ATTITUDES ON ABORTION AND THE ERA

Let us begin our examination of the data by considering the delegates' opinions on the issues of abortion and the Equal Rights Amendment. Attitudes toward abortion were measured in terms of the respondents' reactions to seven questions asking if it should be "possible for a pregnant woman to obtain a legal abortion if . . ."[3]

1. there is a strong chance of serious defect in the baby?
2. she is married and does not want any more children?
3. the woman's health is seriously endangered by the pregnancy?
4. the family has a very low income and cannot afford any more children?
5. she became pregnant as a result of rape?
6. she is <u>not</u> married and does not want to marry the man?
7. the woman wants it for any reason?

Taken together, these items form a Guttman scale with a co-efficient of reproducibility of .96 and a coefficient of scalability of .88. Given this, for each delegate the "yes" responses to these questions were summed to produce a scale ranging from "never approves" (0) to "always approves" (7).

Evaluations of the Equal Rights Amendment were measured in terms of responses to a question concerning whether the individual favored or opposed the amendment. Low scores on the question indicate opposition to the amendment.

Since we were considering political activists known to be interested and involved with the issues of abortion and the ERA, we expected that attitudes would be polarized on the two issues. And, indeed, they are. As indicated in Table 5.1, the delegates are very polarized on the abortion issue. Almost half of the sample falls on one of the two extreme ends of the scale. Overall, attitudes are skewed toward the anti-abortion side, although this is not particularly surprising given our efforts to ensure a sizable conservative portion in the sample. Similarly, as shown in Table 5.2, attitudes toward the Equal Rights Amendment are also polarized, though not quite as much as in the case of the abortion issue. Now, let us turn to a more interesting question: how do the delegates symbolize or define these issues?

ISSUE SYMBOLIZATION

In our theoretical discussions to this point, the focus has been upon how leaders have defined the meaning of the abortion and ERA issues. From this perspective, it was possible to identify the actual symbols—such as the "family" or "equality"—used by political entrepreneurs to define the issues for the public as a whole. Similarly, it was appropriate, and relatively easy, to discuss the nature of those symbols, i.e., whether they are referential or condensational. But, now, in moving from a broad-based historical discussion of the feminist and New Right movements to an empirical analysis of individuals, it is necessary to change perspectives.

Table 5.1   ATTITUDES TOWARD ABORTION
(Activist Sample)

Frequency Distribution of Opinion on Abortion		Percent
Never	0	20.6
	1	27.1
	2	8.4
	3	4.7
	4	3.7
	5	2.8
	6	4.7
Always	7	28.0
TOTAL		100.0
		(n = 107)

Source: Authors' White House Conference Study.

Table 5.2   ATTITUDES TOWARD THE ERA
(Activist Sample)

Attitude	Percent
Strongly Oppose	39.3
Oppose	10.2
Uncertain	1.0
Favor	16.8
Strongly Favor	32.7
TOTAL	100.0
	(n = 107)

Source: Authors' White House Conference Study.

In adopting the individual as the unit of analysis, we must
shift our focus to the individual's orientation toward the issue (i.e.,
how the individual perceives the meaning of abortion and the Equal
Rights Amendment). It was argued earlier that symbols are used
to interpret or represent the substance of an issue, and thus the
meaning of the symbols defines that of the issue. The meaning
of symbols, and thus the issues themselves, can be either cognitive
or evaluative in nature; they may have substantive meaning as well
as strong emotional meaning (Cobb and Elder 1972a, 1973).

In the case of issues of abortion and the ERA, it is expected
that many people will have intense emotional feelings. In some instances, this emotional reaction may be an outgrowth of the substantive meaning that the symbols defining the issue hold for the individual. But, such intense reactions may also be a result of the
issue being linked to certain symbols which, themselves, produce
strong emotional feelings. In particular, it is expected that attitudes toward abortion and the ERA will reflect the linkage of those
issues with consensually valued higher-order, condensational symbols of the sort discussed earlier (e.g., the family, equality). Yet,
it is also likely that these issues are defined in terms of those symbols characterizing the conflict between the women's movement and
that of the New Right (e.g., liberals and women's libbers on the
left, and conservatives and big business on the right). Also, although the meaning of abortion and the ERA may be largely symbolic
for much of the mass public, political activists should associate substantial information with the two issues. Specifically, the stands
that activists take on these issues should be related to their beliefs
about the family. In effect, activists should have what Cobb and
Elder (1973) call an "ideological" orientation toward abortion and
the ERA; the issues should have both cognitive and evaluative meaning.

Measures

In measuring the cognitive meaning of abortion and the ERA,
we developed summated ratings scales of three attitudinal orientations that are linked to the women's movement and that help to define different, often competing, conceptions of the family. The first
scale concerns the definition of appropriate sex roles and focuses
on relationships among family members. The second scale has to
do with the perception of women's status in the labor market and
considers whether society or the individual is responsible for the
status of women vis-à-vis men. The third and final scale was designed to assess the respondents' sense of personal morality as

indicated by their approval or disapproval of such things as homosexual sex and the distribution of pornography. The specific questions used in the construction of each scale, as well as their relia-
bilities, are presented in Appendix C. In the case of all three
measures, low scores indicate "traditional" perspectives while
high scores represent "liberated" attitudes.

In measuring the evaluative meaning of abortion and the ERA,
we did not focus on the higher-order, condensational symbols (i.e.,
family, equality) characterizing the rhetoric associated with the two
issues. Because there should be a relatively high degree of consensus on the importance and value of such symbols, it was expected
that evaluations of such symbols would not help to explain the variation in attitudes toward the issues of abortion and the ERA. Rather,
we explored the symbols of conflict that presumably underlie the
different meanings given the issues of abortion and the ERA.

With this in mind, in measuring the evaluative sources of
meaning we focused upon groups that constitute symbolic represen-
tations of various cleavages in society thought to be important to the
conflict over these issues (Conover and Feldman 1981). Using the
"feeling thermometer" format devised by the Center for Political
Studies, respondents were asked to rate on a scale from zero to one
hundred how "warm" or "cold" they felt toward a randomly arranged
list of two sets of groups in society. The first set of groups are
those related to and composing the "New Left" in general and the
women's liberation movement specifically: liberals, radical students, homosexuals, marijuana users, the women's liberation movement, black militants, and civil rights leaders. The second set of
groups are those thought to represent symbolically the causes of the
Right: big business, policemen, Republicans, conservatives, businessmen, the military, and housewives.

Findings

As illustrated in Table 5.3, the delegates' opinions on abortion
and the ERA are very strongly related to the three cognitive orientations that we argue define different conceptions of the modern American family.[4] Those respondents who favor the ERA and the right to
abortion also tend to adhere to the "new morality," the idea of equal
sex roles, and the belief that women have a lower economic status
because of discrimination. Conversely, delegates who oppose abortion and the ERA have more traditional moral codes; they support
traditional sex roles in the family; and they place responsibility for
women's status squarely on the head of the individual woman. Such
clear-cut and strong relationships suggest three things. First, the

issues of abortion and the ERA hold substantial cognitive meaning for these political activists. Secondly, the cognitive meaning of these issues is strongly rooted in ideas about the family and the roles that men and women play in relationship to that family. Finally, such results are basically consistent with Granberg's (1981) finding that anti-abortion activists have a more conservative view of sex roles than do pro-choice activists.

Table 5.3   THE MEANING OF ABORTION AND THE ERA[a]
(Activist Sample)

| | Attitudes on | |
Indicators	ERA	Abortion
I. Cognitive Variables		
Sex Roles	.79	.75
Women's Status	.75	.62
Morality	.87	.86
II. Symbols of the "Left"		
Liberals	.78	.67
Radical Students	.60	.51
Homosexuals	.57	.52
Marijuana Users	.52	.46
Women's Liberation Movement	.82	.70
Black Militants	.48	.35
Civil Rights Leaders	.44	.36
III. Symbols of the "Right"		
Big Business	−.33	−.20
Policemen	−.51	−.53
Republicans	−.44	−.39
Conservatives	−.69	−.57
Businessmen	−.48	−.34
The Military	−.55	−.48
Housewives	−.58	−.50

[a] Entries are Pearson's Product-Moment Correlations. All are significant at the .01 level.

Source: Authors' White House Conference Study.

Turning to the question of affective meaning, in Table 5.3 we find ample support for the hypothesis that opinions on abortion and the ERA are strongly linked to evaluations of those groups that help define the lines of conflict between the feminist movement and the New Right. Support for the ERA and the right to abortion are very strongly related to positive feelings toward the symbols of the "left." Furthermore, it is important to note that among the symbols of the left it is the symbol of the women's liberation movement itself that is most strongly related to attitudes on the two issues. At the same time, support on the two issues is related to negative feelings toward the symbols of the right.

Two aspects of these findings merit further comment. First, overall, the symbols of the left are more strongly related to opinions on abortion and the ERA than are the symbols of the right. This makes sense given the nature of the political environment that has nurtured the development of the feminist and New Right movements. Over the past 20 years, the political agenda has been dominated by concerns of the various social movements that together comprise the political and social "left." Thus, to the extent there has been conflict over issues it has been in response to the actions of the left and the symbols that represent those activities. Consequently, the "liberal" label and the symbols associated with it have been focused on more heavily in political discourse, and have become more emotionally charged (Conover and Feldman 1981). This pattern may well change, however, if the New Right goes on the offensive and begins to champion issues and symbols of its own design, rather than simply denigrating the symbols of the left. Secondly, it is also apparent in Table 5.3 that the issue of the ERA is more symbolic of the clash between the women's liberation movement and the New Right than is the issue of abortion (at least for the activists considered here). In the case of virtually every symbol, there is a stronger relationship with attitudes on the ERA than with those on abortion.

In summary, as expected, political activists involved in the struggle over abortion and the ERA tend to have an ideological orientation toward the two issues. On the one hand, the issues have substantial cognitive meaning for the delegates: both are strongly linked to beliefs about the role of women inside and outside the family, as well as to more general beliefs about morality. At the same time, the two issues appear to be charged very heavily with emotional meaning; evaluations of symbols of the left and, to a somewhat lesser extent, symbols of the right are clearly related to the delegates' positions on abortion and the ERA. Finally, although the patterns of meaning are very similar for the two issues, opinions on the ERA appear to be more closely linked to the symbols of conflict distinguishing the feminist movement from the New Right.

MOBILIZATION

To this point, we have merely assumed that the delegates to the family conference were political activists—people who had been mobilized by some organization for the purpose of taking collective action on abortion, the ERA, and other family-related issues. In this section, we will examine that assumption empirically by comparing the delegates who represent the views of the New Right with those who are more likely to be sympathetic to the women's movement. In so doing, special attention will be paid to the mobilization of those delegates with a New Right ideology, although nonrightists will also be considered.

Given this, how do we separate the potential New Right delegates from the nonrightists? From our perspective, members of the sample with a New Right ideology may be distinguished from nonrightists according to certain core beliefs, among which are an opposition to the issues of abortion and the Equal Rights Amendment (Crawford 1980; Falwell 1980). Accordingly, a composite variable was formed based on the respondent's attitudes on these two issues. Specifically, the abortion scale was divided into two parts: the "antis" (scale scores of 0-3) and the "pros" (scale scores of 3-5).[5] Similarly, the ERA variable was split into the "antis" (scale scores of 1-2) and the "pros" (scale scores of 3-5).[6]

Based on this division of the abortion and the ERA variables, a composite variable with the following values was formed: (1) antis—respondents who opposed both issues; (2) the moderates—people who favored one issue and opposed the other; and (3) the pros—individuals favoring both issues. Although attitudes toward abortion and the ERA are highly correlated (Pearson's $r = .79$), it is not necessarily the case that the two issues are tapping the same underlying dimension of basic beliefs. Thus, strictly speaking, this composite variable should be considered nominal in nature. Nonetheless, we will treat the variable as being ordinal since preliminary analysis indicates that to do so does not introduce any serious biases into the analysis.

The frequency distribution on this composite variable reveals that the antis (49.5 percent) clearly outnumber the pros (39.3 percent). This is not particularly surprising, however, given our deliberate focus on the unratified states attending the conference. Perhaps somewhat more interesting is the composition of the moderates (11.2 percent); all of them are respondents who favor the ERA but oppose abortion. In essence a stand against the Equal Rights Amendment virtually assures that the respondent will also have anti-abortion sentiments, but the reverse does not hold.

What explains this pattern? If the three groups are compared on a number of variables, we find that the moderates are most distinguishable from the other two groups in terms of their relatively low participation in national politics and their religious background.[7] In contrast to the very conservative positions of the antis and the extremely liberal stands of the pros, the moderates adopt middle-of-the-road positions on the three attitudinal orientations discussed earlier—sex roles, women's status, and morality. Thus, their opposition to abortion seems to stem primarily from strong religious beliefs rather than a broad concern over social issues involving the state of the American family. In support of this interpretation, we find that almost 60 percent of the moderates are Catholic as compared to 23 percent of the antis and only 10 percent of the pros.

The appearance of the moderates in our analysis, then, seems to illustrate the heterogeneity of the anti-abortion movement. For delegates with a New Right ideology, anti-abortion sentiments are part of a broader opposition to "liberal" changes in society; for others an opposition to abortion represents a narrower expression of fundamental religious beliefs. With this in mind, let us explore the degree to which the antis—presumably the New Right delegates— are mobilized as compared to the other two groups.

Bases of Support

Are these delegates drawn from the same groups that we argued earlier were subject to mobilization efforts from both the New Right and the feminist movement? There are two ways of approaching this question. First, it can be determined which groups the delegates represent in an objective sense. Second, the subjective group membership of the delegates can be assessed in order to determine which groups they psychologically represent. In both instances, the major goal of our analysis will be to see if the anti delegates—those having a New Right ideology—represent the groups that we argued earlier were actually being mobilized by the New Right. To a lesser extent, we will also be interested in seeing if the pro delegates are associated with the women's movement.

Measures

Based on our discussion in Chapter 4, we may identify three types of objective measures of the bases of support of the New Right: political, religious, and socioeconomic. Politically, we have argued that the New Right represents a conflict of Republicans vs. Democrats; conservatives vs. liberals; and super-patriots vs. less nationalistic citizens (Crawford 1980; Falwell 1980). Accordingly, the political bases of support are measured by three variables. The first of these, party identification, is based on the traditional CPS seven-point scale which, in our case, runs from Strong Republicans (1) to Strong Democrats (7). Paralleling this measure in its form is a measure of liberal-conservative self-identification that ranges from extreme liberals to extreme conservatives. Although for our purposes these measures of party and liberal-conservative identification are considered to be relatively objective measures of group membership, it should be noted that both measures tap an element of psychological identification as well. Finally, our last political measure is a patriotism scale that ranges from low to high patriotism. The details of all our measurement procedures are presented in Appendix C.

In terms of the religious bases of support, the conflict underlying the emergence of the New Right is thought to pit the religious elements of society against the relatively nonreligious. In more specific terms, we have argued that the New Right is based on a coalition of fundamentalist, born-again Christians and conservative Catholics. Given this argument, two measures of the religious bases of support are used. First, religious preference is measured in terms of a dummy variable coded "1" for Catholics and fundamentalist Protestants, and "0" for the remaining religious preferences. Secondly, the respondents' religiosity is assessed in terms of reported church attendance; the variable has six categories ranging from low to high attendance.

Finally, based on Ladd's (1978) argument that there has been a basic transformation in the traditional lines of social conflict in America, we posited that the emergence of the New Right may be status-based to some extent. To test this possibility, we use the three traditional indicators of socioeconomic status—education, income, and occupation. High scores indicate, respectively, high levels of education, high income, and less prestigious occupations.

The political, religious, and status measures just described will enable us to infer what groups the New Right has drawn from in order to mobilize support. But, if we wish to go a step further and argue that the New Right has actually used the solidary ties of various groups as a means of mobilization, then we must establish that the delegates identify with those groups. Consequently, in order to measure the delegates' psychological identification with various groups in society, they were presented a list of 19 groups and then instructed in the following fashion: "Please read over this list and tell me the letter for those groups you feel particularly close to—people who are most like you in their ideas and feelings about things."

Findings

Are the anti-delegates representative of the groups that we argued earlier compose the New Right coalition? Looking first at the objective measures of the bases of support represented by the delegates, we do find support for our earlier argument. As illustrated by the overall correlations in Table 5.4, all three measures of the political leanings of the delegates are related to their abortion/ERA sentiments. Delegates who identify themselves as Conservatives and as Republicans, and who score high on patriotism tend to hold New Right positions on the issues of abortion and the ERA. Such findings confirm previous speculation on the political make-up of the New Right (Crawford 1980), and support those few studies that have identified elements of conservatism and nationalism in the beliefs of anti-ERA political activists (Arrington and Kyle 1978; Brady and Tedin 1976; Tedin 1978).

Along these lines, it is also interesting to note that liberal-conservative self-placement is much more strongly related to the composite abortion/ERA variable than is party identification. This may reflect the fact that liberal-conservative identifications tend to symbolize the respondent's position on basic social conflicts; liberals favor social change and the groups symbolic of it, while conservatives react negatively to those symbols or groups that challenge tradition (Conover and Feldman 1981). Thus, the very strong relationship of a conservative self-identification with New Right attitudes tends to support our contention that the New Right is a product of conflict over the preservation of basic life-styles and values.

Next, looking at type of religion, we find that there is a relationship between being Catholic or fundamentalist Protestant and holding New Right attitudes on abortion and the ERA. The relationship, however, is a mild one (tau c = -.28). In effect, fundamentalist Protestant denominations and the Catholic religion are one base of support for New Right activists; but, simply belonging to one of those religions does not guarantee New Right sentiments. Instead, religiosity also appears to play a role in determining where the New Right draws its support from; there is a clear, and fairly strong, relationship between frequent church attendance and New Right attitudes (tau c = -.44). Such findings tend to confirm earlier studies that had found both anti-ERA (Arrington and Kyle 1978; Brady and Tedin 1976; Tedin 1978; Tedin et al. 1977) and anti-abortion (Granberg 1981) activism to be related to religion and church attendance.

Finally, let us turn to the status measures. On these measures, the sample is skewed with over half of the delegates reporting incomes over $20,000, some postgraduate work, and a relatively prestigious occupation. Nonetheless, there are moderate relationships

Table 5.4   BASES OF SUPPORT BY IDEOLOGY

Bases of Support	Ideology			Overall Correlations*
	Antis	Moderates	Pros	
I. Political Variables				
Ideological Identification:				
% conservative	80.8%	0.0%	7.5%	-.70
Party Identification:				
% Republican	50.0	25.1	12.0	.31
Patriotism: % highly				
patriotic	45.4	8.3	2.4	-.59
II. Religious Variables				
Religion: % fundamentalist				
or Catholic	64.2	91.7	33.3	-.28
Religiosity: % frequent				
church attenders (every				
week or every other week)	88.7	75.0	42.9	-.44
III. Status Variables				
Occupation: % housewives	32.0	16.7	16.7	-.25
Income: % less than				
$20,000	20.9	25.0	14.3	.16
Education: % no college				
degree	49.1	16.6	9.6	.26
(N)	(53)	(12)	(42)	

* Correlations are Tau B or Tau C coefficients. All are significant at the .05 level.

Source: Authors' White House Conference Study.

110

in the predicted direction between the three status indicators and our composite abortion/ERA variable. As shown in Table 5.4, the anti-delegates tend to be engaged in the less prestigious occupations (tau c = -.25). Most interesting is the fact that 32 percent of the antis are women who work inside the home. This finding tends to confirm Crawford's (1980) argument that "homemakers" are some of the most active "soldiers" in the New Right army. The high rate of housewives among the antis is also similar to the patterns among anti-ERA activists discovered by Tedin et al. (1977) and Arrington and Kyle (1978).

Along the same lines, there is a very modest relationship between income and our composite attitude variable; as income rises the delegate is more likely to be a member of the pro group (tau c = .16). Finally, there is a moderate relationship between education and attitudes on abortion and the ERA; the New Right delegates, although not uneducated, tend to have lower education levels than the nonrightists (tau c = .26). This last finding is especially critical to the viability of Ladd's (1978) thesis since he argues that education is the key factor polarizing the New Intelligentsia and the New Bourgeoisie. And again, it parallels previous profiles of anti-ERA and anti-abortion activists who, though relatively well-educated, were less educated than activists favoring abortion and the ERA (Arrington and Kyle 1978; Granberg 1981; Tedin et al. 1977; Tedin 1978).

To this point, we have demonstrated that the anti or New Right delegates do appear to represent in an objective sense certain groups in society that we argued were subject to mobilization efforts from the New Right. Yet, with the exception of party and liberal/conservative identifications, it is not clear from the data just presented whether the delegates actually identify with the sorts of groups being mobilized by the New Right and the women's movement. In an effort to determine what groups the delegates identify with psychologically, let us turn to our second type of measures.

Presented in Table 5.5 is a profile of the groups that the pro and anti respondents report feeling psychologically close to.[8] First, there are a number of groups that both the pro and anti groups feel close to, suggesting that the New Right and the left are not diametrically opposed in their feelings toward all groups in society. At the same time, however, there are some marked differences in the patterns of psychological attachment characterizing the two groups. Looking first at the anti delegates, we find that they do appear to identify with those groups generally associated with the New Right. With respect to the two issues of interest here, over 85 percent of the antis feel close to the anti-abortion groups while 50 percent report that they identify with ERA opponents. In more general terms, a sizable number of the anti delegates also identify with other groups

Table 5.5   MEASURES OF CLOSENESS TO GROUPS SUBJECT TO MOBILIZATION, BY IDEOLOGY

	Percent Who Feel Close to		Percent Who Feel Closest to	
	Anti	Pro	Anti	Pro
I. Groups Linked with the Women's Movement				
Liberals	7.7	61.7*	0.0	22.0
Women "Libbers"	1.9	38.1*	0.0	2.4
ERA Supporters	3.8	61.9*	0.0	9.8
Pro-Choice	0.0	42.9*	0.0	7.3
II. Groups Linked with the New Right				
Catholics	34.6	4.8*	7.8	0.0
Conservatives	63.5	2.4*	15.7	0.0
Businessmen	34.6	11.9*	7.8	0.0
Housewives	50.0	14.3*	3.9	0.0
ERA Opponents	50.0	0.0*	5.9	0.0
Anti-Abortion	86.5	4.8*	23.5	0.0
III. Other Groups				
Protestants	42.3	33.3	11.8	4.9
Jews	9.6	35.7*	0.0	7.3
Poor People	26.9	31.0	0.0	7.3
Young People	46.2	45.2	2.0	7.3
Older People	50.0	26.2*	2.0	2.4
Whites	38.5	26.2	2.0	2.4
Blacks	21.2	40.5*	5.9	14.6
Women	44.2	59.5	5.9	9.8
Workingmen	40.4	14.3*	3.9	0.0

* = a difference of means test is significant at the .05 level.

Source: Authors' White House Conference Study.

that are commonly associated with the New Right: conservatives, housewives, Catholics, and businessmen.

In contrast, the pro delegates feel psychologically close to those groups generally associated with the feminist movement and more broadly the New Left. Also, reversing the pattern found among the antis, the pro delegates identify more closely with ERA supporters than they do with pro-choice people (62 percent as compared to 43 percent). This may reflect the fact that the pro-choice movement was not quite as salient as the pro-ERA drive, since at the time of the conference in early 1980, the threat to the passage of the ERA may have seemed more urgent than threats to abortion rights. Alternatively, each issue may be most salient to that side which is attempting to alter the status quo: supporters of the ERA and opponents of abortion. Or, the pro delegates' greater closeness to the pro-ERA forces simply may have been a function of the nature of our sample. We also find that substantial numbers of the pro delegates identify with two other groups linked with the Left: liberals and women "libbers."

The differences between the pro and anti delegates become even clearer when we consider which single group each respondent identifies as feeling closest to. Over 40 percent of the pro delegates feel closest to one of the groups clearly associated with the feminist movement: liberals, women libbers, ERA supporters, and pro-choice people. Even more striking is the pattern characterizing the anti delegates' psychological attachment to the corresponding New Right groups: almost 50 percent feel closest to either the anti-abortion people, the ERA opponents, conservatives, or housewives.

In summary, then, in both an objective and psychological sense the anti delegates—those labeled as having a New Right ideology—do appear to be drawn from those groups in society that we argue are most susceptible to mobilization by the New Right. Politically, the antis are mobilized from those segments of the population that are conservative, Republican, and highly patriotic. In terms of religion, the New Right delegates are more likely than the nonrightists to have been mobilized from the highly religious elements of the Catholic Church and the fundamentalist Protestant denominations. Finally, although the class-related bases of support of the New Right are less distinct than the religious and political bases, there is some tendency for the New Right delegates to be drawn from what Ladd (1978) would label the New Bourgeoisie.

The Levels of Mobilization

To this point, we have demonstrated that the anti and pro delegates do tend to represent, respectively, those groups that we

argued earlier were the prime targets for mobilization by the New
Right and the feminist and other "left-wing" movements. Yet, not
all people who are subject to mobilization efforts actually become
mobilized. This is evident in the relatively low levels of mobilization characterizing New Right and feminist organizations nationwide.
A recent Gallup Poll survey (Gallup Report 1981a) reported that only
about 1 percent of the nation's population belonged to anti-abortion
groups; 1 percent were members of pro-choice groups; and 1 percent had joined a group promoting women's rights. What about the
delegates considered here? How many of them have actually been
mobilized by some organization that could legitimately be considered part of either the New Right or the Left?

Measures

As explained in Chapter 2, the concept of mobilization may be
measured in terms of organizational development without there being too much "slippage" between the theoretical conceptualization
and the operational measure. Accordingly, our measure of mobilization will be the percentage of delegates belonging to an organization associated with either the New Right or liberal causes.

In order to tap the full range of their group memberships, the
delegates were asked three questions. First, did they belong to any
organization that represents the interests and viewpoints of the
group that they felt closest to? Second, did they belong to any organization that is involved with or takes stands on issues concerning the family? And finally, of all the groups and organizations
they belong to, which is the most important or the one they are most
involved with? Responses to each question were recorded and later
coded into one of five categories: (1) groups linked with the New
Right; (2) liberal organizations opposed to New Right policies;
(3) churches or church-related groups that are not explicitly identified as being aligned with either New Right or liberal causes; (4)
nonprofessional organizations that are relatively neutral toward the
conflict; and (5) job-related groups.[9]

Findings

By considering the three group membership questions together, we can get some idea of the extent to which the delegates
have actually joined an organization associated with either the New
Right or the left. We find that the delegates with a New Right ideology—the antis—report a relatively high level of membership in New
Right organizations; almost 70 percent belong to at least one such
group. Clearly, this finding supports our treatment of the anti
delegates as members of the New Right in an organizational sense
as well as an ideological one.

In contrast, only 31 percent of the pros—the delegates with a feminist ideology—actually report belonging to a liberal organization of the type that could be expected to be aligned with the women's movement. This finding can be interpreted in two ways. On the one hand, it may indicate that members of the left and the women's movement are simply not as highly mobilized as adherents of the New Right. Alternatively, given the somewhat uncertain nature of the population represented by the delegates, it may be that various organizations associated with the women's movement were simply not well represented at the Minneapolis White House Conference on the Families. Betty Friedan (1981), for one, implies that this might have been the case. Whatever the reason for the comparatively low mobilization of the pro delegates, the finding suggests that we must be cautious in using the pro delegates as a reference group for the women's movement as a whole. While they may constitute a good nonrightist comparison group for the New Right delegates, they are not necessarily representative of the mainline women's groups.

Finally, the moderates—the delegates with neither a New Right nor feminist ideology—tend to belong to liberal organizations with none reporting membership in a New Right group. In fact, proportionately more of the moderates (33 percent) belong to a clearly liberal organization than do the pro delegates (31 percent). This finding, as well, indicates that caution should be taken in our interpretation of the population represented by the pro delegates.

To this point, we have seen that as a whole the anti delegates demonstrate a fairly high level of mobilization by New Right organizations. Yet, group membership alone says relatively little about the importance of the organization to the delegate, and thus the individual's expected loyalty to it. It may be that the anti delegates, though members, are only peripherally involved in the New Right organizations. To examine this possibility, we consider the types of organizations that the delegates label most important to them.

As shown in Table 5.6, the anti, moderate, and pro delegates definitely differ in terms of the type of organization that they are most involved in. Furthermore, an analysis of variance indicates that these differences are significant at the .05 level. Over 50 percent of the anti delegates consider a New Right organization to be the one most important to them. Thus, the anti delegates are representative of the New Right not only in the sense of formal organizational membership but, more importantly, in terms of psychological commitment as well. Looking at the anti delegates who do not consider a New Right organization to be most important to them, we find that they are concentrated in the "church" category (most frequently a fundamentalist one). This suggests that various churches may, indeed, form a network of solidary ties that have been utilized by the New Right in their mobilization networks. Finally, the few remaining anti delegates are dispersed relatively evenly over the other categories of organizations, though it should be noted that a higher percent of the antis than the other groups do not have a "most important organization."

Table 5.6   MOST IMPORTANT ORGANIZATION BY IDEOLOGY
(in percent)

	Ideological Group		
Type of Organization	Anti	Moderate	Pro
New Right	52.8	0.0	0.0
Liberal	0.0	8.3	16.7
Church	20.8	25.0	11.9
Nonprofessional	7.6	25.0	26.1
Job-Related	7.5	33.0	40.5
None Reported	11.3	8.3	4.8
TOTAL	100.0	99.9*	100.0
(N)	(53)	(12)	(42)

* Figures do not total 100% due to rounding.

Source: Authors' White House Conference Study.

In contrast to the anti delegates, the moderates and the pros are more widely scattered across the various categories. Substantial numbers of the moderates consider a church (in most instances the Catholic Church) to be their most important organization. This finding confirms our earlier characterization of the moderates as a relatively religious, apolitical group. In the case of the pro delegates, a relatively small proportion (16.7 percent) consider a liberal organization to be most important. Instead, both the moderates and especially the pros seem much more heavily involved in professional organizations such as the Family Services Association of America and the Family Service agency.

In summary, the anti delegates demonstrate a relatively high level of mobilization in an organizational sense. Many of them belong to New Right organizations, and even more critical, over half of them consider a New Right organization to be their most important group. This finding supports the validity of our treatment of the anti delegates as representatives of the New Right. In contrast, the pro delegates, while representative of the feminist movement in an ideological sense, are by no means a mobilized constituency of the movement in an organizational sense.

Strategies of Mobilization

In Chapter 2, three different strategies of mobilization were outlined. Specifically, it was argued that people can be motivated to join a group out of self-interest, through existing solidary ties, and out of adherence to personal principles. Which of these strategies figured most prominently in motivating the White House Conference delegates? Based on our earlier examination of the New Right and women's movements, we hypothesize that personal principles should dominate the motivational schemes of those delegates joining either a New Right or liberal group. Simply put, given the argument that the conflict between the New Right and the feminist movement is a life-style one rooted in the clash of basic values, it seems reasonable to posit that the respondents have joined New Right and liberal organizations out of a desire to protect the personal principles based on such values. Solidary ties, while also important to the New Right and liberal organizations, are expected to play a somewhat greater role in church-related and nonprofessional organizations, because such groups often serve a social or friendship function in addition to their ideological one. Finally, self-interests, such as those fulfilled through economic benefits, are expected to be a more important motivational factor for the job-related groups—e.g., professional, labor, and business organizations.

Measures

To test these hypotheses, the delegates were asked the following question:

> People join organizations for a number of different reasons. Some join for economic benefits such as improving their job possibilities. Others join groups for friendship and the opportunity to discuss common problems. Still others join organizations for ideological reasons such as the pursuit of a common goal or value. Which of these reasons best explains why you joined
> _____ (Respondent's most important group)?

Where economic benefits were chosen, self-interest is seen as being the underlying motivation; friendship is taken as an indicator of the importance of solidary ties; and joining because of the pursuit of common goals and values is viewed as an indicator of the importance of personal principles.

Findings

As shown in Table 5.7, there is good support for our hypotheses. All members of the New Right, liberal, and church organizations cite personal principles or ideology as being their primary motivation in joining the group. This is strong evidence that these delegates view their activism as a means of pursuing basic goals and values. To use Fireman and Gamson's (1979) terms, the delegates' personal principles led them to value the collective goods sought by those groups and thus out of a sense of responsibility they joined the group. In a more general sense, this finding supports the argument advanced by critics (Fireman and Gamson 1979; Mitchell 1979; Moe 1981; Tillock and Morrison 1979) of Mancur Olson; that is, in certain types of organizations self-interest may not be the major factor in motivating individuals to join the group.

Our confidence in this conclusion is strengthened when the other types of organizations are considered. Ideology continues to play a major role among the members in the nonprofessional organizations, although, as expected, the solidary ties found in friendship also are important in explaining membership. Finally, in the job-related groups, self-interest asserts itself as a significant motivating factor in the delegates' membership calculus. This provides some measure of support for Olson's (1971) argument since the job-related organizations are the ones most similar to the type discussed by Olson in his pioneering work. Nonetheless, even in the job-related groups values and personal principles still assume the dominant motivational role for over half the members.[10]

Yet, although personal principles may be the major reason why a person joins a group, other motivational factors should also come into play. Recall from our theoretical discussion in Chapter 2, in most instances political entrepreneurs are expected to employ mixed strategies in their membership appeals. They may, for example, supplement a primary appeal to personal principles by drawing upon solidary ties. If this is the case, it should be reflected in the reasons that group members offer for their membership. Indeed, this would seem to be the case among the delegates considered here. The fact that almost half of them felt compelled to volunteer a second reason for their membership suggests that they had mixed motivations in joining. Furthermore, when the nature of

Table 5.7   REASON FOR JOINING MOST IMPORTANT ORGANIZATION*
(in percent)

| Reason | Type of Organization | | | | |
	New Right	Liberal	Church	Nonprofessional	Job–Related
Self-interest (economic benefits)	0	0	0	5.9	25.0
Solidary Ties (friendship)	0	0	0	23.5	12.5
Personal Principles (ideology)	100	100	100	70.6	62.5
Total	100	100	100	100.0	100.0
(N)	(28)	(8)	(18)	(17)	(24)

* Analysis of variance indicates that there are significant ($p < .05$) differences across groups in reasons for joining.

Source: Authors' White House Conference Study.

119

those motivations is considered, they coincide with our earlier hypotheses. Specifically, among the New Right, liberal, and church group members, over half offered some mention of solidarity as a second explanation for their group membership.

In summary, our brief examination of the reasons underlying the delegates' group membership provides support for some of the ideas expressed in earlier chapters. Different types of groups appear to employ different strategies of mobilization. As expected, those groups most heavily involved in the New Right conflict do seem to rely on personal principles as a major motivating factor. Clearly, this makes sense if we accept the argument that a value and a life-style conflict underlies the emergence of the New Right. In contrast, as predicted from Olson's (1971) original theory, the job-related groups are based more heavily on economic benefits that appeal to the individual's self-interest. Finally, in many instances organizations do appear to employ mixed strategies of mobilization.

ORGANIZATIONAL ACTIVITIES

Now that we have examined the mobilization process characterizing these various organizations, let us turn our attention to the activities engaged in by those organizations. In particular, our interest lies in exploring two types of activities: those that primarily serve the membership of the group and those intended to affect the "targets of influence" whose decisions determine whether the group will attain its collective goals. With respect to the former, we have already examined the delegates' perceptions as to why they joined the particular organization most important to them. Yet, the mobilization process does not cease once an organization has successfully recruited its initial group of supporters. On the contrary, virtually all organizations must engage in some "maintenance" activities whose purpose is to preserve their current membership through the reinforcement of existing individual loyalties. In this regard, we are interested in determining if the New Right organizations use the same sorts of maintenance tactics as other types of groups.

Even more interesting are the tactics of influence. As explained in Chapter 2, the government is typically the primary target of influence when groups are contending for political power. Certainly, this appears to be the case where the New Right and the women's movements are concerned. Furthermore, in their advocacy efforts neither movement can really be considered to be a political "challenger" in Gamson's (1975) sense of the word; rather, both movements seem to have access to the channels of influence usually open to "members of the polity." Thus, we are led to consider whether the New Right and leftist groups make equal use of those channels of influence. Even more generally, how do the New Right organizations differ from the other types of organizations considered in our study?

Measures

In order to measure the type of maintenance activities engaged in by their most important organization, the delegates were asked whether their group: (1) sponsored workshops and conferences; and (2) published newsletters or pamphlets. With regard to tactics of influence, we were interested in determining the organizations' activity levels in the three broad areas of direct lobbying, lobbying through constituents, and indirect lobbying. Accordingly, the delegates were asked whether their groups had engaged in the following activities: (1) direct lobbying—filing a court suit, testifying at legislative hearings, and personal presentations of argument to elected representatives, agency heads, or other government executives; (2) lobbying through constituents—having an influential member of the organization contact a government decision-maker, instigating a letter-writing campaign, and organizing political protests; and (3) indirect lobbying—contributing money to political campaigns, publicizing voting records of elected officials, releasing research results, and public relations campaigns.

In the case of both types of tactics—organizational maintenance and advocacy—a simple percentage of the <u>delegates</u> stating that their organization used the tactic are reported. Yet, although the data are still based on the individual delegate, it is important to keep in mind that in responding to these questions the delegates are acting as representatives of their respective organizations. In such a role it is expected that the delegates have provided relatively accurate information about their organizations. Certainly, this should be the case given that most of the delegates are in a position where they should be well-informed about the organization's activities; over 80 percent of the delegates naming a most important organization claim to be both a leader in the group as well as very involved in its activities. Finally, given that the delegates are acting in the capacity of spokesperson for their organization, the data provide a broad sampling of a wide range of organizations. Represented are 20 different New Right organizations and seven liberal groups.[11]

Findings

For each of the 12 activities, Table 5.8 presents the percentage of delegates reporting that their most important organization

Table 5.8   ORGANIZATIONAL ACTIVITIES

		% Using Tactic[a]			
Tactic	New Right	Liberal	Church	Nonprofessional	Job-Related
I. Organizational Maintenance					
Newsletters	92.9	87.5	78.9	83.8	96.0
Workshops	89.3	100.0	89.5	77.8	100.0
II. Direct Lobbying					
Court Suit*	39.3	50.0	15.8	27.8	8.0
Testify at Hearings*	78.6	100.0	31.6	27.8	96.0
Personal Presentations*	96.4	100.0	47.4	66.7	88.0
III. Lobbying through Constituents					
Contact by Influential Member*	92.9	100.0	63.2	83.3	92.0
Letter–Writing*	96.4	100.0	47.4	72.2	80.0
Protest*	60.7	62.5	10.5	27.8	28.0
IV. Indirect Lobbying					
Campaign Money	17.9	0.0	0.0	5.6	20.0
Publicize Voting Records*	89.3	87.5	15.8	38.9	56.0
Release Research Results	67.9	75.0	42.1	72.2	84.0
Public Relations Campaign	67.9	100.0	42.1	72.2	64.0
(N)	(28)	(8)	(19)	(18)	(25)

[a] Entries are the percent of delegates who said their most important organization engaged in that activity in the last two years.

* = Analysis of variance indicates significant differences ($p < .05$) across types of organizations for that activity.

Source: Authors' White House Conference Study.

has engaged in the activity. For each activity, an analysis of variance (ANOVA) was run to determine if the overall differences among types of organizations were significant; a star by the activity indicates that the F-test for the ANOVA was significant at the .05 level.

To begin, let us consider the organizational maintenance activities—newsletters and workshops. As we see in Table 5.8, there is very little variance across types of organizations in terms of these two activities. For each type of organization, the delegates reveal a very high use of both newsletters and workshops. To some extent, this is not surprising. All organizations must exert some effort to retain their membership. Providing a newsletter is certainly one relatively economical way of maintaining ties among members. Similarly, sponsoring workshops and conferences acts not only to reinforce existing loyalties to the group, but also to recruit new members. From another perspective, some might argue that the high levels of organizational maintenance activities indicate support for Olson's (1971) theory. As Moe (1980) explains, political entrepreneurs can use an activity such as a newsletter or a group workshop not only as a means of communicating among members, but also as a selective incentive. In effect, the information communicated in these ways takes on a value of its own which acts as a material selective incentive in maintaining group membership.

Let us turn now to the various types of lobbying activities. Beginning with direct lobbying, we find that there are significant differences across types of organizations for all three activities. Of the three activities, as a whole the organizations are the least likely to file a court suit. This supports what Berry (1977) found in his study of public interest groups. Generally, filing a court suit is only undertaken by an organization when it is structured to carry out a lawsuit, and thus the tactic is used most frequently by groups that are set up explicitly to lobby the courts. In the case of the organizations considered here, the liberal groups are most likely to use the courts, although the difference between them and the next highest type of organization—New Right—is not significant. Nonetheless, this slight difference may exist because, on the whole, the liberal advocacy groups are better established than the New Right groups.

Turning to the other direct lobbying tactics, we find that the New Right, liberal, and job-related groups all are more likely than the other groups to testify at hearings. Their greater use of this tactic confirms Berry's (1977) finding that 88 percent of the public interest groups use this tactic. Furthermore, although the tactic is often viewed as ineffective in winning supporters (Berry 1977), it is one major way of getting things on the legislative agenda, a fact that might explain why more of the New Right and liberal groups have used the tactic. Finally, almost all the New Right and liberal organizations have made personal presentations to decision-makers. This is no surprise, however, given that Berry's (1977) study judged this to be the most effective means of direct lobbying.

With regard to the different means of lobbying through constituents, we again find that there are significant differences across organizations in their usage of all three tactics. Of the three tactics, contacting a decision-maker through an influential member is the one that virtually all types of organizations use. Furthermore, the overall percent of groups using this tactic is somewhat higher than the 62 percent level of use that Berry (1977) found among public interest groups. Letter-writing was the constituent lobbying tactic that Berry found to be the most popular among public interest groups, and one that the groups considered most effective. In our sample, as well, a relatively high percent of all types of organizations engaged in letter-writing, with the New Right and liberal organizations topping the usage list. This is to be expected, however, since by their very nature these are advocacy groups that have a cause to push.

Finally, we examine the protest levels of the groups. Berry (1977) found that only about a quarter of the public interest groups engaged in protest activities, specifically political demonstrations. Our study also reveals that a relatively low percent of the church, nonprofessional, and job-related groups have used protest. At the same time, however, more than half of the New Right and the liberal groups are reported to have engaged in protest. One reason for this might be that the New Right and liberal groups are more interested in influencing public opinion than are the other types of organizations. Certainly, the media coverage gained from engaging in protest activities would help in this regard. In addition to increasing media coverage and thus exposure to the public, the New Right and liberal groups may also be using protest as a political resource in sensitizing government officials to their demands and influencing perceptions of the group's power (Berry 1977; Lipsky 1968). Thus, the "channels of access" may not be as open to these groups as we initially thought they might be.

Last, we can examine the methods of indirect lobbying where, in contrast to the other forms of lobbying, there are few significant differences among the organizations. The groups vary little in their use of public relations campaigns and research results; over half of most types of organizations use these tactics. Similarly, there are no significant differences in the organizations' contributions to political candidates; very few of them report giving money to candidates. No doubt, in part this is attributable to the tax laws which make it impossible for many of these organizations to engage in this activity.

Nonetheless, on the face of it, this finding may be somewhat surprising to some given all the talk in the popular media about the
large amounts of money that flowed from the coffers of the New
Right into the campaigns of conservative candidates during the 1980
elections. Yet, it must be remembered that this finding does not
necessarily reflect on the campaign contributions that New Right
organizations make to political action committees (PACs). Indeed,
as discussed in earlier chapters, these organizations appear to be
making substantial contributions to PACs, thus circumventing the
need for any direct contributions to candidates.

A related method of influencing the outcomes of political elections is through publicizing the voting records of incumbent legislators. Again, this is a tactic that the New Right is famous for according to the popular media. This time, our findings bear out
their reputation; almost 90 percent of the delegates belonging to a
New Right organization report that their group has used this tactic.
Yet, at the same time, it is important to note that proportionately
almost as many liberal groups as New Right organizations use this
tactic in contrast to other types of groups.

Summary

We are now in a position to answer the questions posed at the
beginning of this section. Overall, there are very few differences
(and none that are significant) between the activities of the New Right
organizations and those of the liberal groups. [12] These two types of
organizations are alike in the sense that both are composed of advocacy groups attempting to influence the government to adopt policies
favorable to their values and goals. As such, they make very similar use of the tactics available to them. At the same time, while
there is little variation between the New Right and liberal groups,
differences emerge when other types of organizations are taken into
account.

What seems most important in determining the activities of an
organization is the nature, rather than ideological content, of its
goals. If the group is attempting to gain political power and influence a broad spectrum of policy—as some of the New Right and liberal groups are—then it must make use of the wide range of lobbying activities available to it, regardless of whether its goals are
liberal or conservative in nature. In contrast, if the group is only
marginally concerned with attaining political power and influencing
public policy—as most of the church organizations and some of the
nonprofessional groups are—then it need not involve itself in most
types of lobbying activities.

CONCLUSIONS

These data have provided some interesting information about the nature of activists involved in the New Right conflict. Yet, in evaluating our findings it is important to keep in mind the limitations of the data. As noted earlier, the sample is not a large one. Not only has this led us to choose rather simple techniques of analysis, but it also forces us to be somewhat cautious in the conclusions we draw. This is especially true given the added uncertainty about the population represented by these delegates. Our analysis indicates that the delegates with a New Right ideology may be fairly representative of other New Right activists not only in terms of their ideology but also with respect to their backgrounds and organizational involvement. In contrast, the delegates with a feminist ideology seem to be drawn more from professional organizations than from groups associated with the women's movement. Thus, while the nonright delegates provide a good comparison group for the New Right members of our sample, we are hesitant to treat them necessarily as good representatives of the women's movement. With this in mind, let us consider some of our findings.

First, with respect to the issues of abortion and the ERA, as might be expected among activists, attitudes toward these issues are polarized. Even more important to our argument, however, is the meaning the delegates associate with these issues. The delegates' attitudes are based on both substantive information and emotional feelings. With regard to the issues' cognitive meaning, the delegates' attitudes toward abortion and the ERA are definitely related to their beliefs about proper sex roles, women's economic status, and morality. Such findings lend substantial support to our argument that the conflict over these issues symbolizes a more basic conflict over values and life-styles. This conclusion is reinforced by our findings concerning the evaluative meaning of these issues. The delegates' attitudes toward abortion and the ERA are strongly related to their feelings toward various groups that symbolically represent the lines of cleavage separating the New Right and the left. Thus, among these activists at least, the conflict over the issues of abortion and the ERA is defined according to the terms of debate that we identified earlier.

Turning to the mobilization of the delegates, we find further support for the arguments made in earlier chapters. If we divide the delegates into groups having either a New Right ideology, a leftist or feminist ideology, or an ideology somewhere in between, then we find that these groups of delegates are drawn from those elements in society that we contended earlier are most likely to support the New Right and the left, respectively. Furthermore, if we look at

the actual levels of mobilization, we find that those delegates with a
New Right ideology also tend to belong to at least one New Right organization. In contrast, the delegates having a feminist ideology
are more involved in professional organizations than in liberal
groups. Finally, of particular interest to our understanding of what
motivates individual mobilization was the finding that personal principles and values seem to be more important than economic self-
interests. Thus, as we have argued throughout this book, it certainly appears, at least for these activists, that membership in the
New Right is motivated by threats to basic values.

Finally, our analysis considered the organizational activities
of the groups that the delegates felt were most important to them.
Here, because the delegates were acting as spokespersons for their
organizations, our data take on added breadth and significance. In
this portion of the analysis, it was possible to identify the actual
population of organizations represented. Although not all of the New
Right organizations discussed in Chapter 4 were represented, a
sufficient number of them were covered by the data to make this
portion of the analysis especially interesting. We found quite simply that the New Right organizations differ little from the liberal
groups in terms of either their maintenance activities or their lobbying efforts. This is not to say that the New Right groups do not
engage more heavily in political action committees; that is an empirical question that will be dealt with in a later chapter. What it
does suggest is that the nature of an organization's goals, rather
than its ideological stance, determines the nature of its lobbying
activities. New Right and liberal groups alike are more likely than
other types of organizations to engage in certain forms of activities
(such as protests) simply because their goals are more oriented
toward political influence than are those of the other varieties of
organizations.

Thus, based on the examination of our sample of activists,
the conflict over abortion and the ERA does appear to be a life-style
conflict rooted in basic values central to how people view the American family. It is a conflict that has motivated concerned individuals
to join organizations out of a desire to preserve those values and to
protect the family as they know it. Furthermore, it is a conflict
that seemingly is being waged using traditional means of political
influence. What have the effects been of such efforts at political
influence? In the next two chapters, we will attempt to answer that
question.

NOTES

1. The states attending the conference were Arkansas, Illinois, Iowa, Kentucky, Louisiana, Michigan, Minnesota, Mississippi, Missouri, Ohio, Tennessee, West Virginia, and Wisconsin.

2. The interviewers were graduate students in the Department of Political Science at the University of Minnesota. All of them underwent a three-hour training session and conducted several practice interviews. The actual interviews were conducted, whenever possible, without the presence of other delegates of the conference.

3. This series of abortion questions is adopted from the National Opinion Research Center (NORC's) General Social Surveys.

4. We use correlational analysis, rather than regression, because we do not wish to argue that these independent variables—representing various dimensions of substantive and emotional meaning—actually cause variations in attitudes toward abortion and the ERA.

5. This cutting point was selected on the basis of the Guttman scale analysis which revealed that those respondents scoring 0–3 tended to oppose abortion in all cases or to favor it only in the case of some of the so-called "easy" alternatives—health of the woman, rape, and possible birth defect. In contrast, those scoring 4–7 tended to favor abortion in all of the "easy" cases as well as some of the "hard" ones—low income, unmarried, does not want any more children.

6. The one respondent who was uncertain was arbitrarily assigned to the "pro" side.

7. A stepwise discriminant analysis employing all the variables in Appendix C as well as measures of authoritarianism, trust in people, internal-external control, campaign participation, participation in national politics, and participation in local politics was conducted. This conclusion is based on the results of that analysis.

8. The moderates were excluded from this analysis for two reasons: (1) to make the comparison clearer and the discussion briefer; and (2) because the moderates, as a whole, showed little variations on the questions—they tended to say that they felt close to almost all the groups.

9. Groups were coded into categories based first on their name. If there was any doubt on this criterion, then the delegate's description of the goals and activities of the organization were used to determine which category the organization best fit into. The "New Right" groups include: national and local anti-abortion groups, anti-ERA groups, pro-family groups, and other right-wing groups not fitting into those categories. The "liberal" groups include feminist organizations as well as more broadly defined liberal groups

such as the ACLU. The "church" category includes actual churches as well as related organizations. The nonprofessional category covers neutral or traditional women's groups such as the League of Women Voters; racial and ethnic organizations; and community organizations such as the PTA. Finally, the "job-related" category also encompasses three types of groups: professional associations such as the Family Service Association of America; labor unions; and business groups.

10. Although we do find the expected variations across types of groups, the overall importance of values and personal principles may have been exaggerated somewhat due to the social desirability associated with the "common goals and values" response.

11. In very few instances is an organization represented more than once. Furthermore, in virtually all those cases of multiple representation, the delegates are from different states; thus, their experiences are not with the same local chapters. For this reason, it was decided not to limit organizations to only one representative.

12. For each type of activity, a difference of means test was run for the New Right and liberal groups. None of the t-tests were significant at the .05 level.

6 / THE IMPACT OF THE NEW RIGHT ON MASS ATTITUDES AND BEHAVIOR

In Chapter 5, we found that the conflict separating New Right activists from nonrightists stems from differences over basic life-styles and values. Furthermore, we discovered that New Right groups differ little from their left-wing counterparts in their use of traditional lobbying tactics to win political power. Rather than abandoning the traditional methods of lobbying, the New Right seems to have supplemented these methods with new ones—such as the use of PACs and extensive mailing lists—that presumably make the old tactics more effective. Yet, how effective has the New Right really been?

In evaluating the success of the New Right, our focus in this chapter will be on the degree to which the New Right has gained new advantages through indirect lobbying (the success of more direct lobbying efforts will be reviewed in the next chapter). As we saw in the last chapter, a substantial proportion of the New Right groups examined had engaged in various forms of indirect lobbying (i.e., trying to influence public opinion and electoral politics). But it is unclear how successful these efforts have been. In fact, there is a striking split between popular and scholarly writing on the subject.

Journalists argue that single-issue politics is an important new negative development in American politics. For example, in 1978 Newsweek decried the proliferation of single-issue groups and their "me-first" brand of politics that could potentially fragment our political system (1978, p. 48). Similarly, conservative journalist Alan Crawford (1980) decided to write a book exposing the New Right because of the threat he felt it posed to "true" conservatism and the Republic. Second, some recently defeated politicians blame their losses on the New Right. As a result of his experience, one defeated liberal, George McGovern, has formed his own PAC to fight the Right, while former Senator Thomas McIntyre (1979) of New Hampshire has written a book to warn of the danger. Third, New Right strategists are quick to point out their role in the victories of conservative candidates (e.g., Ronald Reagan in the White House). Richard Viguerie, for example, takes credit for a number of victories in the 1980 election. He states that America was always conservative; what the New Right did was to give it leadership (Viguerie 1981, p. 6).

In contrast, many others argue that the impact of the Right in the 1980 elections and in general is highly overrated: the GOP, for example, and several political pollsters say that the role of the Right was minimal and in some cases even harmful to their campaigns (Congressional Quarterly 1980d, p. 3372). For the most part, political scientists studying 1980 campaigns and other contests tend to agree. For example, with respect to the abortion issue, there have been several studies spanning electoral contests from 1976 to 1980 (Morris and Stempel 1978; Traugott and Vinovskis 1980; Hershey and West 1981; Zwier 1981; Penfield and Davis 1981). Although not all of these studies directly assess the impact of abortion on vote choice, the general thrust of their findings is that the impact of the anti-abortion forces specifically and the New Right in general have been overrated.

Thus, most political science studies do not attribute much impact to the electoral activities of pro-life groups and the Moral Majority on the abortion and ERA issues. Yet, politicians and activists on each side, as well as the mass media, perceive the New Right as wielding substantial power at the polls. In this chapter, we will attempt to determine which perspective is the more accurate. Specifically, we will examine changes in public opinion over time, as well as the behavior of the American electorate, in an effort to assess the New Right's impact.

DATA

In assessing the impact of the Right on public opinion, it was deemed necessary to consider changes in public opinion over time. Yet, the question of how to evaluate changes over time is a difficult one complicated by the fact that data relevant to our theoretical approach are limited. Bearing this in mind, a number of decisions were made. First, we chose to use repeated cross-sections rather than panel data. Practically, this decision was dictated by the fact that there were no available panel studies spanning the decade of the

1970s. Furthermore, from a theoretical perspective, although information about individual-level changes may prove useful in understanding changes in aggregate opinion levels (Weber and Uslaner 1981), this was not considered necessary in order to gain an understanding of the overall impact of the New Right on public opinion.

Second, our choice of data was shaped by the need to ensure as much comparability in question wording as possible, so that any changes in public opinion could be considered "real" changes rather than artifacts of our methodology. Question comparability is particularly important in the case of attitudes toward abortion since studies have shown that public opinion on abortion varies considerably depending on the question wording (Schuman and Presser 1981; Schuman, Presser, and Ludwig 1981).

Guided by our decisions to use repeated cross-sections and to stress question comparability, we selected the National Election Studies conducted by the Center for Political Studies (CPS) at the University of Michigan as the best single source of data. But, as is often the case in secondary analysis, the data set does not suit our needs perfectly. Consequently, we have supplemented the CPS studies with data from both the General Social Surveys conducted by the National Opinion Research Center at the University of Chicago and the Gallup survey. Let us turn now to the first part of our analysis: a consideration of attitudes toward abortion and the ERA.

ATTITUDES TOWARD ABORTION AND THE ERA

How have the public's attitudes toward abortion and the ERA changed over the last decade? In the last chapter, we saw that for political activists abortion and the ERA are very polarized issues that evoke substantial cognitive meaning as well as intense emotional reactions. This was precisely what was expected given our argument that a conflict over life-style and basic values underlies the emergence of the New Right. Yet, to what extent has the polarization and symbolization of these issues "filtered into" the attitudes of the mass public? If the New Right has broadened the conflict over these issues in order to enhance its mobilization efforts, then there should be some change in the public's opinions over the last decade or so.

Measures

In measuring attitudes toward abortion, we employ a question that the CPS asked in each election study since 1972. Respondents were instructed to pick the alternative which best agrees with their view on abortion:

1. Abortion should never be permitted.
2. Abortion should be permitted only if the life and health of the woman is in danger.
3. Abortion should be permitted if, due to personal reasons, the woman would have difficulty in caring for the child.
4. Abortion should never be forbidden, since one should not require a woman to have a child she doesn't want.

Although it is less comprehensive than the seven-item set of questions used in the previous chapter's analysis, this question does attempt to get at the potential variations in opinion associated with the so-called "hard" and "soft" abortion items discussed earlier. Thus, it should provide us with an acceptable estimate of attitudes on the issue.

In measuring attitudes toward the Equal Rights Amendment, we were less fortunate. The CPS did not ask about the issue until 1976. Thus, using the CPS data we would be limited in our ability to assess changes in the distribution of attitudes on the ERA. Consequently, we rely on Gallup Poll surveys which ask respondents simply whether they favor or oppose the amendment.

Findings

In evaluating attitudes toward abortion and the ERA, several things are important. First, to what extent have opinions become more crystallized on the issues? If the conflict has indeed broadened to include a substantial portion of the mass public, then we would expect the number of people without an opinion to decline over time. Second, to what extent have attitudes become more polarized? If the issues have become more symbolic in their meaning, then attitudes should also have become more polarized. Third, and finally, which side is favored by public opinion? If the New Right has been successful in its indirect lobbying efforts, then there should be some shift in public opinion toward its position.

Taking the abortion issue first, Table 6.1 shows that surprisingly few people are uncertain about their opinion on abortion; in every year except 1976 less than 2 percent express no opinion. Thus, the public seems very familiar with the abortion issue, but that does not appear to be a function of the New Right conflict since opinionation has been high throughout the decade. Likewise, there has been relatively little change since 1972 in the distribution of opinion; in each year a majority of the public adopts a moderate position on abortion, and the pro-choice extremists outnumber the anti-abortion extremists. Thus, the public's attitudes have definitely not become more polarized. Nor have there been any sizable shifts in opinion toward the anti-abortion side.[1] On the contrary, according to the CPS data, what little movement there has been is toward the pro-choice side. Thus, in 1980, as in 1972, a majority of the public is <u>un</u>willing to ban all abortions although many are willing to put some restrictions on the right. In summary, then, the conflict over abortion at the activist or elite level does not seem to have had much impact on the mass public's attitudes.

Table 6.1 ATTITUDES TOWARD ABORTION
(in percent)

Attitude	1972	1976	1980
Never Permit	10.9	10.7	9.5
Life Only	45.6	43.7	43.5
If Care Difficult	16.9	15.9	17.5
Never Forbid	23.8	26.0	26.8
Other	.9	1.3	.8
Don't Know	1.8	2.4	1.9
Total	99.9	100.0	100.0
(N)	(2692)	(2380)	(2400)

* Percentages do not total 100% due to rounding.

<u>Source</u>: CPS National Election Studies.

Given that people's reactions to abortion are quite sensitive to question wording, it is important to note that other national polls using different questions also report a pattern of general stability in the aggregate distribution of opinion, as well as a basic opposition to forbidding all abortions (for a review of some of these data, see Granberg and Granberg 1980; Uslaner and Weber 1979). For example, over the years the Gallup Poll has asked the following question at regular intervals:

Do you think abortions should be legal under any circumstances, legal under only certain circumstances,
or illegal in all circumstances? (Gallup Report 1981b,
p. 21).

As in the case of the CPS data, the Gallup Polls report a very
high level of opinionation on the abortion issue; at no point in time
do they find that more than 5 percent have no opinion. Similarly,
they find that attitudes have not become more polarized. Instead,
a substantial portion of the population (between 50 and 55 percent)
occupies a middle-of-the-road position in which they are willing to
allow abortion in at least some circumstances. Thus, although
there may be some variations in the distribution of opinion depending
on question wording, the overall pattern of aggregate stability and
favorability toward a limited right to abortion does not seem to vary
much across data sets.

Turning our attention to attitudes toward the ERA, we find that
awareness of the amendment reached its peak during 1980 when
only 9 percent of the population reported not having heard or read
about it (see Table 6.2). Since that election year, awareness has
dropped off some (down to 88 percent). Thus, opinionation does
appear to be lower for the ERA than for abortion. But, support for
the amendment has remained fairly steady and has even increased
slightly in recent months, among those respondents who have heard
or read about it. At the same time, opponents of the ERA have
made some gains, but not at the expense of support for the amendment. Instead, until quite recently, the anti-ERA forces have
apparently been winning over some of those people that had heard
about the amendment but who had been undecided in their feeling
toward it. But, even this trend seems to be grinding to a halt as
the memories of the 1980 election fade from the public's mind.
According to the Gallup Poll (1981c), in 1981 it is the supporters of
the ERA who have gained in numbers. Similar findings emerge
from an April 1982 Harris survey (Opinion Outlook 1982a) that found
63 percent of the population in favor of the ERA and only 34 percent
opposed. Thus, while less opinionated on the issue of the ERA, the
public does seem to have reacted more to the rhetoric of both the
New Right and the women's movement.

Overall, the distribution of attitudes on the issues of abortion
and the ERA provide little evidence that the heated conflict between
New Right activists and feminists has spread to the mass public. On
the issue of abortion, opinionation has been high for the entire decade
and the aggregate distribution of attitudes has changed very little.
While a majority of the public is willing to put some limits on the
right to abortion, relatively few are willing to make all abortions

illegal. Similarly, while opinionation is lower on the Equal Rights Amendment than for abortion, it has been increasing over the decade. Yet, this increase in the number of people who take a stand on the issue has not resulted in a substantial shift in attitudes; in 1982, as in the early 1970s, Americans still favor the Equal Rights Amendment. But, even though neither the New Right nor feminists have been able to alter substantially the distribution of opinion on abortion and the ERA, it is still possible that they have influenced the meaning that those issues hold for members of the mass public. Let us consider that possibility now.

Table 6.2 ATTITUDES TOWARD THE ERA
(in percent)

Attitude[a]	1975	1976[b]	1978	1980	1981
% Who Have Heard Or Read About the Amendment:	91	90	90	91	88
Favor	58	57	58	58	63
Oppose	24	24	31	31	32
Don't Know	18	19	11	11	5

a Attitudes toward the amendment are based only on respondents who had heard or read about it, unless otherwise noted.

b Attitudes based on all respondents. Reprinted with permission.

Source: The Gallup Report #190 (July 1981), p. 24. Reprinted with permission.

ISSUE SYMBOLIZATION

In the previous chapter, we found that activists involved in the controversy over abortion and the ERA tend to have "ideological" orientations toward the two issues. In contrast, it is anticipated that the mass public will tend to have "reactive" orientations toward the issues. That is, abortion and the ERA should hold relatively more symbolic or evaluative meaning than cognitive meaning (i.e., people will react more on the basis of emotions than substance). Finally, if the New Right has been successful in altering the meaning of these two issues, then we should find that their meaning increases over time; substantively their meaning should broaden and become ambiguous while at the same time their evaluative meaning becomes stronger.

Measures

With regard to our dependent variables, attitudes toward abortion are measured in terms of the CPS four-item question described in the previous section. Attitudes toward the ERA are based on the CPS's simple disapprove-approve question in 1976 and in 1980 unless otherwise noted.[2]

As in the last chapter, the cognitive meaning of the issues is measured in terms of three attitudinal orientations that concern competing definitions of the family, and the role of women both within and outside the family. In 1972, 1976, and 1980, attitudes toward sex roles are measured by the same 7-point scale that ranges from "1" which represents the conservative response that a "woman's place is in the home" to "7" which represents the idea that women should have an equal role with men. In all three years, attitudes toward women's economic status are measured by an additive scale composed of various questions about women's status in society and the impact of discrimination on that status. Although the precise questions composing that scale differ from year to year, we feel that they are comparable enough for our purposes. Again, the scale ranges from traditional to liberated responses.

Finally, there were no questions on the CPS surveys suitable for measuring personal morality, a variable that we found to be quite important to the meaning of abortion and the ERA among activists. Consequently, to help compensate for this serious omission, we used the NORC surveys from 1972 to 1980. In each of those years, they asked a series of questions on morality that, although not perfectly comparable, do allow us to form an acceptable morality scale.[3] Again, low scores indicate a "traditional" or conservative sense of morality while high scores represent a more "liberated" perspective. More detailed information about these measures is provided in Appendix D.

With respect to the symbolic or evaluative meaning of the issues, the same measurement technique employed in the last chapter is used here. In each of the three CPS studies, the respondents were asked to rate various groups on the "feeling thermometer." For our purposes, six of these groups are taken to be symbols or representatives of the "left": liberals, the women's liberation movement, radical students, marijuana users, black militants, civil rights leaders, and environmentalists. Similarly, seven of the groups represent elements of the "old" and "New Right": big business, businessmen, Republicans, conservatives, policemen, the military, and evangelical groups.

The Meaning of the Abortion Issue

Let us begin by considering the current meaning of the abortion issue for the mass public and how that meaning has changed over the last ten years. Presented in Table 6.3 are the correlations of the abortion measure with the various indicators of cognitive and evaluative meaning for 1972, 1976, and 1980.[4] Contrary to expectation, in each of the three years, the measures of substantive meaning demonstrate, on average, a stronger relationship with abortion attitudes than the measures of symbolic meaning. Yet, to fully understand this pattern it is necessary to look at the pattern of change across years as well.

In terms of the cognitive meaning of abortion, the three indicators behave differently. As in the activist data, morality demonstrates a strong and consistent relationship with abortion attitudes. In contrast, the relationship between beliefs about sex roles and abortion has increased modestly over the same time period. This is balanced by the decrease in association recorded by women's status (although that might be due to the fact that we perforce used different items across the years to form this scale). Thus, overall there is a general sense of stability in the cognitive meaning of abortion. What changes there have been seem to have tied the meaning of the issue more closely to ideas about sex roles and the family, while at the same time divorcing the issue from beliefs about women's economic status and the role of discrimination in society.

If we look at the evaluative measures of meaning, slightly more change may be detected over the time period. Focusing first on the symbols of the left, we find that evaluations of most of the groups associated with left-wing activities in the 1960s—radical students, black militants, and civil rights leaders—become less related with abortion attitudes as the decade of the 1970s wore on.[5] As these groups became less relevant to defining the left in American society, they also became relatively unimportant to defining the meaning of abortion for the mass public. In contrast, more current and general symbols of the left show an increase over time in their relationship with abortion attitudes. In particular, the correlation for the women's liberation movement climbs from .08 in 1972 to .20 in 1980, making it the symbol that is most strongly related to abortion attitudes.[6]

Table 6.3 THE MEANING OF ABORTION

Indicator	Year[b] 1972	Year[b] 1976	Year[b] 1980
I. Cognitive Variables			
Morality[a]	.32*	.38*	.32*
Sex Roles	.24*	.28*	.33*
Women's Status	.31*	.33*	.19*
II. Symbols of the Left			
Women's Liberation Movement	.08*	.16*	.20*
Liberals	.06*	.09*	.12*
Radical Students	.12*	.09*	.06*
Marijuana Users	.32*	.32*	—c
Black Militants	.12*	.06*	-.00
Civil Rights Leaders	.14*	.07*	.05*
Environmentalists	—c	—c	-.02
III. Symbols of the Right			
Big Business	-.07*	-.13*	-.07*
Businessmen	—c	-.14*	-.05*
Republicans	-.11*	-.11*	-.12*
Conservatives	-.08*	-.13*	-.14*
Policemen	-.17*	-.14*	—c
Military	-.22*	-.21*	-.18*
Evangelical Groups	—c	—c	-.25*

a Data taken from the NORC General Social Survey for this variable only.

b Entries are Pearson's Product-Moment correlations.

c Data not available.

* = ($p \leq .05$).

Source: Calculated by authors from data in CPS National Election Studies.

With respect to the symbols of the right, we find a somewhat similar pattern. Evaluations of those groups linked with the traditional or "old" right—big business, businessmen, Republicans, and policemen—either remain the same or decline slightly in their relationship with abortion attitudes.[7] Evaluations of conservatives— a general symbol of both the old and New Right—increase in their relationship with abortion attitudes. Similarly, the symbol of the military which plays a role in the thinking of the new and old right is consistently one of the stronger correlates of abortion sentiments, with its power declining only slightly over time. Finally, the clearest symbol of the New Right—evangelical groups—shows one of the stronger correlations with abortion attitudes.

In summary, then, the issue of abortion continues to hold substantial cognitive meaning for the mass public: a meaning that has changed only slightly over the last decade. As some previous studies had indicated, ideas about personal morality and proper sex roles within and outside the family are important to the abortion issue (Barnett and Harris 1982; Blake 1971; Clayton and Tolene 1973; Finner and Gamache 1969; Granberg 1977/78; Granberg and Granberg 1980; Singh and Leahy 1978; and Westoff and Westoff 1971). While the substantive meaning of abortion has changed relatively little, its symbolic meaning has undergone more distinct transformations. The older symbols of the left and the right have become relatively unimportant to defining the meaning of abortion, while the symbols more closely related to the New Right and the current feminist movement have become more important to defining the issue. This suggests that, to a certain degree, the New Right conflict has had an impact on how the public views the issue of abortion.

The Meaning of the ERA Issue

To what extent does the ERA issue resemble the abortion issue in the meaning it holds for members of the mass public? By comparing Tables 6.3 and 6.4, it is apparent that in each year our measures of both cognitive and evaluative meaning are more highly related to attitudes on ERA than on abortion. Overall the issue of the ERA holds more meaning for the mass public than the abortion issue. Yet, more important, the patterns of change characterizing the issue of the ERA are considerably different than those for the abortion issue.

With regard to the measures of cognitive meaning, we find consistent increases in their correlations with attitudes on the ERA.[8] The women's status measure, in particular, goes from a

Table 6.4 THE MEANING OF THE ERA[a]

Indicator	1976	1980
I. Cognitive Variables		
Sex Roles	.36*	.40*
Women's Status	.22*	.32*
II. Symbols of the Left		
Liberals	.25*	.36*
Women's Liberation Movement	.38*	.52*
Radical Students	.17*	.18*
Marijuana Users	.11*	—[b]
Black Militants	.18*	.20*
Civil Rights Leaders	.21*	.32*
Environmentalists	—[b]	.22*
III. Symbols of the Right		
Big Business	-.10*	-.05*
Businessmen	-.04*	-.04
Republicans	-.08*	-.17*
Conservatives	-.15	-.19*
Policemen	-.11*	—[b]
Military	-.09*	-.06*
Evangelical Groups	—[b]	-.10*

[a] Entries are Pearson's Product-Moment Correlations.

[b] Data not available.

* = $(p \leq .05)$.

Source: Calculated by authors from data in CPS National Election Studies.

141

correlation of .22 to .32. This is in direct contrast to the abortion issue where beliefs about the status of women in society became less relevant over time. This pattern indicates that the cognitive or substantive meaning of the ERA is broadening and reflecting clearer lines of conflict as time wears on. In effect, the conflict between the New Right and the women's movement has resulted in the ERA being linked to a wide array of beliefs about the status of women within and outside the family.

With respect to the evaluative measures of meaning, we find strong support for our earlier hypotheses. In particular, evaluations of all of the groups or symbols of the left have become more highly related over time to attitudes on the ERA. Whereas in the case of abortion, the older symbols of the left—black militants, civil rights leaders, radical students—had become virtually irrelevant to the issue by 1980, the opposite is true for the ERA. Furthermore, evaluations of the symbols or groups most symbolic of the New Left—the women's liberation movement and liberals—are quite highly related to ERA attitudes by 1980. Similarly, although the symbols of the right are not as closely tied to ERA attitudes as those of the left, the correlations are still stronger than they were in the case of abortion. [9]

Thus, the meaning of the ERA as an issue has changed over the last few years. Substantively, the issue has become more firmly linked in people's minds with their beliefs about the role of women inside the family and in the society at large. Others have reported similar findings for the mass public (e.g., Bokowski and Clausen 1979; Huber, Rexroat, and Spitze 1978; Jelen 1982; Tedin 1980; Volgy 1979). Yet, the significance of such findings has not been adequately noted. From our perspective, the expansion of the cognitive meaning of the ERA signals a clear advantage for the New Right. It is this expansion of the substantive meaning of the ERA that has made it possible to exaggerate the consequences of the amendment, a tactic that the New Right has used successfully (Tedin 1980). Furthermore, at the same time that the cognitive meaning of the issue was broadening and becoming more general, so was the evaluative meaning becoming stronger. Over the past few years, the ERA has come to be strongly linked with other groups symbolic of the social changes that have swept the country in the last 15 years. In essence, by 1980, the issue of the ERA had come to be a very emotional one capable of evoking intense feelings associated with the other symbols of social conflict in our country today.

BASES OF SUPPORT

In Chapter 5, we explored the various bases of support that the New Right and its opponents had drawn upon in their mobilization

efforts. Our empirical results tended to confirm the conclusions
we had reached in our historical overview of the emergence of the
New Right. The New Right clearly draws upon certain segments of
society in its mobilization efforts. Politically, the rightists tend to
be patriotic, conservative, and Republican; they are more likely to
be regular church-goers of either the Catholic faith or some fundamentalist Protestant denomination; and they tend to have slightly
less education and somewhat lower incomes than nonrightists. Yet,
to what extent are these bases of support crystallized at the mass
level? In the case of both abortion and the ERA, previous research
provides an initial answer to this question.

Previous Research

Of the two issues, the correlates of abortion attitudes have received considerably more attention with respect to the mass public.
Specifically, regarding the political bases of support, numerous researchers have noted that liberal-conservative self-identifications
are modestly related to positions on the abortion issue, with liberals
adopting the pro-choice stance (Baker, Epstein, and Forth 1981;
Granberg 1977/78; Granberg and Granberg 1980; Peterson and Mauss
1976; Singh and Leahy 1978). Yet, at the same time, researchers
have failed to uncover any relationship between party identification
and abortion attitudes (Baker, Epstein, and Forth 1981; Welch 1975).

With respect to the religious bases of support, Protestants
have been found to be consistently more supportive of a right to
abortion than Catholics, but the differences between the two are influenced by other factors and substantially smaller than traditionally
assumed. More important than religious preference per se is religiosity; as church attendance increases, so does opposition to abortion, particularly among Catholics and with respect to the "soft"
alternatives (Baker, Epstein, and Forth 1981; Barnett and Harris
1982; Blake and Del Pinal 1980; Granberg 1977/78; Granberg and
Granberg 1980; Peterson and Mauss 1976; Tedrow and Mahoney 1979;
Singh and Leahy 1978).

Finally, in terms of the status-related bases of support, a
higher socioeconomic status is usually associated with the pro-choice
position, although the strength of the relationship varies with the
indicator. Specifically, income and occupational status tend to be
only modestly related with abortion attitudes; higher levels of education, in contrast, typically are moderately to strongly correlated
with support for a right to abortion (Baker, Epstein, and Forth 1981;
Barnett and Harris 1982; Blake and Del Pinal 1980; Granberg
1977/78; Granberg and Granberg 1980; Skerry 1978; Singh and Leahy
1978; Tedrow and Mahoney 1979; and Welch 1975).

In contrast to the abortion issue, the scholarly research on the correlates of <u>mass</u> attitudes toward the ERA is quite limited both in volume and scope. With respect to <u>political</u> correlates, there is some evidence that an overall liberal political perspective tends to be associated with support for the ERA while a conservative outlook is related to opposition of the amendment (Huber, Rexroat, and Spitze 1978). In terms of <u>religion</u>, the Huber, Rexroat, and Spitze (1978) study finds that Protestants as a whole tend to be slightly less supportive of the ERA than Catholics, while Jelen (1982) notes that religious preference has little impact on ERA attitudes. Finally, with regard to <u>social status</u>, Huber, Rexroat, and Spitze (1978) discover little relationship between having a high income and support for the ERA, and only a slight link between education and support for the amendment.

In summary, particularly in the case of abortion, previous research provides some evidence that the distinctions in the bases of support identified for the abortion and ERA activists also exist to a lesser extent for the mass public. Yet, not at all clear from previous research is whether these distinctions are becoming more well-defined over time.[10] Let us consider that possibility.

Measures

With only a few exceptions, the measures of the various bases of support, political, religious, and social status, parallel those employed in Chapter 5. Similarly, the details of our measurement procedure are once again explained in Appendix D. Two measures of the political bases of support are employed: party identification (ranging from strong Democrat to strong Republican) and liberal-conservative identification (ranging from extremely liberal to extremely conservative). Three measures of the religious bases of support are used: religious preference (coded "1" for fundamentalist Protestant and Catholics, and "0" for all others), church attendance (high to low), and evangelical identification (a three-point scale ranging from nonevangelical to highly evangelical). Finally, three measures of social status are included: education (low to high), income (low to high), and subjective social class (a seven-point scale ranging from "0" lower class to "7" upper class).[11]

Bases of Support: The Abortion Issue

Let us begin our analysis by considering the bases of support for the various sides of the abortion issue. Presented in Table 6.5 are the Pearson product-moment correlations between abortion attitudes and the measures of the bases of support for the mass public in 1972, 1976, and 1980.

Table 6.5 BASES OF SUPPORT FOR THE ABORTION ISSUE[a]

Variables	Mass Sample		
	1972	1976	1980
I. Political Variables			
Liberal-Conservative	-.12*	-.16*	-.26*
Party Identification	.06*	.06*	.01
II. Religion Variables			
Preference	-.23*	-.23*	-.20*
Church Attendance	.27*	.31*	.33*
Evangelical	—b	—b	-.41*
III. Status Variables			
Education	.30*	.33*	.28*
Income	.20*	.25*	.21*
Subjective Social Class	.19*	.18*	.15*

[a] Entries are Pearson's Product-Moment correlations.

[b] Data not available.

* = $(p \leq .05)$.

Source: Calculated by authors from data in CPS National Election Studies.

Beginning with the political bases of support, we see that liberals and conservatives are becoming more distinctive in their abortion attitudes over time, with the liberals becoming more supportive of the right to abortion and the conservatives more disapproving. If we accept the argument that liberal-conservative identification is symbolic of the basic social cleavages in our society, then this finding suggests that the conflict over abortion is becoming more associated with those cleavages as time goes on. At the same time, abortion still resists becoming a partisan issue on the mass level; in 1980 there is no significant relationship between party identification and abortion sentiments.

Turning to the indicators of the religious bases of support, we find that church-going fundamentalist Protestants and Catholics are more opposed to abortion. Furthermore, for these two indicators the correlations are relatively stable over time. Thus, the entanglement of the abortion issue with the New Right does not seem to have resulted in a broadening over time of religious-based attitudinal cleavages on the issue.[12] Yet, at the same time, the sizable correlation of evangelical identification with anti-abortion attitudes ($r = -.41$) suggests that, in 1980 at least, there is a substantial difference in abortion attitudes between evangelical Christians and nonevangelics. Whether or not this cleavage has increased in recent years, we cannot say. Nonetheless, if we accept the arguments of the mass media and some scholars (Fairbanks 1981; Lipset and Raab 1981; Patel, Pilant, and Rose 1982), this last finding would seem to herald the emergence of the evangelical right as a significant element in the New Right coalition.

Finally, with respect to the measures of status, we find modest distinctions between status groups in their positions on abortion. Specifically, the higher the education, income, and subjective social class then the greater the support for abortion. Yet, while there are distinct status-based differences in abortion attitudes among the mass public, there is no indication that the differences are becoming more well-defined over time. Thus, while the New Right and the women's movement have solid class bases to draw upon for mass support, they have not succeeded in strengthening those bases with respect to the issue of abortion.

Bases of Support: The ERA Issue

Turning to Table 6.6 we find the same information about the bases of mass support on the ERA issue. Beginning with the political bases of support, we see that liberal-conservative distinctions are becoming more important over time in defining the public's attitudes toward the ERA. Furthermore, these differences are considerably stronger than in the case of abortion. In addition, unlike the abortion issue, partisan differences on the ERA are increasing; by 1980 there is a moderate relationship between identifying with the Democrats and favoring the ERA. Thus, the political bases of support and opposition to the ERA have become more well-defined over the last few years, to the point that they are now considerably more distinct than they are for the abortion issue.

This pattern is reversed when the religious bases of support are considered. Whereas there is a stable and moderately strong religious cleavage on the abortion issue at the mass level, there is a much weaker religious split over the ERA. There were no discernible differences in ERA attitudes between the coalition of fundamentalist Protestants and Catholics and other religious preferences in 1976; and by 1980, there is only a very small difference.

In terms of religiosity, there is a small, but growing, distinction between the frequent church-goers and those who do not attend religious services, with the more religious tending to oppose the ERA. Finally, there is a moderate relationship between identification as an evangelical Christian and opposition to the ERA. But, again, the cleavage between the evangelicals and the nonevangelicals over the ERA is not nearly as strong as in the case of abortion.

Table 6.6 BASES OF SUPPORT FOR THE ERA ISSUE

Bases of Support	Mass Sample[a]	
	1976	1980
I. Political Variables		
Liberal-Conservative	-.26*	-.35
Party Identification	-.12*	-.25*
II. Religion Variables		
Preference	-.02	-.05*
Church Attendance	.14*	.20*
Evangelical	—b	-.21*
III. Status Variables		
Education	-.01	.01
Income	-.06	-.01
Subjective Social Class	-.04*	..01

a Entries are Pearson's Product-Moment correlations.

b Data not available.

* = $(p \leq .05)$.

Source: Calculated by authors from data in CPS National Election Studies.

Finally, let us briefly examine the social bases of support characterizing the ERA issue. Here, again, we find substantial differences between the issues of the ERA and abortion. Whereas there are stable and moderate status-based distinctions between the mass supporters and opponents of abortion, there are no such differences in the case of the ERA. In 1976 and again in 1980, there are no real discernible differences in ERA sentiments in terms of either education, income, or subjective social class. Not only does this contrast with mass attitudes on abortion, but it also varies significantly from the pattern characterizing the activists on the ERA issue, as discussed in the previous chapter. In effect, while both the New Right and the women's movement have succeeded in drawing upon certain social strata in the mobilization of activists, they have been unable to develop the same constituencies of attitudinal support at the mass level.

MASS BEHAVIOR

To this point, we have found that neither the New Right nor the women's movement has been especially successful in terms of either polarizing public opinion, changing the meaning of abortion and the ERA, or establishing clear bases of mass support on those issues. However, we have yet to consider the actual impact on mass behavior that the New Right conflict may have had. Even if neither the New Right nor the feminist movement has established a substantial mass constituency, their indirect lobbying efforts need not be failures. The small, strongly motivated bands of activists that exist on each side of the abortion and the ERA issues could combine with less active members of the public, who, nonetheless, hold extreme attitudes on these issues, to form an "issue public" capable of exercising substantial influence on public policy vis-à-vis the electoral process.

There are a variety of methods that New Right organizations might use in an attempt to influence the outcome of an election. But, according to Richard Viguerie (1981), four key elements lie at the heart of the New Right's electoral strategy: single-issue groups, multi-issue conservative groups, coalition politics, and direct mail campaigns. How successful is the New Right's use of such elements of electoral politics? What advantages have they gained through the voting booth?

In assessing the New Right's influence on electoral politics, we focus on the extent to which the New Right has succeeded in mobilizing issue constituencies among the mass public. We assume that, in part, the New Right's strategy depends upon encouraging the mass public to take greater notice of certain issues and the candidates' stands on those issues when they go to the polls. From this perspective, we will first consider the degree to which "single-issue" politics does indeed benefit the New Right. Then, we will examine the 1980 elections in an effort to determine the general role of the New Right, and the more specific roles of the abortion and the ERA issues.

The Levels of Single-Issue Voting

Of the four strategic elements mentioned by Richard Viguerie (1981), none is more closely tied to the issues than that of the single-issue interest group. The electoral strategy of single-issue interest groups is a very simple one: candidates are to be rewarded or punished based solely on their stands on a particular issue. The single-issue interest group pours its resources, both human and financial, into convincing the public of the importance of the issue at stake and the necessity of casting their votes with that issue foremost on their minds. Furthermore, abortion and the ERA, perhaps more than any other issues, have been the focus of this single-minded electoral strategy (Newsweek 1978, p. 54). Yet, how much single-issue voting has there been on the issues of abortion and the ERA over the last few years?

Measures

The measurement of single-issue voting is a more difficult task than one might suppose. The root of the problem lies in assessing the voters' intentions; do they vote a particular way because of the candidates' stands on a single, identifiable issue? Two basic approaches may be taken to identifying the voters' intentions. The first is to ask the voters directly whether their intention was to single-issue vote. Alternatively, a much more indirect method is for the researcher to infer what the voters' intentions might have been in making a particular vote choice. From our perspective, the first method is a better way of determining whether a voter purposely acted in a single-minded fashion in voting for a particular candidate. Yet, it is by no means a perfect method; voters may have other reasons than the one stated for voting the way they did, reasons that they may not be able to articulate or that they may have even forgotten. Nonetheless, direct questioning should provide some estimate as to the levels of single-issue voting that characterize the abortion and the ERA issues.

Having decided upon a direct method of assessing single-issue voting, we collected several different estimates of single-issue voting for both abortion and the ERA. It is important to recognize that all of the estimates refer to "potential" or "hypothetical" single-issue voting. In addition, comparisons of these estimates may be hampered by technical factors. For one thing, the samples from which the data were collected differ in their nature: one is national; another is statewide; still others are limited to a single city. Clearly, an issue may be more strongly disputed in one of these locales and presumably this may result in a higher level of single-issue voting.

There are also variations in question-wording that may affect the level of single-issue voting. First, the questions differ in terms of the candidates referred to: one question is quite general in that it deals with an unspecified candidate; another refers to presidential candidates; and still another concerns congressional candidates. Second, there are variations in terms of the type of voting considered: some questions ask if respondents would vote against a candidate simply because of his or her stand on a particular issue; others ask if they would vote for a candidate only because of his or her position on an issue. Finally, with respect to abortion, the questions differ in terms of how they frame the issue: some ask about a woman's right to abortion while others focus on a constitutional amendment to ban all abortions. Thus, because of these variations, we must use some caution in interpreting the data.

With this in mind, we focused on the following three sources in obtaining our estimates of single-issue voting. First the White House Conference delegates studied in Chapter 5 were asked the following two questions:

> Do you think you would vote for a candidate for public
> office based only on his or her stand on abortion/the
> ERA ?

Second, a random sample of 1,228 residents of the state of Minnesota was asked the two above issue-voting questions as well as the same abortion and ERA questions asked of the activists.[13] Because of the identical question wording and the close time proximity, these two samples should provide us with a rough estimate of how single-issue voting differs between the mass public and political activists. Our third major source of information is a Harris poll conducted during February 1982.[14] It does not ask about the ERA, and the question wording on abortion differs significantly from that of the activist sample and the Minnesota poll. Specifically, respondents were asked:

> Now, suppose in the Congressional elections this year,
> you found a candidate in your district whose view you
> mostly agreed with. Then suppose that same candidate
> took a position on a constitutional amendment to ban
> legalized abortion that you disagreed with completely.
> Would you certainly not vote for that candidate, prob-
> ably not vote for him, or could you still vote for him ?
> (Opinion Outlook 1982b, p. 1).

For our purposes, respondents reporting that they "certainly" would not vote for the candidate are considered to be potential single-issue voters. In addition to these three surveys, findings from several other polls will also be briefly reviewed.

Single-Issue Voting on the ERA

First, let us consider single-issue voting on the Equal Rights Amendment. Before doing so, however, it is important to recognize the uncertain context surrounding the ERA during the early 1980s. In the majority of states, the ERA was a settled issue by this time: a fact that should have worked to depress single-issue voting on the issue, especially where candidates for state and local offices were concerned. Yet, at the same time, debates over the rescission of the amendment, the extension of the ratification deadline, and heated controversies in unratified states such as Florida and Illinois, all conspired to keep the ERA in the voters' minds as an unresolved issue, at least at the national level. And, thus, potentially there could have been substantial single-issue voting on the issue, particularly where candidates for national office were involved. For example, although a president may not play a direct role in state ratification battles, his or stand could potentially have a significant influence on public opinion and thus an indirect effect on the outcome of such fights. This makes single-issue voting at the presidential level more likely. With this in mind, let us begin by examining the levels of single-issue voting on ERA characterizing our activist and mass samples.

As illustrated in Table 6.7, there is a striking difference between the activists and the mass public in their willingness to single-issue vote on the ERA. Ignoring the direction of their attitudes for the moment and focusing on those respondents with an opinion, we find that 28.2 percent of the activists as compared to 5.6 percent of the mass public in Minnesota report that they would have voted for a candidate simply because of his or her stand on the ERA. Thus, single-issue voting certainly appears to be a tactic of indirect lobbying endorsed by political activists, but embraced considerably less strongly by the mass public, at least with respect to the ERA issue. While we did not expect single-issue voting to be extremely widespread on the ERA, we did anticipate slightly higher levels given the increased symbolism of the issue in recent years. Why, then, do relatively few voters report a willingness to single-issue vote on the ERA?

In part, the relatively low level of single-issue voting may be a reflection of reality; the ERA was ratified relatively early by Minnesota and has not been the topic of much debate since then in that state. Thus, the issue simply may not have been "hot" enough in 1980 to inspire much single-issue voting. On the other hand, the apparent level of potential single-issue voting may have been artificially depressed by the question-wording that asked if a person would vote for an unspecified candidate simply because of the candidate's stand on the ERA. Evidence bearing on this matter is provided by a 1980 survey (Sigelman 1981) of Lexington, Kentucky, which revealed that 21 percent of the public would "vote against a candidate for President on the basis of his position on the Equal Rights Amendment" (emphasis added). [15] It is impossible to determine if this substantially higher level of potential single-issue voting is produced by the change in question wording or whether it reflects real differences between the electorates of Minnesota and Kentucky, a state where the ERA was controversial enough that the legislature rescinded its ratification of the amendment. [16] Nonetheless, these findings do suggest that a modest portion of certain publics may still have been willing to single-issue vote on the ERA as late as 1980, particularly where a candidate for national office was involved.

TABLE 6.7 LEVELS OF SINGLE-ISSUE VOTING ON THE ERA

	% of sample who favor/oppose the ERA	x	% of those who favor/oppose and would vote for a candidate because of the ERA	=	% of public/ activists gained by a candidate taking the same stand
Minnesota					
Sample, 1980					
Favor:	60.9	x	5.9	=	3.6
Oppose:	25.2	x	7.8	=	2.0
Activist					
Sample, 1980					
Favor:	50.5	x	11.5	=	5.8
Oppose	49.5	x	45.2	=	22.4

Source: Calculated by authors from unpublished data in the Minnesota Poll, April 1980, and the authors' White House Conference Survey.

Also evident from Table 6.7 is that the supporters and opponents of the ERA differed in their willingness to single-issue vote.
At the activist level, far more opponents of the ERA were willing
to single-issue vote than were supporters of the amendment. In
part, this may be a function of the nature of the sample; as we
learned in the last chapter, opponents of the ERA tended to be
more representative of the New Right than supporters were of
feminist organizations. Yet, at the same time, the size of the dis-
parity between opponents and proponents in their willingness to
single-issue vote suggests that there may be a real difference in
the tactics of indirect lobbying that activists on the two sides were
willing to endorse.

Finally, and most important to understanding the effect of
single-issue voting on electoral outcomes, we can consider the net
impact of single-issue voting on the ERA. If we just focus on the
voting behavior of political activists, we find that a candidate
would have been hurt much more than helped by adopting a pro-ERA
stand; there would have been a net loss of almost 20 percentage
points for the pro-ERA candidate among our activists. But, such
activists make up only a small portion of the voting public. Unless
an electoral race were especially close, it is not at all clear that
the anti-activists, even if they were united in their tactics, would
have mustered enough strength to defeat the pro-ERA candidate.
This is certainly likely to have been true in a state like Minnesota
where single-issue voting among the general public would have
produced a small net benefit for the pro-ERA candidate, simply
because in absolute numbers there were more ERA supporters even
though proportionately there were fewer pro-ERA single-issue
voters. Thus, only in relatively close elections and only in conservative states does it seem likely that single-issue voting could
have actually benefited the anti-ERA candidates. But, of course,
it is in precisely those same states where the ERA encountered its
greatest opposition.

In summary, the data available on single-issue voting on the
ERA suggest several things. First, single-issue voting was clearly
a tactic used by activists and presumably encouraged among their
followers, although the levels of single-issue voting were considerably lower among the mass public than among the activists. But
then again, the activists are more likely to get involved in political
campaigns, and thus potentially they have more direct influence on
the candidates. Secondly, although differences in question wording
make it difficult to estimate how much variation really existed,
the level of single-issue voting on this issue probably varied from
state to state depending upon the status of the amendment, and
from election to election according to whether it concerned a

national office (where the office-holder's stand on ERA might have a symbolic value) or a lower-level office.

Thirdly, and most important, in all but the most conservative states single-issue voting on the ERA had the potential to hurt rather than help the anti-ERA candidate. This is true simply because pro-ERA sentiments tended to outweigh negative attitudes among the mass public in most states. As a consequence, opponents of the ERA who encouraged single-issue voting had to be especially careful in adopting that strategy; in order for the tactic to succeed, the anti-ERA single-issue voters must have heavily outweighed the pro-ERA single-issue voters. Even then the net gain for the anti-ERA candidate may not have been worth the risk. Once the New Right encouraged single-issue voting, there was always the danger that nonrightists would embrace the strategy every bit as much as the rightists, thus causing the tactic to backfire. Finally, paradoxically, single-issue voting on the ERA may have its greatest impact on electoral outcomes in the elections of the fall of 1982, four months after the deadline for ratification of the amendment. If staunch supporters of the ERA in states like Florida keep their promises and are successful in encouraging single-issue voting among electorates that have favored the ERA in the past, then state legislators who cast the negative votes that sealed the ERA's fate may find themselves tossed out of office.

Single-Issue Voting on Abortion

Now, let us turn to an examination of single-issue voting on the issue of abortion. Here, we find considerably more information than in the case of the ERA simply because the abortion issue is a current issue, relevant to virtually all state and national electorates. Yet, despite the greater availability of information about single-issue voting on abortion, it is still difficult to estimate the levels of this activity because the abortion issue can be framed in so many more ways than the ERA. With this in mind, let us review the information provided in Table 6.8.

First, let us focus on the overall levels of single-issue voting on abortion (again measured in terms of the total percent of the sample having an opinion). As illustrated in Table 6.8, among the activist sample we find a slightly lower level of single-issue voting on abortion than for the ERA (21.9 percent as compared to 28.2 percent on the ERA). Yet, at the same time, in the mass sample of Minnesotans, we find a higher level of single-issue voting on abortion (10 percent on abortion as compared to 5.6 percent on the ERA). For the mass sample, this difference may well reflect the fact that abortion was, and continues to be, a hotly debated issue in Minnesota, whereas the ERA was not. Further evidence is

Table 6.8 LEVELS OF SINGLE-ISSUE VOTING
ON THE ABORTION ISSUE

	% of sample who favor/oppose right to abortion	x	% of those who favor/oppose and would vote for a candidate because of the abortion issue	=	% of public/ activists gained by a candidate taking same stand
Minnesota Sample, 1980					
Favor:	47.5	x	6.5	=	3.1
Oppose:	52.5	x	13.2	=	6.9
Activist Sample, 1980					
Favor:	39.2	x	5.0	=	2.0
Oppose:	60.8	x	32.8	=	19.9

	% of those who favor/oppose constitutional amendment to ban abortions	x	% of those who favor/oppose and who would vote against a candidate because of their stand on the amendment	=	% of public lost by a candidate taking the same stand
National Sample, 1982					
Favor:	33	x	32	=	11
Oppose	61	x	30	=	18

Sources: 1. Minnesota data—Calculated by authors from unpublished
data in Minnesota Poll, April 1980.
2. Activist data—Authors' White House Conference Study.
3. National sample—Harris Survey, February 12-17, 1982
cited in Opinion Outlook 2 (March 29, 1982b): 1-2.
Reprinted with permission.

provided by the previously noted survey of Lexington, Kentucky, a
locale where both the ERA and abortion were relevant issues. In
that poll, single-issue voting was again greater for abortion than
for the ERA (30.2 percent on abortion as compared to 20.9 percent
on the ERA).[17] Thus, despite the fact that the ERA is the more
symbolic of the two issues, the abortion issue appears to evoke
more single-issue voting.

Additional information about the levels of single-issue voting
on abortion are provided by the Harris poll summarized in Table
6.8, as well as several surveys whose figures are not included in
that table. The Harris survey, conducted in 1982, focuses on single-
issue voting with respect to a congressional candidate's stand on a
constitutional amendment to ban legalized abortion. Within this
context, the poll reveals that 29 percent of those holding an opinion
would single-issue vote. Along the same lines, a series of three
polls conducted by Market Opinion Research (MOR) for the National
Abortion Rights Action League reveals an even higher level of single-
issue voting; on average, about 35 percent of the respondents—citizens of Springfield, Massachusetts; Des Moines, Iowa; and Seattle/
Tacoma, Washington—would single-issue vote when the question is
one of a candidate's support or opposition for a constitutional amendment to ban abortions (Opinion Outlook 1981, p. 7). Thus around
one-third of the public seems willing to single-issue vote on abortion
when the question concerns extreme measures such as a constitutional ban on abortions. Finally, it is interesting to note that, according to the Harris survey, the level of single-issue voting on
abortion is higher than that for virtually any other issue including
busing, gun control, and prayer in the schools (Opinion Outlook
1982b).

Why is the willingness to single-issue vote on abortion so
relatively high? In part, the answer lies in the behavior of that portion of the public holding anti-abortion attitudes. In virtually every
instance, the opponents of abortion are more willing to single-issue
vote (sometimes by very wide margins) than are those members of
the public adopting the pro-choice position. In our sample of activists, proportionately anti-abortion single-issue voters outweigh the
pros by a six to one margin. Similarly, in percentage terms, there
are twice as many anti-abortion as pro-choice single-issue voters
in the Minnesota sample (13.2 percent as compared to 6.5 percent).
In the previously mentioned surveys conducted by Market Opinion
Research, the number of single-issue voters among the opponents
of abortion climbs even higher; in the three cities, on average,
about half those respondents favoring a constitutional amendment
to ban abortions would single-issue vote while about 30 percent of
those opposing the amendment would do the same (Opinion Outlook
1981, p. 7). Finally, the nation-wide Harris poll produces the

closest margin between the proponents and opponents of abortion; 32 percent of those respondents favoring a constitutional ban on abortions would single-issue vote, while only slightly fewer of the proponents (30 percent) would do the same (Opinion Outlook 1982b). Thus, opponents of abortion have adopted single-issue voting as a tactic more than those taking the pro-choice position, so much so that their high numbers have helped push up overall levels of single-issue voting on the abortion issue.[18]

What is the potential impact on electoral outcomes of single-issue voting on abortion? As in the case of the ERA, the impact of single-issue voting with respect to abortion is likely to vary depending upon the distribution of opinions in the electorate and the closeness of the election. Yet, unlike the ERA which is a relatively straightforward issue from the perspective of the single-issue voter (the candidate either favors or opposes the amendment) single-issue voting on abortion is complicated by how the issue is framed. When the issue is posed in the extreme form of a constitutional ban on abortions, then the anti-abortion candidate tends to suffer a net loss as a consequence of single-issue voting. For example, in the national Harris survey, the candidate favoring a constitutional amendment to ban abortions would lose about 7 percent of the electorate as a consequence of that stand. Similarly, in the three MOR surveys, candidates supporting a constitutional ban on abortions would lose about 25 percent of the voters because of their stand while candidates opposing the amendment would lose only about 12 percent—a net loss of 13 percent for the anti-abortion candidate (Opinion Outlook 1981, p. 7). In effect, on extreme measures such as a constitutional ban on abortions, the anti-abortion single-issue voters suffer the same fate as those opposing the ERA: although proportionately there are more single-issue voters among the opponents of abortion, in actual numbers there are more pro-choice single-issue voters.

But, single-issue voting becomes a more viable strategy for the anti-abortion side when the issue is framed in terms of less extreme, more popular policy measures. In both the Minnesota and activist samples, for example, the respondents are simply asked whether or not they would vote for a candidate because of his or her stand on abortion; no specific policy measures are mentioned. In both cases, it is the anti-abortion candidate that enjoys a net gain from single-issue voting. Along the same lines, the three MOR surveys reveal that on two policy measures that are more popular than a constitutional amendment to ban abortions—a "human life" law and a "states rights" amendment that would allow the stricter abortion law to apply when federal and state statutes differ—the anti-abortion candidate may not be hurt as much, and might even be helped, by single-issue voting. For example, on the states' rights amendment, the anti-abortion candidate would have a net loss of 11 percent in Des Moines, but a gain of 3 percent in Springfield (Opinion Outlook 1981, p. 7). Thus, in electorates where anti-abortion sentiments run relatively high, an anti-abortion candidate backing a moderate policy measure might enjoy a net small gain as a consequence of single-issue voting. In a close election that gain could conceivably represent the margin of victory.

Implications

Single-issue voting is a method of decision making that has not been embraced wholeheartedly by the American public—at least not with respect to the issues of abortion and the ERA. Despite the substantial symbolic meaning that it evokes, the ERA apparently did not stimulate large numbers of the public to single-issue vote. Similarly, although not quite the symbolic issue that the ERA represents, abortion nonetheless evokes strong sentiments from a substantial portion of the public. Yet, in no survey considered here, not even among the activists, does single-issue voting begin to approach the 50 percent level. Thus, single-issue voting is not rampant, not even on two of the most divisive issues of the last decade.

At the same time, we cannot dismiss the potential effects of the single-issue voting that could occur. On the ERA, and especially abortion, there are significant if not overwhelming numbers of people who claim they are ready to support or discard a candidate simply because of his or her stand on the issue. Who are these single-issue voters? First, if our activist sample is an accurate indication, single-issue voting is not simply the province of the politically unsophisticated. On the contrary, on both abortion and the ERA it seems likely that knowledgeable, politically sophisticated activists form the core of the single-issue voters. This politically informed body of single-issue voters is joined by members of the mass public who are acting on the basis of their own extreme attitudes or who are attracted by the symbolic nature of the issue or both.

Secondly, proportionately there are more single-issue voters among the opponents, rather than supporters, of abortion and the ERA. Furthermore, this is true not only in the mass public but in our activist sample as well. The New Right activists see single-issue voting as a much more viable and powerful tactic of indirect lobbying, while the pro-ERA and abortion activists tend to spurn the method. This difference between pro and anti-activists in their willingness to single-issue vote seems to be a message that has

filtered down to the masses, where single-issue voting is also endorsed more frequently by those sympathetic to the New Right. In
effect, there appears to be an elite-mass linkage in the use of
single-issue voting. Thus, the journalists who view the New Right
as wielding substantial power through its tactic of targeting candidates are vindicated to some degree: defeating candidates through
the single-minded voting of their supporters is a tactic that the New
Right seems to rely on more heavily than the left.

Yet, advocating single-issue voting and using it effectively
are two different things. It is in this distinction that we find evidence for the claim that the New Right is not an especially powerful force in recent American elections. In most electorates the
distribution of opinion favors the ERA, and to a lesser extent the
right to abortion. Consequently, although there may be proportionately fewer pro single-issue voters, in actual numbers (where
it really counts) there are typically more than enough pro single-
issue voters to cancel out the effects of the anti single-issue voters.
Potentially, then, in many elections single-issue voting, the tactic
favored by the New Right, may actually hurt the New Right candidate. This is especially likely to be the case for the Equal Rights
Amendment and for unpopular abortion measures such as a constitutional ban on abortions.

To this point then, our evidence suggests that the New Right's
tactics of using single-issue voting to put pressure on elected officials may not be as potent a weapon as originally thought. Yet,
there are clearly problems with our data. All of the evidence on
single-issue voting is hypothetical in nature; it deals with the potential, as opposed to actual, behavior of voters. In real-life
elections, single-issue voters on one side of an issue may be more
likely to vote than those on the other side, thus altering the
potency of the strategy. Alternatively, voters may not be as
single-minded in their decisions as they have said they would be.
Whether voters actually follow through on their intentions to single-
issue vote may be influenced by the importance of other factors:
party ties, the candidate's images, and other issues. Furthermore, with regard to issues the candidates play an important role
in establishing the agenda for an election. By stressing certain
issues, candidates may distract the voters from single-issue
voting on issues they originally thought important. Such may have
been the case in the 1980 elections. With this in mind, let us
briefly consider the role the issues of abortion and the ERA, and
the New Right in general played in those elections.

The 1980 Elections

The 1980 elections provided a major testing ground for the New Right. Based strictly on the election outcomes, the New Right's plunge into electoral politics seems to have been a success. Ronald Reagan, the champion of the New Right, marched into the White House with one of the largest margins of victory in this century. In the House 33 Democratic incumbents, including eight members holding key leadership positions, lost their seats; and to the surprise of everyone the Republicans took control of the Senate. Yet, to what extent was the New Right actually responsible for these Republican victories? Did these newly elected Republican candidates win because the New Right succeeded in molding a conservative constituency? Although we lack both the space and data necessary to provide definitive answers to such questions we are able to briefly address them.

With regard to the congressional elections, a variety of sources suggest that, while the New Right certainly played a role in the Republican victories, it could not take all or even most of the credit. Both political analysts (Jacob 1981) and Republican party officials (Congressional Quarterly 1980d, p. 3372) argued that the Republican party, not the New Right, was the major architect in its own revival. In effect, the downfall of so many Democratic congressmen was not produced by the electorate embracing the ideology of the New Right, but rather by the combined effect of "fresh but experienced candidates, generous doses of party financing, a popular presidential candidate atop the ticket and a throw-the-bums-out mood" (Congressional Quarterly 1980d, p. 3372). This is not to deny that the New Right had any effect, but it does suggest that its influence was primarily financial (i.e., the use of PACs and especially the National Conservative Political Action Committee to provide monetary aid to "deserving" candidates) (Jacob 1981).

With respect to the Senate races, the New Right was quick to accept responsibility for the defeat of four of the six liberal Senators that had been targeted by NCPAC: Bayh of Indiana, Culver of Iowa, McGovern of South Dakota, and Church of Idaho. Yet, while New Right money certainly was used against these defeated Senators, it is again not clear that the New Right deserves credit for the Republicans' victories (Lipset and Raab 1981). Republican party officials, and in some instances the winning candidates themselves, said that "the New Right's role was minimal and in some cases harmful to their campaigns" (Congressional Quarterly 1980d, p. 3372). Who, then, deserves credit for these important Republican victories? Politicians see the strong, united Republican party campaign as being a major factor, while political scientists (e.g., Jacob 1981) also cite Reagan's coattails, idiosyncratic factors, and "excessive" seniority as possible explanations.

With respect to the 1980 Presidential election, the evidence suggests that Reagan's win was also not a consequence of the "arousal of a conservative mandate" spearheaded by the New Right (Pomper 1981, p. 87). Instead, Reagan's victory—or perhaps we should say Carter's loss—in the election was a consequence of Carter's failure to hold on to his own natural constituencies; across-the-board, members of the groups composing the traditional Democratic coalition abandoned Jimmy Carter for Ronald Reagan in 1980 (Pomper 1981). Furthermore, this wholesale desertion of Carter appears to have been brought on primarily by concerns over Carter's image; stunned by the crisis in Iran and worn down by the slumping economy at home, the electorate ultimately lost faith in Carter's competence to act as president (Kinder and Abelson 1981; Miller and Shanks 1981; Miller and Wattenberg 1981; Petrocik et al. 1981). Although Carter's declining image may have been foremost on many voters' minds, there were, nonetheless, issues such as defense spending and the economy (Miller and Shanks 1981; Pomper 1981) that had an independent effect on the voters' decisions (Lake 1982). But, neither of these issues was solely a New Right concern. Given this, then, what role did abortion and the ERA play in the 1980 presidential election?[19] Were these issues really of minor importance, as these studies suggest?

The Importance of Abortion and the ERA

Based on the voters' own reports, abortion and the ERA were not very important issues in the 1980 election. For example, a CBS/New York Times poll conducted just after the Reagan-Anderson debate in September 1980 reveals that neither abortion nor the ERA was foremost on the voters' minds. When given six issues to choose from, only 17 percent of the respondents said that abortion would be among the top three issues in deciding how they would vote for president, while only 14 percent picked the ERA as being among their top three issues. In contrast, over 40 percent mentioned government spending, military strength, or oil as one of their top three issues, while over 30 percent included income taxes in that category (CBS News/New York Times 1980). Thus, although they were important to a small percentage of people, for the electorate as a whole abortion and the ERA simply were not that important in determining presidential vote; other issues were definitely considered more urgent.

The relative unimportance of abortion and the ERA becomes even clearer when the data collected in the CPS National Election

Study is considered. Based on an open-ended question that asked people to name the most important problems currently facing the nation, abortion and the ERA ranked quite low: less than 1 percent mentioned either issue as being among the most important problems facing the country. Thus, given the relatively low level of importance accorded abortion and the ERA, it is unlikely that many people single-issue voted on either issue.

Knowledge of the Candidates' Issue Positions

Not only was the public not particularly interested in abortion and the ERA, but the two major presidential candidates themselves were not especially active in publicizing their views on these issues once the nominating conventions were over, a fact that may help explain the public's low evaluation of the importance of the issues. Prior to the convention, as is usually the case, both Carter and Reagan were forced to take stands that would appeal primarily to their respective party stalwarts (Page 1978). Thus, Reagan came out against the Equal Rights Amendment and favored a constitutional amendment to prohibit abortions, while Carter adopted the opposite stands. These relatively distinct positions were reflected in the party platforms (Plotkin 1981).

But once the candidates had won their respective party nominations, it was imperative that they "soften" their rhetoric, if not their actual stands, so that they might appeal to a broader base in the general election. As Gerald Pomper (1981, p. 78) notes, Reagan's "opposition to the Equal Rights Amendment was replaced by endorsement of statutory enactment of the same principle, and his endorsement of a constitutional amendment to ban abortion was replaced by silence." Meanwhile, Carter's pro-ERA stand received little attention from his camp and his pro-choice position on a constitutional amendment to ban abortions was blurred by his statement that "personally" he opposed abortion (Congressional Quarterly 1980a). As a consequence of the candidates downplaying their positions, the voters received less information about the issues and what information they received tended to make the candidates' stands on these issues more ambiguous. Thus, as the election drew near, it became less likely that the candidates' stands on either abortion or the ERA would affect very many people's decision-making processes.

This seems especially true when one actually considers the degree to which the public was knowledgeable about the candidates' stands on those two issues. As illustrated in Table 6.9, a CBS/ New York Times poll conducted in September 1980 indicates that a substantial portion of the electorate either had no idea where the

Table 6.9   PERCEPTIONS OF CANDIDATES' ISSUE STANDS
           BY PRESIDENTIAL PREFERENCE

| | Presidential Preference | | |
Candidates' Issue Positions	Carter Voters	Reagan Voters	All Voters[a]
ERA			
Carter			
favor	71%	76%	71%
oppose	12	9	10
no answer	17	15	19
Reagan			
favor	27%	36%	30%
oppose	44	49	46
no answer	29	15	24
Constitutional Amendment to Ban Abortions			
Carter			
favor	24%	25%	24%
oppose	45	40	41
no answer	31	35	35
Reagan			
favor	35%	36%	34%
oppose	27	40	32
no answer	38	24	34
n = 810			

[a] Includes Anderson voters.

Source: CBS News/New York Times Poll, September 1980, pp. 11, 13.

two major candidates stood on abortion and the ERA, or they misperceived the candidates' positions on those issues.[20] First, we
find a substantial portion of the electorate—between one-fifth and
one-third depending on the candidate and issue—unable to say what
are the candidates' positions. Thus, in terms of the level of
knowledge alone, a number of voters were not sufficiently informed
to take either abortion or the ERA into account in making their
vote choice.

The number of people who could have accurately single-issue
voted drops even further when the levels of misperception are taken
into account. Overall, misperception was lowest for Carter's position on the ERA; only 10 percent of those asked thought that he
opposed the amendment. At the same time, it was highest for
Reagan's position on a constitutional amendment to ban abortions;
32 percent of those asked mistakenly thought that he opposed such
an amendment. Interestingly, for both abortion and the ERA, misperception is highest for the potential Reagan voters' perceptions
of their own candidate. On the ERA, 36 percent of the potential
Reagan voters thought that he favored the amendment. Even more
surprising is the fact that there were more potential Reagan voters
(40 percent) who actually misperceived his position on a constitutional amendment to ban abortions than there were potential voters
who accurately perceived it (36 percent).

When the level of information is taken in conjunction with the
level of misperception, it becomes clear that the number of people
who accurately perceived a candidate's position and thus could have
accurately single-issue voted on either abortion or the ERA is
limited: 71 percent for Carter on the ERA, 46 percent for Reagan
on the ERA, 41 percent for Carter on abortion, and 34 percent for
Reagan on abortion. It seems unlikely, then, that Reagan's victory
could be termed a conservative mandate on either of these two
issues.

1980 Presidential Vote Choice and Abortion
and ERA Attitudes

Finally, we can consider the actual relationship between
presidential vote choice in 1980 and attitudes on abortion and the
ERA. In so doing, however, we must exercise considerable caution in interpreting our findings. For one thing, the correlations
we present are based on only a portion of the original CPS 1980
National Election Study sample; respondents who had no opinion on
the issue in question were eliminated from the analysis. Thus the
resulting correlations overestimate to some extent the true overall impact of the issue on the electorate's vote. Secondly, even if

we find correlations between attitudes on these issues and vote choice, this does not necessarily mean that issue voting has occurred. Processes other than issue-voting (such as projection and persuasion) can produce correlations between vote choice and issue positions (for further explanations see Brody and Page 1972). Without the use of panel data, we cannot begin to untangle the causal ordering between vote choice and the voter's own issue position. Furthermore, even if the causal direction were established, other issues and party identification may still help to account for the relationship between the voters' issue positions and their vote choice. With these qualifications in mind, let us briefly examine the relationships between attitudes on abortion and the ERA and vote choice.

As we can see from Table 6.10, there is no significant relationship between attitudes toward abortion and vote choice in the 1980 presidential election. Those people favoring the right to abortion voted for Reagan almost as frequently as those who opposed abortion. In fact, a lower proportion of abortion supporters than of opponents actually voted for Carter. These findings are not particularly surprising given the relatively low importance of the abortion issue, the voters' lack of information about the major candidates' stands on the issues, and the relatively high level of misperception about the major candidates' positions on the issue.

In contrast to the abortion issue, there is a relationship between vote choice and the respondent's position on the Equal Rights Amendment. Those who opposed the amendment are clearly more likely to have voted for Reagan than for Carter. Similarly, while the difference is not quite as large as in the case of the opponents of the amendment, substantially more ERA supporters gave their support to Carter than they did to Reagan. Why are attitudes toward the ERA related to vote choice while attitudes toward abortion are not?

In part, the answer may be that voters had both more information and more accurate information about the candidates' stands on the ERA than on abortion. This may be because the ERA refers to only one policy measure that candidates either favor or oppose; in contrast there are a number of different abortion measures that candidates might address, some they may favor and others they might oppose. Thus, ambiguity might have been inherently less on the ERA than on abortion, making it easier for voters to base their decision on the candidates' stands on the ERA.

A second factor that helps explain both the relationship between vote choice and attitudes toward the ERA as well as the higher level of information about the ERA is that the amendment is more closely linked than abortion to the partisan cleavages separating the Democrats and the Republicans. As a consequence, party cues may be used to infer the candidates' stands on the ERA, thus raising the voters' apparent knowledge on the issue. Similarly, the link between party identification and attitudes on the ERA may account for some of the relationship between vote choice and attitudes toward the ERA. Indeed, further analysis indicates that this is the case; the correlation (gamma) between vote choice and ERA attitudes declines from .55 to .38 when party identification is controlled for. Yet, at the same time, it is important to recognize that there remains a moderate relationship between vote choice and ERA attitudes that is independent of party identification.

Table 6.10 1980 PRESIDENTIAL VOTE CHOICE BY ATTITUDES TOWARD ABORTION AND ERA (in percent)

Vote Choice	Abortion			ERA	
	Anti[a]	Pro[b]		Anti	Pro
Reagan	53.5	49.3		71.8	38.6
Anderson	4.3	13.9		5.1	11.8
Carter	42.2	36.8		23.1	49.6
Total	100.0	100.0		100.0	100.0
(N)	(507)	(424)		(351)	(502)
	Tau c = -.001			Tau c = .32	
	(p > .05)			(p < .01)	

[a] Anti-abortion attitudes = never permit or permit only if woman's life in danger.

[b] Pro-abortion attitudes = permit for personal reasons or always permit.

Source: Calculated by authors from data in CPS National Election Studies.

This residual relationship may reflect some issue voting on the part of the electorate, although without further analysis we cannot say how much issue voting might have occurred. Our earlier findings on the relative unimportance of the ERA issue suggest that not many voters picked between Reagan and Carter solely on the basis of the ERA. What, then, accounts for the relationship of the ERA and vote choice? We posit that, to some extent, the relationship is a product of the strong symbolic meaning of the issue that links it in the voters' minds to a variety of other issues and symbols that we have not controlled for. Thus, the ERA itself may not have caused many people to vote for either Carter or Reagan, but it is nonetheless related to that decision because of its symbolic ties to those factors that were important.

CONCLUSIONS

We are now in a position to assess the impact of the New Right conflict on the mass public's attitudes and behavior toward the issues of abortion and the ERA. In terms of the distribution of opinion, there has been a remarkable stability in attitudes toward the ERA and especially abortion. In effect, neither the feminists nor the New Right has succeeded in greatly shifting the weight of public opinion from where it was in the early 1970s; moderate support for the ERA and for abortion in some circumstances. In terms of their meaning, there has been some change in both issues though especially the ERA; the symbolic meaning of abortion has both narrowed and become somewhat more emotional, while the symbolic meaning of the ERA has broadened considerably and become more intense. Thus, for the public as a whole, the ERA is the more symbolic of the two issues.

These changes in the meaning of the two issues have been paralleled by shifts in their mass bases of support. Like the meaning of the issue, the bases of support underlying attitudes toward abortion have changed relatively little; the religious cleavages on the issue are the only ones that have become noticeably more distinct over time. In contrast, for the ERA both the political and religious bases of support are more pronounced now than previously. In summary, then, the New Right conflict has had some effect on mass attitudes toward the ERA and a noticeably smaller influence on abortion attitudes.

The impact of the New Right conflict on mass behavior toward abortion and the ERA is more difficult to assess. If we focus on potential single-issue voting, the much publicized tactic of the New Right, then we find only limited evidence that the New Right has the ability to target and subsequently defeat any candidate of its choosing. The elites in various New Right single-issue groups have apparently succeeded in conveying to their mass constituencies the efficacy of single-issue voting; there are proportionately more potential single-issue voters among the opponents of the ERA and abortion. Yet, for many electorates encouraging single-issue voting

is a dangerous tactic for the New Right. Because most publics
favor the ERA and the right to abortion in at least some instances,
it takes proportionately fewer single-issue voters on the pro side
to outweigh the votes of the New Rightists. Therefore, if an electorate is encouraged to vote single-mindedly on the basis of an
issue such as abortion, the tactic could backfire and lead to the
defeat of the New Right candidate. Thus, the New Right's potential
power to target and defeat candidates through single-issue voting is
perhaps not as great as the New Right would have us believe.

Similarly, if we examine actual elections for evidence that
the New Right has succeeded in mobilizing a conservative constituency, then we again find only marginal support for the contention
that the New Right is an extremely powerful force in determining
electoral outcomes. There is little evidence that the 1980 presidential election constituted a conservative mandate; and there is
even less evidence that two of the most symbolic issues of the New
Right—abortion and the ERA—had any substantial effect on whether
most Americans voted for Reagan or Carter in that election. Nor
does it appear that the numerous Republican victories in the 1980
congressional and senatorial races are attributable to the New
Right.

Yet, if we measure the New Right's power in terms of the
amount of money that conservative PACs raised and spent in the
1980 elections, then—as journalists and some defeated liberal
candidates have implied—the New Right does appear powerful indeed. But, on the other hand, if we measure the New Right's power
in terms of its impact on mass attitudes and its shaping of mass
behavior, then—as various political scientists have suggested—the
New Right's power does not appear as great. Despite all of the
money it has poured into various campaigns and the subsequent
victories of conservative candidates, the New Right does not seem
to have succeeded in converting the mass public into a conservative, mobilized constituency, at least not with respect to the issues
of abortion and the ERA. Thus, indirect lobbying through the voting booth has <u>not</u> "bought" the New Right all that it had hoped for;
it has helped to elect certain candidates, but it has failed to produce a clearly conservative mandate for those new officeholders to
act upon. Perhaps, however, simple <u>fear</u> of the New Right's electoral tactics (i.e., targeting) may have had the desired effect of
encouraging elected officials to temper their policy stances and
change their behavior. Alternatively, the New Right may have been
more successful in its direct lobbying efforts. Let us turn to the
next chapter where we consider that possibility.

NOTES

1. Weber and Uslaner (1981) note that the lack of change at
the aggregate level may be somewhat misleading since the analysis
of panel data reveals that there have been some individual level
changes that tend to cancel each other out when viewed only from
the aggregate. From our perspective, it is the aggregate opinion
levels that are most important since they provide the best measure
of the overall impact of the New Right.

2. We have reversed the order of the responses to the original CPS question so that the analysis would be more consistent
with that in previous chapters.

3. For the NORC data, abortion is measured in terms of the
same series of seven questions employed in Chapter 5.

4. With respect to our methods of analysis, we once again
rely only on correlation (rather than regression) analysis, since
we definitely do not wish to argue that the various dimensions of
meaning actually determine positions on the two issues. But
over time comparisons of correlations can be misleading. Since
correlations are affected by the variance in the variables, a change
in a correlation over time could possibly be an artifact of substantial changes in the variance of the variables involved. For example, a decrease in the variance of a variable would tend (ceteris
paribus) to depress the correlation. In our case, however, there
were only relatively minor changes in the variances of most of the
variables used to assess the meaning of abortion and the ERA.
Furthermore, those correlations involving variables whose variances had increased or decreased tended to change in the opposite
direction of what would be expected (i.e., increases in the correlations among variables whose variances had decreased). Where
this is not the case, it will be noted. Nonetheless, these findings
should be viewed with some caution.

5. For the correlation involving "civil rights leaders" part
of this decline may be a function of the fact that the variance for
that variable had decreased from 29.26 in 1972 to 23.7 in 1980.
But in the case of "black militants," the variance actually increased
slightly over the same time period, while the variance remained
virtually the same for "radical students" from 1972 to 1980.

6. This is despite a decrease in the variance for the "women's
liberation movement" feeling thermometer.

7. Of these, the "republican" feeling thermometer was the
only one whose variance declined noticeably over the time period.

8. The ERA question was not asked on the NORC surveys in
1976 and 1980; thus we cannot provide comparable data for the
relationship between ERA attitudes and morality. However, they

did ask about the ERA in 1977. Using the same morality measure employed in the analysis of abortion attitudes, we find that ERA attitudes are correlated with morality: Pearson's r equals .23. In effect, the more traditional the morality, the greater the opposition to the ERA.

    9. Of the feeling thermometer variables, "black militants" and "big business" were the only ones whose variances increased noticeably over time.

    10. Granberg and Granberg (1980) and Barnett and Harris (1982) do provide some over time analysis of the bases of support underlying abortion attitudes.

    11. The variances for these variables remained virtually the same over the time period, thus reducing the possibility that any changes in the correlations were a statistical artifact.

    12. Barnett and Harris (1982) find that the relationship between church attendance and attitudes toward abortion remained stable between 1974 and 1977 for women, but that it increased slightly for men over the same time period.

    13. During April 1980, these data were collected via a telephone poll on one of the surveys compiled by the ongoing "Minnesota Poll" which is sponsored by the Minneapolis Tribune. Trained interviewers were employed. Samples of this size have a sampling error of approximately ± 3.5 at the 95 percent confidence level. Our special thanks to Stephen Coombs and the Minneapolis Tribune for making these data available.

    14. The Harris Survey results appeared in Opinion Outlook, 2 (March 29, 1982b: 1).

    15. These data were collected in a telephone survey of a random sample of 460 residents of Lexington, Kentucky, conducted during the first week of November 1980. Trained student interviewers were used. We thank Lee Sigelman of the University of Kentucky for the use of these data.

    16. The ERA issue is particularly complicated in Kentucky. Although the legislature rescinded their ratification of the amendment, Lieutenant Governor Thelma Stovall, acting in the governor's place while he was out of the state, vetoed the legislature's rescission. Thus, the status of the ERA in Kentucky is particularly ambiguous.

    17. These data, again, were collected and made available by Lee Sigelman.

    18. A comparison of these data with earlier surveys suggests that the levels of single-issue voting on abortion have increased in recent years, particularly among opponents of the issue (Jaffe et al. 1981, pp. 107-108).

19. We focus on the presidential election for two reasons: (1) its symbolic value as a gauge of public sentiment; and (2) the unavailability of data at the state level. In so doing, we acknowledge that these issues may have been more critical to issue-voting for state and congressional candidates.

20. The CPS data were not used for this analysis for several reasons. First, and most important, the CPS did not ask the voters where the candidates stood on the ERA. Instead, they asked about the voters' perceptions of the candidates on the equal rights scale. Secondly, the abortion measure used by the CPS is a more difficult one to place candidates on than simply asking about their stand on a constitutional amendment. Were we to have conducted the same analysis using the CPS data, it is expected that there would have been less information and more misperception of the candidates' stands, given that ambiguity might have been greater with regard to how the CPS framed the issues of abortion and equal rights for women.

7 / THE "PRO-FAMILY VS. PRO-FEMINIST" CONFLICT IN THE STATES

Many of the important family-related conflicts between feminists and the New Right have taken place at the state and local levels: for example, the ERA ratification battles in state legislatures and the various efforts by state legislatures and city councils to restrict abortion access. These two social movements are in large part organized at the subnational level, the feminists employing a federal structure and the New Right a grassroots structure. Thus, to understand the emergence of the New Right as a counterforce against feminism as well as to explain the outcome of the abortion and ERA conflicts, it is necessary to study both social movements at the state level. Furthermore, the formation of political interest groups out of the feminist and New Right movements is shaped by the political and social context in which the groups are embedded. Thus, we need to examine how the state's political system facilitates the emergence of groups and shapes their ultimate success.

In this chapter we shall first consider the rise of the pro-family Right in the 50 states. Can our theory of social movements help us to predict those states in which the New Right will appear? In the second, and more speculative, section of the chapter we will consider the pro-family sector's success in blocking the ratification of the ERA and in restricting abortions. Is the pro-family movement responsible for those policy outcomes or can they be explained on other grounds?

PREVIOUS RESEARCH

No state-level empirical research has yet been conducted to describe the numbers and types of New Right groups in the 50 states nor to explain the variation in mobilization. Certainly, the observations of journalists (e.g., Fitzgerald 1981a; Crawford 1980) suggest that states undergoing rapid social change, or disintegration from the New Right's perspective, would be prime candidates for mobilization. Also in the past the fundamentalist, Bible Belt South has proven to be fertile ground for similar movements such as the anti-evolution and prohibition movements. Still, no systematic analysis at the state level has been undertaken, primarily because of the absence of reliable state-by-state data on group mobilization.

Research on the success of the New Right at the state level is similarly nonexistent. There are, however, individual case studies and comparative state studies analyzing state actions on the ERA and on abortion that have implications for our study of the New Right. Of these, consideration of state ratification action is more extensive than is study of state abortion restrictions. Studies of individual ERA activists (e.g., Brady and Tedin 1976; Arrington and Kyle 1978; Miller and Linker 1974; Tolchin and Tolchin 1974; Dodson 1982) were, of course, carried out in states and thus provide us with some knowledge of the reasons for success and failure in Texas, North Carolina, Utah, Connecticut, and Illinois, respectively. Boles' study (1979) concludes that ad hoc group activity is the explanation for the ERA's failure in Georgia, Texas, and Illinois.

Although not concerned with the New Right specifically, three comparative studies of ERA ratification efforts in all 50 states are more relevant to our efforts (Bell no date; Wohlenberg 1980; Daniels and Darcy 1982). These treat ratification of an amendment as a diffusion process. Daniels and Darcy (1982) find that ERA's diffusion pattern is similar to that of other amendments, implying that interest groups had little effect. Bell found that socioeconomic and political variables were not related to ratification after control variables were introduced. His highest predictor was Gray's welfare innovation index, suggesting that ERA is treated like other innovations in the welfare field. Wohlenberg reports a similar conclusion: Walker's innovativeness score is highly related to ratification. He further found that religious conservatism, political conservatism, and previous action on extension of voting rights to women and 18-year-olds were related to state actions on the ERA. Together these articles imply that the political, religious, and cultural environment might shape the New Right's success in blocking ratification.

Though less extensive in volume, case studies of anti-abortion groups (e.g., Margolis and Neary 1980 in Pennsylvania; Steinhoff and Diamond 1977 in Hawaii) emphasize the impact of single-issue tactics. Thus far, comparative state studies have sought to explain abortion rates, not abortion restrictions as we are doing (e.g., Johnson and Bond 1980; Hansen 1980).

In summary, previous research yields a mixed picture on the New Right's mobilization and success at the state level. Case studies in individual states tend to emphasize the impact of anti-ERA or anti-abortion groups in deterring ratification or regulating abortions. Comparative state studies, in contrast, generally rate political variables as less important than other types of variables. None of these studies, however, included interest groups as political factors. Thus, the New Right's strength and success is still an open question.

THE MOBILIZATION OF THE PRO-FAMILY MOVEMENT

Social Movement Theory

The theory outlined in Chapter 2 can help us to answer the two questions posed for this chapter. In this section we examine our theory's implications for the rise of the New Right; that is, its relation to identifiable grievances, to solidarity networks, and to outsiders. A later section considers our theory's implications for understanding the movement's success, where success is defined as defeating the ERA and restricting abortions. Our primary focus is the pro-family sector of the New Right because it is these groups that have worked throughout the 1970s specifically against ERA and abortion. The pro-family sector cooperates with the secular and religious sectors of the New Right but, as explained in Chapter 4, the latter two sectors focus on collective goods other than the family and consequently are active on a broader range of issues than ERA and abortion.

We are seeking to explain mobilization, which is defined as the process by which a group goes from being a collection of individuals to being a set of active participants pursuing a collective goal. Thus, we will need evidence that social movement organizations exist in each state. Once we have assessed the level of mobilization, we will need to consider those contextual factors that influence it: preexisting grievances and discontents, the presence of solidarity networks, urgency, and outside forces. The motivations for individuals to lead or to join groups (i.e., self-interest, solidary benefits, or ideological principles) are not considered in this chapter because we are not working with data on individuals. Rather, our measures are at the state level, allowing us to investigate how conditions in the states facilitate mobilization on the Right. Let us consider each of the contextual factors briefly.

Theorists of both the collective behavior and the resource mobilization perspectives agree that shared grievances play a role in the transition from movement to organization. In Chapter 4 we identified some of the grievances of the New Right's pro-family sector: from their perspective, high divorce rates, high abortion rates, and women working outside the home all indicate the breakdown of the traditional American family. If pro-family groups spring up in states with high rates of divorce, abortion, and working women, we shall infer that such preconditions of social disorganization facilitate pro-family mobilization.

Furthermore, the resource mobilization perspective argues that certain conditions increase the likelihood of mobilization: when the sense of urgency is high, defensive mobilization is made easier; consequently, both objective and subjective measures of necessity would be valuable. We assume that where the rates of disorganization have increased over time, family breakdown would appear to be a greater threat. Hence, we will want to use measures from the early and late 1970s and the rate of change in these measures to give an objective basis for assessing the necessity for collective defensive action. In addition, the number of feminist groups, their activities, and increases over time in feminism are perceived as threats to the American family as outlined in Chapter 4. Thus, we will develop measures of feminism's subjective threat to the family as an impetus to pro-family mobilization.

Another factor that tends to lower the cost of mobilization (thereby increasing the likelihood of forming organizations) is the presence of other organizations offering solidarity and support to the fledgling social movement organization. We would expect, therefore, that the existence of relevant conservative political and religious groups within a state would furnish a mobilization network for pro-family organizations. In particular, the presence of large numbers of fundamentalist Protestants or Catholics should help the anti-abortion effort.

Finally, our argument also pointed to the influence of the outside environment on a group's mobilization potential, especially the government and the media. While we do not have systematic evidence on the reaction of governmental actors or media figures in the states, we do expect that the mainstream political culture of a state might be a useful proxy variable expressing states' tolerance for organizing on the Right. According to Daniel Elazar's (1972) description of America's three political subcultures, the traditionalistic culture, with its stress on the preservation of order, would most tolerate pro-family mobilization.

In summary, we expect to find that our theory of mobilization is useful in explaining the level of pro-family mobilization in states. The propositions articulated in Chapter 2 are applicable at several levels of analysis: individual, group, and state. We have empirically confirmed how these principles operate for the elite (Chapter 5) and the mass (Chapter 6). In this chapter we seek the same demonstration for the preconditioning and contextual factors at the state level. In a practical sense the state level findings may have even more import than do the individual level results because the distribution of individuals across states will determine the outcome of the family battle.

Data and Measures

The first, and most difficult, task is to measure the level of mobilization and organization among the pro-family sector of the New Right. While the size of membership would be an obvious choice, our solicitation of major national groups on the Right (and the Left) produced very few who would give us membership data by state. Further, the claims of nationwide membership by several organizations appear to be so inflated that membership data may not be reliable at all. Instead, we decided that the existence of a family group organized for political action as a lobby or PAC would be the best available measure of the level of mobilization. If a group is sufficiently organized that it lobbies in the legislature against feminist legislation or raises and disburses campaign funds, we infer that people have been mobilized. The number of groups representing the pro-family position in a state is then our indicator of mobilization.[1]

Very recently data on interest groups have become available due to the reforms enacted by states in the wake of the Watergate era campaign reforms at the federal level. Nearly all states now require legislative lobbyists to register; we were able to acquire these registration lists from 46 of the 50 states.[2] The number of pro-family groups registered for the purpose of lobbying is a reliable indicator only if state laws are roughly similar and if enforcement is comparable. Our analyses of all the groups (not just the pro-family groups) satisfy us that numerical differences among the states are not due to substantive differences in the laws but rather indicate real differences in the organizational life of states.[3] The specific groups coded into the pro-family category were anti-ERA and anti-abortion groups and other groups whose titles indicated a concern with traditional family and morality. Further, most though not all states now require registration of political action committees whose purpose is to raise and expend campaign funds. These lists were obtained from 40 states.[4] Our lists are for those groups active in the 1980 elections, either legislative races or statewide campaigns.

The outcome of this data collection and coding procedure for pro-family groups and, by way of comparison, for feminist groups provides several results of note. Given all the media attention to this phenomenon, the relatively small number of pro-family groups is striking. When the lobby groups and PACs are added together, the average number of pro-family groups per state is only 4.6. There are some states with no groups active on pro-family issues: Hawaii, New Mexico, and South Carolina. One implication of these small numbers is that the amount of variation is small for either measure. Since the numbers of groups are so small, it appeared best to combine the two measures of mobilization (PACs and lobby groups) into a single measure of pro-family mobilization in each state.[5] The feminist network, in contrast, is better organized at the state level. Feminists average 9.9 groups per state. Two states (Idaho and Utah, to no one's surprise) have no organizations classified as feminist. California has the most with 39 feminist groups. Feminism also relies more on lobbying groups and less on PACs while the pro-family sector relies on PACs more than lobby groups.

Preconditions

As indicated in the theoretical discussion, the objective conditions that the pro-family sector identifies as indicators of the breakdown of the traditional family are divorce, abortion, and women working outside the home. On the basis of Chapter 4's description of the preconditions leading to the New Right's emergence, we need data from the first half of the 1970s. Thus we use the divorce rate per 1000 in 1970 and in 1975 to measure marital breakup (see Appendix E for sources).[6]

To measure the rate of abortion, we elected to use abortions per 1,000 women aged 15-55 by state of occurrence in 1974. State of occurrence rather than state of residence was used because we assume people react to the abortions they see or hear about in their community. They have no way of knowing whether these abortion-seeking women are residents.[7] Another dimension of the abortion grievance might be the lack of restrictions on the performance of abortions. Opponents presumably feel safer when the legislature has passed such laws and more threatened when there was no response against Roe. To measure this aspect of preexisting discontents we use the degree of restrictiveness of abortion laws passed by states in 1973-1975 as calculated by Johnson and Bond (1980) (see Appendix E for explanation). They include 17 types of restrictions in their measure (e.g., parental consent) and adjust for the severity of each state's law.[8]

Finally, the measure of women working outside the home is simply the percentage of women in the labor force in 1976. [9]

Objective Measures of Threat

As argued above, defensive mobilization is more likely where valued goods are threatened because this creates a sense of urgency. We propose to measure the threat to the family (or the necessity for taking action) first in an objective sense. The most recent rates of divorce, abortion, and working women as well as restrictions on abortion are objective indicators that the family is still threatened. Thus, we use data for divorce in 1979, abortion in 1980, women in the labor force in 1979, and abortion restrictions in 1979. The abortion restrictions in 1979 were obtained from the Alan Guttmacher Institute and scored by the authors in the Johnson and Bond fashion (see Appendix E for further detail).

Another component of threat is the rate at which family break-up is getting worse, that is the rate of increase in divorces, abortions, and women leaving the home to join the labor force. Thus, we computed the percentage rate of change (new rate - old rate/ old rate) as an objective measure of urgency. [10] An additional threat measure is the percentage increase in the metropolitan population between 1970 and 1980. The move from the farm to the city implies a certain amount of breakdown in traditional family life and more generally a sense of social disorganization. [11]

Subjective Measures of Threat

The feeling that valued public goods are threatened and that a solution is urgently needed also has a subjective dimension. As argued earlier, feminism has been intimately linked with the breakup of the nuclear family. Thus, the rise of feminism would be perceived as threatening to the family unit. An increase in feminism over time should therefore contribute to a sense of urgency about taking action. Our measures of subjective threat from feminists parallel our measures of New Right mobilization: the sum of feminist PACs and feminist groups registered as lobbying groups. [12]

Measuring the increased feminist threat is somewhat more difficult. We elected to construct a measure of feminist mobilization in 1974 as our base point from which to calculate the percentage rate of change in feminist mobilization (1980 total - 1974 total/1974 total). The 1974 measure is the sum of groups belonging to the state's ERA ratification council, other feminist groups, and abortion providers listed in the Women's Almanac (Gager 1974). The relative increase in feminist groups from 1974 to 1980 is taken as another subjective measure of threat.

Solidarity Networks

The alliance of pro-family groups with the secular New Right, the Religious Right, and to a lesser extent the Old Right is well-documented in Chapter 4. Thus, the validity of using conservatism and religion to represent a solidarity network is established. Our measures of conservatism derive from the same list of registered lobby groups. We first isolated the "cause" groups (those articulating a particular issue; not business, labor, etc.) and then coded the number of those groups expressing a conservative orientation. Such groups primarily are from the secular Right but are relatively few in number, averaging 3.9 groups per state. We also measured the strength of the Old Right by counting all business-oriented groups. This is a considerably larger set of groups, averaging 59.5 percent of all groups. In the states of Arizona, Hawaii, Louisiana, Pennsylvania, South Carolina, and Utah, over 70 percent of all registered lobbyists represent business. We elected to use the percentage of all groups that are business-related.[13]

Since fundamentalist denominations oppose abortion on principle and many oppose the ERA as well, they would be expected to furnish solidarity to emerging pro-family groups. Our measure of fundamentalism is the percent of the state's population belonging to an evangelical or fundamentalist church.[14] Similarly, the Catholic Church has opposed abortion (though not the ERA) and would be expected to facilitate pro-family mobilization. We use the percentage of the state's population belonging to the Catholic Church as our measure.

The measures of the Religious Right are interesting in that the average across states is quite similar: 16.5 percent of the population belong to churches classified as liberal; 14.8 percent belong to fundamentalist denominations; 20 percent are Catholic adherents. The range, however, is very different for the three types of religion: the maximum liberal religious state (North Dakota) has 40.7 percent of the population adhering; the maximum fundamentalist state (Utah) has 75.9 percent adherents; the maximum Catholic state (Rhode Island) has 63.6 percent Catholics. Thus, Catholics and fundamentalists may be strategically located so as to have a greater impact than liberal adherents.

Environment

Our measures of the outside environment are not quite congruent with our theory which is about the role of government and the media. Lacking data on these specific factors, we will substitute data on the mainstream culture or environment. That is, we expect that where the mainstream culture is opposed to ERA and abortion, governmental actors and media figures will be more tolerant of pro-family organizing efforts. Our first measure of culture is Elazar's (1972) categorization of political culture where the traditionalistic culture should be most tolerant of pro-family mobilization. Our index is coded so that moralistic culture is high and traditionalistic is low.

Our second environmental measure is a simulated measure of public opinion regarding abortion developed by Uslaner and Weber (1980), using the Munger-Weber simulation techniques. It expresses the percentage in 1972 that were opposed to abortion on demand in the first three months of pregnancy. We expect that early public attitudes against abortion "on demand" are likely to create a climate of opinion wherein pro-family groups flourish.

Our third environmental measure focuses on state governmental actions on abortion prior to the Roe decision, specifically whether the state had repealed (four had) or reformed their laws (14 had) or still outlawed abortion (32 did). If governmental actors had formally expressed their approval of abortion choice through repeal or reform, we expect that they would be intolerant of pro-family organizing later on. This variable is coded such that a high score represents repeal. It is negatively correlated ($r = -.22$) with the index of opinion disapproval, as it should be.

Findings on the Rise of the Pro-Family Movement

The measures described above can help us to evaluate the reasons for the level of pro-family mobilization in states at the end of the 1970s. Initially, we will be looking at the bivariate correlations (Pearson's product-moment). We shall expect fairly modest levels of association because there are surprisingly few pro-family groups, and hence little variation to be explained.

Table 7.1 summarizes the findings regarding various explanations for the rise of pro-family groups. First, let us look at the preexisting discontents. Clearly, the existence of pro-family groups is related to the initial rate of abortion in states ($r = .31$). The emergence of this New Right sector, nonetheless, is not related to other aspects of familial breakdown such as divorce, women working outside the home, or even the lack of restrictions on abortion. Thus, the mobilization is precipitated, it seems, by only one dimension of family crisis.[15] It appears to be the use of abortion, rather than just its existence (judging by the low correlation with restrictive laws) that is threatening.

When we examine the intercorrelations of the indicators of family breakdown (data not shown), we can further understand the

Table 7.1   CORRELATIONS OF TOTAL PRO-FAMILY AND
            FEMINIST GROUPS WITH OTHER FACTORS

Factors	Groups Pro-Family	Feminist
Preconditions		
Abortion rate, 1974	.31*	.35*
Divorce rate, 1970	.09	.10
Divorce rate, 1975	-.01	.03
Women in labor force, 1976	.01	.14
Abortion restrictions, 1975	-.08	-.01
Objective Threat		
Abortion rate, 1980	.32*	.34*
Divorce rate, 1979	-.06	.03
Women in labor force, 1979	-.03	.04
Abortion restrictions, 1979	-.09	-.04
Change in abortion rate, 1974-1980	-.25	-.16
Change in divorce rate, 1970-1979	-.24	-.06
Change in women in labor force, 1976-1979	-.09	-.17
Change in metro population, 1970-1980	-.10	.01
Subjective Threat		
Total number of feminist groups, 1980	.61*	a
Change in number of feminist groups, 1974-1980	.65*	a
Solidarity Network		
Number of conservative groups, 1980	.27*	a
Percent of business groups, 1980	-.34*	a
Percent fundamentalist church members, 1974	-.06	a
Percent Catholics, 1974	-.15	a
Environment		
Moralistic political culture	.04	a
Percent opposed to abortion, 1972	.05	a
Abortion reform pre-Roe	.05	a

* Significant at .05 level.

a Data not applicable.

Source: Calculated by authors.

pattern under discussion. The abortion rate and the divorce rates are uncorrelated ($r = -.03$ in 1970 and $-.06$ in 1975). The only statistically significant positive correlation is between the abortion rate and working women and that is just barely significant ($r = .23$). Thus, there does not appear to be a syndrome of family breakdown at the state level, though of course there may be at the individual level.

We see a similar pattern when we look at the next set of measures, those purporting to capture the more recent threat from family breakdown. Once again, the abortion rate is significantly associated with the rise of the family Right in that where abortion rates are high, more groups appear. Still, other measures of threat to the present family are not related to the appearance of groups.

Turning to the set of measures that portray the change in objective threat, none of the relationships is significant, though the change in the abortion rate from 1974-1980 and the change in the divorce rate from 1970-1980 are nearly significant. That is, those states in which abortion and divorce rates have increased the most have more pro-family groups. Still, it does not appear that urgency stemming from objective necessity is a powerful motivation for the emergence of groups.

Paralleling our findings for the early 1970s, by the end of the 1970s no syndrome of family breakdown at the state level has appeared. The indexes of abortion, the divorce rate, and the percentage of working women at the end of the decade were uncorrelated, with the exception that the abortion rate and working women were significantly correlated at .26 (data not shown). Further, none of the change measures were positively correlated among themselves. Rather, Table 7.1's results suggest that the subjective threat posed by feminism is what increases pro-family mobilization. Both measures of feminism are highly correlated with pro-family groups: where the number of feminist groups is high, there are more pro-family groups.[16] In particular, where feminist groups have increased the most, pro-family groups are especially great in number ($r = .65$).

Now it may be argued that the absolute number of groups in a state is contributing to the correlation between feminist and pro-family groups. Indeed, when the total number of registered lobby groups is introduced as a control, the zero-order correlation of .36 drops to .19, so to some extent this charge is true.[17] Nonetheless, we believe that the presence of feminism in the states precipitates the rise of the pro-family sector. Note that the partial correlation is still positive, though no longer significant, and the highest correlation in Table 7.1 is that between the number of pro-family groups and the percentage change in feminist groups, a measure not subject to the size of scale problem. Thirdly, a heavily populated group environment probably offers many liberal groups besides feminists and thus more reason for counterorganization by the Right. On theoretical grounds we take Table 7.1's correlations as evidence that the pro-family sector is a defensive mobilization effort against the feminist movement, rather than a movement founded primarily on objective grievances and discontents.

Next it is of interest to determine if feminism is related to any of the objective grievances the New Right has. Perhaps the Right blames feminism for family breakdown by viewing their covariation and imputing causality. Taking first the relation of total feminist groups with the early indicators of family breakdown, the only significant and positive correlation exists with the 1974 abortion rate. Thus, where the early abortion rate was high, feminist groups appeared at the end of the decade in larger numbers. This may help to explain why the abortion rate was the only significant correlate with the pro-family Right among the first set of variables. The Right associates abortion with feminism and reacts to both by forming counterorganizations. By the end of the decade, the abortion rate remained the only indicator of family breakdown to be correlated with the number of feminist groups. In like manner, none of the change scores was correlated with the total number of feminist groups.

Finally, we want to look at the constituent network where pro-family groups have sprung up. First of all, there is a correlation of some significance between the number of pro-family groups and the number of secular New Right conservative groups. This suggests that the pro-family sector of groups is being assisted by the broader New Right network. However, the network does not extend to the business community seemingly as the correlation with the percentage of business groups lobbying the legislature is negative. The pro-family sector does not appear to be fostered by the Old Right. Moreover, the oft-claimed association between fundamentalism and the pro-family Right does not exist at the state level. That is, states with many pro-family groups do not generally have a high percentage of fundamentalist church members. There is a slightly stronger negative correlation with the percentage of Catholics, again indicating that the pro-family Right is not assisted by the number of Catholics in a state.

What these findings indicate to us is that the pro-family movement may be more of a new movement than it is usually understood to be. At the state level it does not have extensive links with business, fundamentalists, or Catholics. These aggregate level results, however, do not imply anything about the linkages at the mass or

elite levels explored in the last two chapters. The state level results may mean that the pro-family sector is less potent than the
media claims. If it is linked only with the more recent conservative groups, and not the older Right, then the pro-family movement
will presumably have more difficulty in pressing its claims in the
political arena.

Another aspect of the context from which pro-family groups
emerge is the mainstream culture. Here the question is whether
groups tend to appear in environments that are reinforcing or opposing. We first look at the correlation between moralistic political culture and the number of pro-family groups. The correlation
reported in Table 7.1 is near zero, indicating that the type of political culture does not influence the emergence of pro-family groups.
We might also reasonably expect that if the pro-family Right is a
straightforward translation of public opinion into group strength,
then the percent opposed to abortion would be related to the number
of pro-family groups. However, that is not the case as indicated by
the near-zero correlation. Finally, the near-zero correlation between pro-family groups and early abortion reform also indicates
that governmental actors are not affecting mobilization. Hence, we
conclude that the mainstream culture is neither facilitating nor re-
tarding the growth of pro-family organizations.

Our last task is to combine selected indicators whose bivariate
correlation coefficients were significant into a single regression
equation.[18] Table 7.2 reports the results of the multivariate analysis in which 42 percent of the variance is explained. The number of
feminist groups is the only statistically significant variable. It appears then that the pro-family movement is primarily a reaction to
the subjective threat posed by the feminist movement rather than to
objective preexisting or existing conditions of the family. These results suggest that what we are analyzing is an anti-feminist rather
than a pro-family movement.

Table 7.2   REGRESSION RESULTS FOR TOTAL PRO-FAMILY
            GROUPS WITH SELECTED VARIABLES

Predictor	Beta
1980 Abortion Rate	.098
Total Conservative Groups	.167
Feminist Groups	.553*
R^2 = .42	

* = Significant at .05 level.

Source: Calculated by authors.

Conclusions about the Rise of the Pro-Family Right

The data examined above lend support to our contention throughout the book that the New Right is primarily a countermovement engaged in a symbolic protest over the American family. There is little reason to believe, on the basis of these findings, that pro-family groups are formed as people react to family breakdowns in their immediate environment. If this were the case, the rate of group formation would be related to indicators of family distress. There is one striking exception to this general finding, however, and that is the abortion rate. Pro-family groups appear most frequently in those states experiencing a high rate of abortions.

Even the abortion rate has a highly symbolized effect, however. The groups are not formed in reaction to a sense of urgency about the increase in abortions. Rather, even the abortion rate is indirectly linked to the countermovement in that the abortion rate was initially highest in those states with large numbers of feminist groups in 1974. The link between feminism and abortion was thus forged in the minds of the members of the New Right and still persists as a motivation for counterorganization. The multivariate analysis underscores this interpretation.

Unless and until the pro-family Right is more tied to other elements of conservatism at the state level, it may be short-lived. Pro-family groups tend to appear where there are groups working for other New Right causes but not particularly where Old Right interests are powerful or where fundamentalist churches are strong. Thus, even if the national New Right organizations are using the mailing lists of "the electronic church" or the Old Right, this has not yet been translated into similar patterns of cooperation and co-optation within the states. The latter is crucial for impact on state politics where family issues are often determined.

THE SUCCESS OF THE PRO-FAMILY RIGHT

Having gained an understanding of the origins of pro-family groups in the states, we can now turn to an examination of their possible effect upon the two central issues of the family conflict: abortion and the ERA. What is the power of this sector of the New Right movement at the state level? And what is the power of the feminist movement when comparably organized? The theory articulated in Chapter 2 primarily focuses upon the origin of groups, rather than upon their effects, but the basic elements of the theory can give some guidance about what to expect, as can the literature cited earlier in this chapter.

Social Movement Theory

As mentioned in Chapter 2, Gamson (1975) has conceptualized movement success as having two dimensions: acceptance and gaining new advantages. Acceptance as members of the polity, it seems to us, has already been achieved by the pro-family Right. They are recognized by other members of the polity as legitimate representatives for pro-family interests. Consequently, it will be more fruitful in this section to concentrate upon their success in gaining new advantages. For us, this will mean state legislatures' enactment of the pro-family Right's goals: the defeat of the ERA and the restriction and eventual elimination of legal abortion.

Along with most political scientists we would expect that the number of groups pressing the same claim will affect success. In particular, the number of pro-family groups relative to the number of feminist groups in the state will determine achievement of collective goals. Where the organizational advantage goes to the pro-family Right, we expect them to be more successful than the feminists. Further, we assume that the New Right will be more successful in obtaining new advantages where its solidarity network is strong, in part because the need for selective incentives is lower. Given our findings above that pro-family groups are not related to most indicators of their likely constituency network, we should also entertain the hypothesis that it is the solidarity network itself that is obtaining the enactment of new legislation. Furthermore, it will be of interest to see the effect of mainstream culture upon the enactment of pro-family goals. We expect that the environment of traditionalistic culture would aid in achieving their goals.

Data and Measures

The stated goals of the pro-family sector are concrete: the defeat of the ERA and the abolition of abortion lead its list of goals just as the ERA's passage and the right to choose an abortion are among the leading objectives of the feminist movement. Thus, our first indicator of New Right success is the nonratification of the ERA. By the 1982 deadline 35 states had ratified the ERA; four of these had rescinded their action;[19] 15 had not ratified. This variable is coded so that a high score equals ERA failure. A second indicator is the severity of selected abortion restrictions passed by the state legislature by 1979. As explained further in Appendix E, this is the authors' updating of the Johnson and Bond measure; a high score indicates a high degree of restrictiveness. Our third indicator is whether the state legislature joined in calling for a constitutional convention to outlaw abortions (coded 1). Twenty-one states have directly called for an HLA; eight have asked Congress to call a convention for the passage of such an amendment; 21 have taken no action (coded 0). These three types of acts will be our dependent variables.

The absolute level of pro-family power will be tapped by our familiar variable, the sum of registered groups and PACs. Their relative power will be measured by the percentage of all groups and PACs active on family or women's issues that are pro-family. This measure then compares the relative strength of pro-family and feminist groups. We also look at the absolute power of feminist groups as indicated by the total number of feminist groups and PACs and by the number of such groups in 1974. The power of the pro-family Right's constituency network is captured by the percentage of all cause groups that are conservative, the percentage of all registered groups that are business, as well as the percentage of the population belonging to fundamentalist churches, or to the Catholic Church—all measures used in the last section. The broader culture will be expressed once again by the state's political culture, early public opinion against abortion, and passage of abortion reform prior to the Roe decision.

Findings on the Success of the New Right

We first want to see if the enactment of laws achieving the goals of the pro-family sector can be attributed to pro-family groups. The absolute number of such groups is definitely not linked to actions against ERA or against abortion. In fact, what relation there is in Table 7.3 runs in the opposite direction; that is, where there are more New Right groups, the ERA is more (not less) likely to have been ratified, abortion is less restricted, and the HLA was not called for. None of these correlations is significant, however.

Of more importance to our argument is the relation between goal achievement and the percent of all family/women's groups that is pro-family. Again, there is little relationship with ERA ratification, a slightly positive relationship with abortion restrictions, but a sizable positive correlation with the call for the HLA. That is, where the Right does achieve success, it is on a symbolic aspect of the abortion issue. Asking Congress to call a constitutional convention to deal with the abortion issue or passing a resolution in support of an amendment not yet passed by the Congress pays respect to the pro-life symbol but does nothing tangible to stop the act of abortion.

Table 7.3   CORRELATIONS OF ACHIEVEMENT OF PRO-FAMILY GOALS WITH OTHER FACTORS

Factors	Failed to Ratify ERA	Pro-Family Goals Abortion Restrictiveness	Called for HLA
Pro-Family Power			
Total Pro-Family groups, 1980	-.04	-.09	-.15
Percent Pro-Family groups, 1980	-.05	.10	.38*
Conservative Network			
Percent conservative groups, 1980	-.09	.09	.16
Percent business groups, 1980	.33*	.24*	.20
Percent Fundamentalist, 1974	.64*	.21	.18
Percent Catholic, 1974	-.48*	-.10	.07
Feminist Power			
Number feminist groups, 1980	.22	-.04	-.32*
Number feminist groups, 1974	.53*	.34*	.10
Mainstream Culture			
Moralistic political culture	-.54*	-.11	-.08
Opposition to abortion, 1972	.53*	.27*	.38*
Abortion reform pre-Roe	-.03	-.25*	-.37*

* Significant at .05 level.

Source: Calculated by authors.

Next we turn to those elements commonly linked with the pro-family Right: conservative cause groups, business groups, fundamentalist church members, and Catholics. We previously found that the rise of pro-family groups was related to the other New Right groups but not to the remaining three types of groups. Thus, if we find the latter three types of groups to be linked to enactment, we shall infer that they proceed independently of the pro-family Right. In fact, Table 7.3 shows that the percentage of other New Right conservative groups has little association with enactment of pro-family goals.

Other highly significant relationships do show up in Table 7.3, however. States dominated by Old Right business interests tend to vote against the ERA, to restrict abortions, and to a lesser extent to favor the HLA. These correlations are consistent with feminist leaders' repeated charge that big business defeated the ERA. There are even more strongly positive associations between the percent of the population adhering to fundamentalism and successful ERA opposition. Those states which have not ratified the ERA are particularly high on fundamentalism; to a lesser extent, fundamentalist states tend to be the ones that voted for the HLA. Recalling the negative correlations between the pro-family sector, the Old Right, and fundamentalism, we might say that in business-dominated and fundamentalist states pro-family groups did not need to organize to attain their objectives: anti-feminist organizations were already in place. The pro-family Right was free to organize in other states and thus to maximize its efficiency across the states. Consequently, its defensive power was enhanced.

The percentage of Catholic adherents presents a mixed picture. The percentage of Catholics is negatively related to ERA failure and, contrary to expectations, not related to abortion opposition. The negative coefficients for ERA point to the uneasy alliance between Catholicism and the New Right where the two may agree on the abortion question but not on other issues, and may reflect differences in the views of lay Catholics and the Catholic hierarchy.

Next we focus on the strength of the movement the pro-family sector is challenging: feminism. The total number of feminist groups and PACs in 1980 appears to be positively but weakly related to the failure of the ERA.[20] Looking at the data, this seems to happen because feminists have recently started a number of organizations in the 15 unratified states and naturally have not concentrated on the already ratified states. The negative relationship with the HLA is more straightforward: where feminist groups are abundant, the HLA is less successful. The number of feminist groups in the states circa 1974 is quite strongly and positively associated with

ERA failure and restrictions on abortion. Again, this does not mean that feminists in the early 1970s advocated these two goals. Rather, it appears that early organization by feminists set off a process whereby anti-feminists organized in reaction and these countergroups were more powerful than the original feminist groups.

The powerful effect of other conservative interests, though not directly linked to pro-family groups, suggests that the mainstream culture measures may be important to look at. We see that indeed those states failing to ratify the ERA tend to be the traditionalistic states and not the moralistic ones. Yet there is little association for the two abortion measures. Early public opinion against abortion "on demand" is positively and significantly associated with all three dependent variables. Where public opinion was initially opposed to abortion, it translated into more restrictions on the performance of abortions, into passing the call for the HLA, and into defeating the ERA.

Concomitantly, the states that had already reformed or repealed their abortion laws prior to the Roe decision passed fewer restrictions than other states and did not pass the HLA. These findings suggest that broader aspects of the culture, not just specific pro-family organizations, may explain pro-family success. In particular, the coefficients for abortion opinion and prior abortion laws emphasize the importance of interstate variations in public opinion toward abortion. Though opinion is highly favorable across the nation, there seem to be quite striking opinion differences from one state to another and these, in turn, have impact in the legislative arena. For example, a 1981 statewide poll in Mississippi found that 72 percent support banning all abortions except when the life of the mother is endangered (Comparative State Politics Newsletter 1982, p. 16).

Finally, we turn to the multivariate analysis to sort out the relative effects of the variables. The first set of results (Table 7.4) is for abortion restrictiveness where a modest amount of variance is explained (24 percent) by a subset of four predictors selected in a stepwise procedure. None of the variables is statistically significant, suggesting that although most factors analyzed here have some role in determining the outcome of the abortion issue at the state level, many other factors not measured in our analysis must be taken into account as well.

To ascertain the relative effects of these variables upon the ERA's failure and the call for the HLA, we must shift gears a bit. Regression analysis is not particularly appropriate here because the ERA variable is trichotomous and the HLA variable dichotomous. Accordingly, we conducted a stepwise discriminant analysis in which all of the possible independent variables were employed as predictors.

Those predictors passing the minimum Wilks Lambda criterion (.001) for entry became part of the discriminant function(s).

Table 7.4   STEPWISE REGRESSION RESULTS FOR ABORTION RESTRICTIVENESS

Predictor	Beta
Percent business groups, 1980	.299
Number feminist groups, 1974	.236
Abortion reform pre-Roe	-.172
Opposition to abortion, 1972	.173
$R^2 = .24$	

Source: Calculated by authors.

The results of this exercise are given in Table 7.5 where the first two columns pertain to the ERA. Since we are attempting to discriminate between three groups—ratifiers, rescinders, and non-ratifiers—the analysis derived two functions. The first function is more important than the second one in discriminating between the groups, as indicated by the size of the canonical correlations. Since the squared canonical correlation may be interpreted in variance-explained terms, we can say that the first function alone accounts for 71.7 percent of the variance, while the second function by itself explains 41.5 percent of the variance. Together, the two functions correctly classify 83.8 percent of the states, indicating that the degree of explanatory power is quite good.

The discriminatory power of the two functions lies in somewhat different areas. An examination of the group centroids reveals that the first function primarily distinguishes between the unratified states and the rest whereas the second function discriminates between the rescinded states and the rest. We would expect this pattern since most of the ratifications occurred relatively early in the 1970s and the rescissions a little later on. The total structure coefficients allow us to determine which predictors are most crucial for distinguishing between the three groups of states. These coefficients indicate how closely related each variable is to the discriminant function itself and they are unaffected by multicollinearity (Klecka 1980). The composition of the first function reveals that fundamentalism, the presence of feminist groups in 1974, a traditionalistic political culture, and early opposition to abortion are the

Table 7.5   STEPWISE DISCRIMINANT ANALYSIS RESULTS FOR PRO-FAMILY GOALS

Predictor	ERA Structure Coefficients		HLA Structure Coefficients
	Function 1	Function 2	
Pro-Family Power			
Total Pro-Family groups, 1980	-.00	-.12	-.57
Percent Pro-Family groups, 1980	-.42	.80	.41
Conservative Network			
Percent conservative groups, 1980	-.13	.06	.31
Percent business groups, 1980	.27	.09	.06
Percent Fundamentalist, 1974	.59	.46	.05
Percent Catholic, 1974	-.37	-.38	.21
Feminist Power			
Number feminist groups, 1980	.40	-.22	-.98
Number feminist groups, 1974	.69	.04	-.12
Mainstream Culture			
Moralistic political culture	-.65	-.01	.17
Opposition to abortion, 1972	.57	.46	.10
Abortion reform pre-Roe	.04	-.31	-.30
Group Centroids			
Ratified	-.77	-.43	
Rescinded	-2.02	2.50	
Unratified	2.45	.29	
Canonical Correlation	.847	.644	.683
% Correctly Classified	83.8		89.2

Source: Calculated by authors

most helpful variables in separating the unratified states from the rest. Those states failing to ratify tend to be fundamentalist, had many feminist groups in the early 1970s, opposed abortion, and are traditionalistic in culture. These findings support those of Wohlenberg (1980) as he pointed to the importance of religious and cultural conservatism in explaining the failure of the ERA. The second set of structure coefficients includes fundamentalism and abortion opposition as important predictors but offers the proportion of pro-family groups as the most crucial variable in separating the rescinding states from the rest. Thus, it appears that once the amendment is passed in the legislature, pro-family organization is necessary to change the amendment's status.

The results in column three of Table 7.5 show that nearly all (89.2 percent) of the states can be classified into those asking for the HLA and those that did not. This set of predictors explains 46.5 percent of the variance (obtained by squaring the canonical correlation). By far the best predictor is the number of current feminist groups. It has the largest structure coefficient, indicating that where the HLA is not called for, feminist groups are large in number. Thus, feminist organization seems to have a strong repressive effect upon anti-abortion legislation. Overall, the most important finding is that the pro-family movement is not vitally important in accounting for three of these victories, though it was crucial for the act of rescission.

Conclusions about Pro-Family Success

The picture emerging from these state level data is that the pro-family sector of the New Right movement cannot lay claim to many successes. Rather, their attainment of pro-family goals in the state legislative arena is due to some extent to traditionalistic culture and fundamentalist churches. Feminists, on the other hand, have shown signs of successful organization against the HLA. However, sometimes as in the case of the ERA, early feminist mobilization may be counterproductive. The mass public's support or opposition to abortion has been consistently relevant at a modest level so that public sentiment may be having more impact within states than previously realized.

IMPLICATIONS FOR THE CONFLICT
OVER THE AMERICAN FAMILY

The overwhelming impression one draws from these two sets of results is that the pro-family phenomenon has been overrated.

First, there are relatively few pro-family groups active at the state level, especially when compared to the number of feminist groups. Our data clearly indicate that feminists, not the pro-family side, had the organizational advantage at the state level in the early 1980s. The second clear impression left by these data is that the few pro-family groups that do exist in the states cannot claim much success. When they do, it is on the more recent act of rescinding the ERA in four states and not on abortion. Rather, the explanations for stopping the ERA's adoption lie to some degree in traditionalism and fundamentalism. Consequently, the outcome of the fight over the American family will be decided in part by whether fundamentalism and traditionalism are on the rise. Fundamentalists constitute a small percent of all religious adherents (14.8 percent) but their churches are growing more rapidly than liberal denominations (Guth 1981; Phillips 1982). Their increase in membership combined with their move into social activism will ensure their continued impact as a political force. Traditional political culture, however, is likely to decline. Migration into the South and West is eroding the cultural base found there.

Feminist power appears to be most effective in stopping the HLA call in state legislatures, suggesting that the future may bring more feminist victories than were true for the ERA fight. Together these findings help to flesh out those at the elite and individual levels. They particularly reinforce our contention that the Right's protest is against feminism and is an effort to regain status. Finally, our findings show that it is the state-by-state variations in public opinion that are important. Despite nationwide public support for the ERA and for abortion rights, there are differences by state which, when translated into state legislative action, shaped the fate of the ERA and may determine the outcome of the abortion fight.

NOTES

1. This measure is not "per capitized" because the number of groups is quite small. Also it is not clear whether the base should be the state's population, the number of legislators, or just what.

2. Alabama, Nevada, Rhode Island, and West Virginia are excluded either because they did not respond to repeated requests or because their lists are available only for inspection in the office.

3. Also, we have to assume that there were family issues on each state's legislative agenda to attract lobbyists to register. Given the intensity of the abortion conflict in most states and the ERA conflict in some states and the range of other pro-family issues, this appears to be a safe assumption.

4. The excluded states are Colorado, Maine, Mississippi, Nevada, New Jersey, North Dakota, Ohio, Oklahoma, Tennessee, and Virginia. Again these states either do not have such a law, never responded to our request, or provide lists only for inspection in the office.

5. There were several additional considerations in our decision to use the summary measure of pro-family mobilization. On the one hand, the PAC data are obviously important as a measure because our data show that the pro-family side relies more on PACs and less on lobbying while feminists rely more on lobbying and less on PACs. Also the PAC phenomenon is relatively recent (since the 1978 election) and might best indicate the recent rise of the New Right. The lobby data, on the other hand, are from more states and may be more reliably reported than the spending data. Overall, we think that the deficiencies of one measure are cancelled out by the advantages of the other, even though the number of cases is reduced to the 37 states on which information is present on both measures. The correlation of the two is only .12 so that it is not likely that we are just counting the same organization twice. In our analyses the sum of the two measures and the PAC measure alone produced nearly the same results. We will note any important differences as we go along.

6. The divorce rate averaged 3.8 in 1970 and 5.3 five years later. New York and New Jersey, bastions of eastern liberalism, had the lowest divorce rates.

7. We chose 1974 because it was the first year that the effects of the Roe decision would be fully felt. We use estimates of the Alan Guttmacher Institute (AGI). They tend to be somewhat higher than the estimates of the government's Abortion Surveillance Unit. The average was 14.5.

8. The scores ranged from 0 (no restrictions) to 27.

9. We would have preferred data from the first half of the 1970s but to our surprise 1976 was the first year the Labor Department made these calculations available on a state-by-state basis. The mean was 47.9 percent.

10. There are several problems with change measures, including the tendency for the original measure and the change measure to be correlated.

11. We expect that pro-family adherents respond to the rate of growth in cities, not to the absolute level of metro population. Hence, we use only the rate of change measure.

12. These data were obtained in the same manner as were the New Right data and pertain to 1980. The measures of feminist PACs and lobby groups are not highly correlated (r = .07).

13. The raw number of business groups would be too closely tied to the total number of groups.

14. The religious data are from Johnson et al.'s (1974) census of church membership by state and county in 1971. Denominations were classified as being either Catholic, liberal Protestant, evangelical Protestant, or fundamentalist Protestant. The latter two categories were later combined because the percentage of evangelicals was so small. One distinction between fundamentalist and liberals is doctrinal: fundamentalists emphasize the Bible's literal inerrancy; liberal Protestants do not. Mead (1975) was used as the source for the doctrine of each denomination. Furthermore, our classification took into account the church's official position on abortion and the ERA as well as membership in the National Council of Churches (for liberals).

15. Interestingly enough, the number of PACs is even more strongly correlated with the abortion rate than is the total number of groups, suggesting that the most recent increase in New Right groups is a reaction to the exercise of abortion rights by millions of women.

16. The correlation between pro-family groups and feminist PACs is somewhat higher ($r = .51$) than with feminist groups ($r = .43$).

17. Since this correlation is for lobby groups only, the number of cases is 46, rather than 37.

18. The 1974 abortion rate was omitted due to its high correlation with the 1980 abortion rate. Likewise, change in feminist groups was omitted because of its high intercorrelation with the number of feminist groups. Essentially, we are left with one indicator from each of the important sets of indicators.

19. Kentucky is an ambiguous case because the state legislature voted to rescind their earlier approval but the rescission was vetoed by Lieutenant Governor Thelma Stovall while the governor was out of the state. We count Kentucky as a ratified state. The ERA analysis should be regarded with some caution because of the unfortunate overlap between unratified states and states that do not register (or report) interest groups. Five of the 15 unratified states and one of the four rescinding states are not included in our 37 case data set.

20. Since the percentage of feminist groups is simply the complement of the percentage of New Right groups, we do not analyze that measure.

8 / THE FUTURE OF SOCIAL MOVEMENTS AND SOCIAL MOVEMENT THEORY

We undertook this effort in order to better understand the conflict between the emerging New Right movement and the feminist movement. In particular, we were interested in determining the roles of the abortion and ERA issues in those movements. Our theoretical discoveries have, perhaps, the most long-term relevance. But, at the same time, our substantive findings should hold the greatest immediate interest. Let us consider each briefly.

THEORETICAL IMPLICATIONS

Until relatively recently, an examination such as ours of the New Right and feminist movements would have drawn heavily on the collective behavior paradigm. From such a perspective, extremist behavior is an "irrational" manifestation of social disorganization and individual pathology. Yet, while it might be psychologically soothing for opponents of each movement to view New Rightists or feminists as "nuts" or "lunatics," it seems hardly accurate upon closer examination.

Closer to the mark, in our judgment, is the viewpoint of those positing a resource mobilization perspective. The works of Tilly (1978), Oberschall (1973, 1978), Gamson (1975), and Fireman and Gamson (1979) have been particularly useful. They suggest that people become involved in social movements, not as a consequence of irrational fears or social isolation, but as a result of self-interest, group loyalties, and personal principles. These motives certainly seem to have been operative in the mobilization of both the feminist and New Right movements.

The mobilization of early feminists, for example, was based upon some appeal to individual self-interests. Yet, perhaps more important were the other organizations to which these early feminists belonged: labor unions, civil rights organizations, and left-wing student groups. Drawing upon the loyalty of women to such groups and using the communication networks provided by those organizations, feminist organizers like Friedan and Firestone were able to launch successful mobilization efforts that gave birth to the organizations of the women's movement. Appeals to the personal principles of potential supporters reinforced these successes, urgently evoking principles such as justice and equality.

The organization of the New Right also fits the theory outlined by the resource mobilization theorists. Furthermore, as in the case of the feminist movement, our examination of the mobilization of the New Right leads us to conclude that self-interests have played a relatively minor role in the organizational development of the New Right. Because of the free-rider effect, we tend to discount the possibility that people have joined New Right organizations just so that they can receive the tangible benefits that would be provided if the New Right's goals were met. Nor, in our examination of a variety of New Right groups do we find the presence of substantial material selective incentives that could induce people to become active. Instead, as in the case of the feminist movement, we learn that New Right organizations have relied extensively on existing group loyalties and personal principles in their mobilization efforts. For example, New Right entrepreneurs have very successfully linked the goals of the Catholic Church and various fundamentalist Protestant churches to those of the New Right movement, thus facilitating mobilization. Similarly, they have tied the goals of the New Right to personal principles and values, such as traditional family life, and thereby increased the probability that people would join the movement out of a sense of personal responsibility.

Even so, the resource mobilization perspective is not without its problems. From our vantage point, perhaps its major difficulty is the relative neglect of emotions and feelings. In abandoning the collective behavior paradigm and its view of social movement adherents as overly emotional, irrational individuals, theorists went too far. In their zeal to establish the normalcy and rationality of social movement activists, theorists sterilized the role of emotions in such movements (e.g., McCarthy and Zald 1977).

Some theorists have addressed this problem to a certain extent by removing group loyalties and personal principles from a utilitarian framework. In effect, rather than viewing solidarity and personal principles as "soft" selective incentives appealing strictly to self-interest, these elements were depicted as separate motivating factors in the mobilization process (Fireman and Gamson 1979). Yet, the impact of emotions on mobilization was still implicit; the focus continued to be on the role that substantive demands played in attracting movement supporters. Neglected in this approach were the mechanisms through which social movement organizers and potential constituents communicated about the substantive goals of the movement. In essence, some theorists adopting the resource mobilization perspective paid little attention to the pivotal role that issues play in mobilization.

From our viewpoint, issues are key factors in the social movement process. Issues represent the demands of a movement; they give form to the grievances that fuel the growth of a movement. As the resource mobilization perspective implies, the substance of an issue is critical to defining the goals of a movement and thus to the success of its mobilization efforts. But what is not evident from the resource mobilization literature is the fact that political elites must define an issue's substance if they are to communicate it to potential supporters. By defining an issue's substance, political entrepreneurs establish its public meaning; in effect, the meaning of any issue can be changed simply by altering the manner in which it is defined. Here lies the key to understanding the emotional appeal of social movements such as the New Right: an issue defined in a dry, unemotional fashion by one side in a conflict can be turned into a highly emotional issue by the other side simply by the way it is defined or symbolized. Thus, the notion of issues provides an explicit means for capturing the emotionality present in appeals to personal principles, group loyalties, and even self-interest.

The pivotal position of issues in the social movement process is clearly illustrated by the roles that the issues of abortion and the ERA have played in the feminist and New Right conflict. At the elite level, these two issues have become the symbolic battleground on which feminists and New Rightists have gone to war. From the perspective of feminists, both issues embody the demand for a woman's right to equality and independence. But the New Right has fought vehemently against "different" abortion and ERA issues. The issues of abortion and ERA that the New Right opposes do not concern the principles of equality and independence championed by the women's movement; rather, they are issues of morality, God, and family life. For all intents and purposes, then, the New Right and the feminist movement have been debating and battling over two different ERA's and two different abortions. There is no common ground for resolution of these issues because the two sides are not talking about the same things. Given this, it is no surprise that the conflict has become more intense and bitter as the years have worn on.

In summary, then, both the New Right and the feminist movement provide ample support for the resource mobilization perspective, particularly that version advanced by such theorists as Tilly
(1978) and Fireman and Gamson (1979). Yet, a close examination
of each movement also suggests the importance of a symbolic
politics in which the role of issues and the emotional responses
they often evoke is preeminent. By recognizing the importance of
issues to social movements, a "marriage" has been formed between
the rational actor of the resource mobilization perspective and the
more emotional actor of the symbolic politics approach. In the
spirit of the New Right, we hope that it is a long-lived marriage!

SUBSTANTIVE IMPLICATIONS

Our findings not only have theoretical implications, but they
also have practical significance as well. By understanding where
the New Right and feminist movements have been we can gain some
insight into where they are going. As we have seen, the issues of
abortion and the ERA have a rich past stretching far back into
American history. Yet, they are issues that also have a potentially
very interesting future—a future that is intertwined with that of the
feminist and New Right movements.

The Future of the ERA

It seems odd to talk about the future of the ERA when it has
only just "died." But, it is an issue that seems to have many lives.
Within weeks of the June 30, 1982 deadline marking its defeat,
supporters of the ERA had succeeded in having the amendment
reintroduced in Congress. Furthermore, the wording of the proposed amendment is precisely the same as the just defeated amendment. What are the chances of the new ERA?
Some people—including feminists—question whether the reintroduction of the ERA so soon after its defeat was a good idea.
Certainly from the viewpoint of mobilizing feminists and others
sympathetic to the movement, the theory we advanced earlier indicates that now is the time to act. In many ways, the ERA has just
become a lost good, to use Morrison's (1979) terminology. Although feminists never really "had" the ERA to lose, neither had
they ever really lost it—until June 30, 1982. Within such a context, the sooner feminists act to regain the ERA, the greater the
success they should meet in mobilizing people for that purpose. For
a lost good is a sort of chameleon: when it has only been recently

lost it tends to resemble a threatened good and thus mobilization efforts should be easier; when it has been lost for a long time, it is like a new good and mobilization efforts become harder. Thus, symbolically now is the time for feminists to act. Organizationally, too, now is also the time to act while the pro-ERA organizations created in the unratified states still exist.

Yet, unfortunately from the feminist perspective, now is also the best time for the New Right to challenge the ERA. Like the feminists, their anti-ERA organizations are still intact. Similarly, as victorious as they are, memories of the threat posed by the passage of the ERA are still fresh in the minds of the anti-ERA activists. And the fact that the wording of the new amendment is the same as the old one only serves to help the anti-ERA activists. Thus, the New Right stands poised to mobilize a new fight against yet another ERA. Therefore, were feminists to wait before reintroducing the ERA, they might stand a better chance of "winning the war," but they would also have a more difficult time in "mounting the attack."

Now seems as good as time as any, then, for the feminists to try for a new ERA. The advantages gained by waiting, such as potentially less opposition, may well be offset by the disadvantages that would occur; that is, it might be considerably harder to mobilize the pro-ERA forces sometime in the future. Given that feminists have gone ahead and started the process over, what can they do different this time around?

For one thing, they must draw upon the mass public for greater support in their efforts. As we have seen, the ERA has the support of the people nationally and in many state electorates as well. Furthermore, the issue is already a very symbolic one. Feminists must bring some of this mass sentiment to bear on state legislators. This can be done in two ways. On the one hand, feminists need to defuse the negative symbolization given the issue by anti-ERA activists. On the other hand, pro-ERA activists would do well to adopt one of the New Right's favorite strategies: encouraging single-issue voting. As we saw earlier, if the pro-ERA forces embraced single-issue voting to the extent that their opponents have in the past, then in most states they could potentially have success in targeting anti-ERA legislators for defeat.

There is some indication that this is precisely what feminist organizations intend to do. For example, in a recent fund-raising letter, NOW sought money so that it could "support pro-ERA candidates in a massive, unprecedented way" and defeat its enemies (National Organization for Women, personal communication 1982). As Eleanor Smeal explained, "we've been lied to, talked down to, and insulted so much by a handful of reactionary legislators that the dignity of the women's rights movement simply requires that these holdovers from another age be defeated" (National Organization for Women, personal communication 1982). Thus, perhaps feminist organizations have learned a valuable lesson from the defeat of the ERA that will help in this next stage of their battle.

The Future of the Abortion Issue

In many ways, the future of the abortion issue is even more uncertain than that of the ERA. With the ERA, the tactics of influence adopted by each side were essentially predetermined by the fact that they were dealing with a constitutional amendment; thus, the way to defeat the ERA was to prevent its ratification in a set number of states. The tactics called for in the case of the abortion issue are not nearly so clear-cut, at least not from the perspective of the New Right. The feminists' strategy has been, and will continue to be, to protect the rights that they now have.

The strategy of the New Right has evolved over time. Initially, its members relied on scare tactics, protest, and even violence in their fight against abortion. Such tactics gained the attention of the public and legislators alike, but it is not clear that they had any substantive impact. In the next phase, anti-abortion activists concentrated more heavily on direct lobbying of legislators at both the state and national levels. Nationally, their efforts resulted in the elimination of federal funding for abortion. At the state level, they also enjoyed some success; but in many instances, the success was short-lived as state and national courts struck down the new anti-abortion statutes almost as fast as the states passed them. Out of this frustrating experience the New Right came to recognize clearly that they had one formidable enemy in the anti-abortion fight that was missing from the ERA struggle: the Supreme Court. This awareness has molded the current nature of the battle over abortion. If abortion is to be eliminated, then anti-abortion activists must find some way to overcome the constitutional precedent established by Roe v. Wade in 1973.

Currently, anti-abortion activists are proceeding in several directions in their attempts to undo the Roe v. Wade decision. Two of their strategies will be discussed here. The first, and most direct, is a constitutional amendment to ban abortions. At this time, it seems unlikely that the drive for such an amendment will be successful. Even if the anti-abortion activists were to succeed in getting such an amendment through Congress, it would still require state approval. And as the experience of the ERA has shown, it can be a very difficult task to get the requisite number of states to ratify an amendment, even when it has popular support—which a constitutional ban on abortions does not. Recall from our discussion of single-issue voting on abortion, such a constitutional amendment is an extremely unpopular measure that already evokes more single-issue voting on the pro-choice side than on the anti-abortion side. It seems reasonable to assume that if an anti-abortion amendment were submitted to the states for ratification, feminists would not dawdle in organizing against the amendment. A well-organized opposition to the amendment combined with its unpopularity among the mass public should make it difficult if not impossible for anti-abortion activists to succeed in adding such an amendment to the constitution. If such an amendment is doomed to fail, then the New Right may turn to a "human life" bill.

A "human life" bill would declare that life begins at conception, thus, presumably bringing unborn fetuses under the protection of the Constitution. From the viewpoint of the anti-abortion activists, such a bill has several attractive features. First, because it is simply a bill to be passed by Congress, rather than a Constitutional amendment, the battle is potentially smaller in scope and duration. The short duration is desirable for several reasons: if the anti-abortion forces are successful, it means getting rid of abortion sooner; and the chances of success are higher because the pro-choice side has less time to mobilize against the threat.

The second, very attractive feature of a "human life" bill is that it need not make any mention of abortion. As a consequence, its meaning is less well-defined than that of the abortion issue itself. Thus, proponents of such a bill have more leeway in symbolizing the bill in more neutral terms than the abortion issue has been defined. At the same time, opponents of the bill would be faced with the task of finding something objectionable about declaring all human life to fall under the purview of the Constitution. Therefore, from our perspective, pursuing the passage of a human life bill seems to be a more viable strategy for the New Right than is pressing for a Constitutional amendment to ban abortions. Of course, were such a bill to pass eventually its constitutionality would be questioned. Once again it would be up to the Supreme Court to make a decision on the abortion issue.

The Future of the New Right

To this point, we have seen that the success of the New Right has been mixed. On the level of the mass public, the New Right seems to be considerably less powerful than the media and the New Right itself would have us believe. As we have seen, the pro-family

sector of the New Right has encountered little success in altering
the public's stands on two issues most symbolic of their goals: the
ERA and abortion. Nor has the New Right succeeded in mobilizing
a conservative constituency capable of providing a clear conservative direction to the flock of newly elected Republicans. The New
Right is a social movement that has not especially flourished at
the mass level. But, then again, while broad-based mass support
might be nice, it is not necessarily essential to securing the success of the New Right's policy goals.

It may be that actually having a mass constituency is less
important than having the image of substantial mass support. In
the real world, it may not matter whether the New Right is responsible for the victories of various conservative candidates.
Just as the voters may be swayed by candidate images, so might
elected officials and candidates be manipulated by images of constituent preference and response. Furthermore, to the extent that
candidates and observant incumbents attribute electoral outcomes
to New Right activities and money, they may alter their behavior
and thereby policy. Thus, perceptions of successful indirect lobbying may be more important in securing the passage of the New
Right's policy goals than the actual success of such efforts.

It is also possible that the New Right's direct lobbying of
legislators has been instrumental in the passage of favorable legislation at both the state and national levels. It is possible, but it
is not necessarily reality. As we saw in Chapter 7, at the state
level the pro-family sector of the New Right cannot take full credit
for defeating the ERA or passing abortion restrictions. Of course
our analysis was based on the strength of the New Right in terms
of numbers, and not in terms of the actions they had taken. It
could be that in defeating the ERA and passing state abortion restrictions, a few New Right groups, though small in number, were
able to exercise power disproportionate to their size. Thus, while
we cannot rule out the possibility that New Right groups have exercised their power in defeating the ERA and passing abortion restrictions, we also cannot claim that they have demonstrated such
power.

This is not to say, however, that the New Right is not a formidable social movement. At the elite level, the New Right has
forcefully demonstrated an organizational capability that is unprecedented among right-wing and left-wing movements in the
United States. They have revolutionized the politics of special interests. With their careful cultivation of extensive mailing lists
and their astute use of political action committees, the New Right
has developed into one of the most powerful financial forces popu-
lating the American political scene. Clearly, when power is

measured in terms of money-raising capabilities, the New Right is
a powerful movement indeed. Yet, the translation of monetary clout
into political influence is not necessarily a direct one. The New
Right's money can help it elect conservative legislators, but unless
those legislators perceive that their constituents share in the New
Right's philosophy, their votes on the highly symbolic issues so
important to the New Right will not be ensured. Thus, therein lies
one of the key tasks confronting the New Right if it is to enjoy all
the success that it desires: it must mold a more formidable mass
constituency, or at least a more formidable image of one.

If it moves to develop a broader base of mass support, the
social sector of the New Right will clearly be entering into its second phase. Until recently, it has been a countermovement caught
up in the defense of the values that it perceived to be threatened.
Yet, in 1980, with the election of Ronald Reagan and so many other
Republicans, the New Right had the potential to become an offensive
movement, focused on gaining new goods rather than protecting
threatened ones. The economic sector of the New Right accepted
the challenge and plunged head-on into its second stage as an offensive movement. By the summer of 1982, New Right economic
theories had taken hold in high places everywhere except the Federal
Reserve Board. And, the New Right was working hard to overcome
that obstacle by demanding the resignation of the board's chair,
Paul Volcker, and the end of the Fed's independence. But, until
recently, the trials and tribulations of the economic facet of the
New Right had pushed the social sector into the background.

In 1982, however, the social wing of the New Right also
seems to have finally entered its offensive, second stage. This
shift from defensive to offensive mobilization is represented in symbolic terms by the taking of the name "pro-family." In terms of
more concrete actions, key New Right leaders such as Phyllis
Schlafly have gone on the offensive. In 1982, she opened a Washington office, signaling that she would be expanding her single-issue
ERA campaign to other issues. She promised to work against sex
education ("the principal cause of teen-age pregnancy"), feminist
influence in school textbooks, and the nuclear freeze ("the atomic
bomb is a marvelous gift from a wise God") (quoted in Minneapolis
Tribune 1982, p. 5A).

Perhaps the best example of the New Right's transformation
to offensive mobilization is the Family Protection Act. Instead of
just opposing liberal legislation, the New Right introduced legislation to protect the traditional American family. Its original sponsor
was Senator Paul Laxalt (President Reagan's campaign manager),
joined by Senator Roger Jepsen in the 1982-83 Congress (Jepsen
having been the New Right's candidate in Iowa). This bill seeks to

reestablish prayer in public schools, forbids federal funding for school textbooks that portray women in other than traditional roles, repeals federal laws against child and spouse abuse, and prevents sex-mixed sports, among other things.

As the New Right moves into an offensive mobilization stage in which it proposes its own solutions, its efforts provoke feminists and liberals into reaction. The Family Protection Act and other proposals have become the rallying point for anti-Right coalitions among feminist and liberal groups. Essentially, we are repeating the experience of ten years ago when feminist successes propelled the Right into defensive action. Today it is New Right successes that are provoking a reaction from the Left: a reaction that has transformed the women's movement.

The Future of the Women's Movement

Like the New Right, the women's movement is also entering into its second stage. As Betty Friedan (1981) has recently argued, this second stage will be less focused on women's liberation and more focused on human liberation. From Friedan's perspective, a key factor in this second stage will be the renewed interest of feminists in the family. Thus, we have come full circle, returning to that institution, the family, that is inextricably linked to the status of women in our society.

Not only does it appear that the focus of the women's movement is shifting, but it also is possible that their tactics may change as well. The success of the New Right and feminism's partial failures in the early 1980s have altered the feminist movement's acceptance of certain tactics. Feminist groups are imitating the single-issue tactics of their opponents, including their fundraising through direct mail. Since 1980 a number of anti-right groups and PACs have been formed that represent a new kind of coalition on the Left. These organizations feature women's rights prominently in their literature. They include: PRO-PAC started by Gloria Steinem, Representative Pat Schroder, and Representative Cardis Collins; Norman Lear's People for the American Way; Interchange; the National Committee for an Effective Congress; Senator Ted Kennedy's Fund for a Democratic Majority; Senator George McGovern's Americans for Common Sense; and Independent Action.

These groups, along with Common Cause and the ACLU, are using new symbols in attempting to organize a defensive mobilization against the New Right. Their literature tends to depict the Right, especially the pro-family attack on feminism, as an extremist attack upon all civil liberties guaranteed by the Constitution.

In order to preserve freedom and basic human rights, patriots must organize against the Right, they contend. They are attempting to knock off anti-feminist and anti-abortion opponents such as Senator Jesse Helms and Senator Orrin Hatch.

The outlines of such an anti-Right defensive strategy and the pro-family/pro-person philosophy advocated by Friedan are just beginning to take shape, but their adoption could bring about a significant change in the women's movement. Whether this change takes place, however, depends to some extent on the actions that feminists take on the ERA. As mentioned earlier, feminists are already hard at work on a new ERA campaign. And while now may be the time to act if there is ever going to be an Equal Rights Amendment added to the Constitution, it is not altogether clear that a new ERA campaign is the most efficient and productive place to be expending feminist energies. Indeed, the defeat of the ERA represents a tremendous symbolic blow to the women's movement; and as such, it is difficult for feminists to accept. Yet, the substantial investment of feminists' energies in a new ERA might also be costly in the sense that it could well divert valuable resources away from the pursuit of more attainable goals. The demise of the ERA could free feminists from an ideological battle conducted in condensational terms and enable them to concentrate upon smaller-scale, incremental changes that can be advocated in referential terms. Thus, one clear decision that feminists must make in terms of tactics is whether to continue to pursue equal rights in the form of an ERA, or to give up that objective and seek equality in a more incremental fashion.

Finally, not only is the women's movement entering a second stage in terms of its focus (the family and the individual) and its tactics (anti-right organizations and perhaps an emphasis on incremental changes), but there is also the potential for the women's movement to be entering a second stage in terms of its power. In recent years, women have begun to distinguish themselves from men in terms of several policy areas: "compassion" issues such as the role of government in providing jobs and "force" issues like defense spending and the threat of war (Public Opinion, 1982). Notably, women still do not differ much from men in terms of so-called women's issues such as abortion. What are we to make of these emerging attitudinal differences between the sexes?

One interpretation is that the women's movement has made women more independent of men politically (Friedan 1982). Now women are more confident and more willing to take a stand different from men. Implicit in such arguments is the possibility that women are about to develop into a powerful political force. Yet, one key element is missing that would allow such a transformation to take place: group consciousness. Women must not only become more confident in themselves, individually, but there must also be the recognition that by working together, women as a whole can exert a tremendous influence on the course of this nation's politics. Whether this step will truly be taken in the second stage of the women's movement remains to be seen. But, if the women's movement does harness the potential that it has, then more than just the New Right and the women's movement will have entered into a second stage: America, itself, will also have made that jump.

APPENDIXES

A / NATIONAL AND STATE ORGANIZATIONS OPPOSING ERA

RELIGIOUS RIGHT
American Association of Christian Schools
Catholic Daughters of America
Catholic League for Religious and Civil Rights
Christian Crusade
Christian Coalition for Legislative Action
Christian Voice
Christian Voters Victory Fund
Christian Women's National Concerns
Church of Christ (several congregations)
Esther Action Council (Methodist)
General Association of Regular Baptist Churches
Knights of Columbus
Lutheran Church, Missouri Synod
Moral Majority
Mormon Church
National Christian Action Coalition
National Council of Catholic Laity
National Council of Catholic Women
Rabbinical Alliance of America
Rabbinical Society of America
Religious Roundtable
Southern Baptist Convention

PRO-FAMILY RIGHT
American Family Institute
American Women Against Ratification of ERA
American Woman Already Richly Endowed

Association of the W's (Women Who Want to be Women)
Citizens for Constructive Education
Citizens for Educational Freedom
Citizens for God, Family and Country
Concerned Women for America
Eagle Forum
Family America
Family and Freedom Institution
Females Opposed to Equality
Happiness of Motherhood Eternal
Happiness of Womanhood
Home Administrators, Inc.
International Anti-Women's Liberation League
International Women's Year Grass Roots Majority
Intercessors for America
League of Housewives
League of Large Families
Library Court Group
Morality in Media
National Committee of Endorsers Against ERA
National Right to Life Committee
Pro America
Pro Family Forum
Pro Family United
STOP ERA
United Families of America
Viva La Difference Committee
Women for Responsible Legislation
Women of Industry
Women's Christian Temperance Union

A

OLD RIGHT
American Conservative Union
American Independent Party
American Party
Congress of Freedom
Daughters of the American
    Revolution
John Birch Society
Ku Klux Klan
Leadership Foundation
Liberty Lobby
National States' Rights Party
We the People
Young Americans for Freedom
Young Republican National
    Federation

SECULAR NEW RIGHT
American Legislative Exchange
    Council
Committee for the Survival of
    a Free Congress
Conservative Caucus
Conservatives Against Liberal
    Legislation
National Conservative Political
    Action Committee

OTHER
American Legion (many states)
Communist Party USA
Farm Bureau (many states)
Men International
Men's Rights Association
National Coalition for
    Accountability
PTA (many states)

Republican Party
Veterans of Foreign Wars

STATE GROUPS
American Legion (Minnesota)
Citizens Against ERA (Ohio)
Citizens Against the Draft
    (Florida)
Citizens Organized for the
    Protection in Education of
    Children (Ohio)
Committee for Retention and
    Protection of Women's
    Rights (Mississippi)
Committee to Preserve
    Women's Rights (Texas)
Committee to Repeal the ERA
    (Texas)
Concerned Parents Committee
    (Wisconsin)
Concerned Women for America
    (California)
Daughters of the Colonial Wars
    (Virginia)
Equal Rights Amendment Steer-
    ing Endeavor (Indiana)
Farm Bureau (Virginia)
Federation of Republican
    Women's Clubs (Alabama,
    Connecticut, Florida)
Feminine Anti-Feminists (Ohio)
FLAG (Family, Life, America,
    God) (Arkansas)
General Federation of Women's
    Clubs (Virginia, Illinois,
    Michigan, Florida, Arizona,
    New York City)
Gi Gi Gals Galore Against the
    ERA (Florida)

212

Grandmothers United Against the ERA (Ohio)

Homemakers' United Efforts (Arizona)

Housewives and Motherhood Anti-Lib Movement (Ohio)

Humanitarians Opposed to Degrading Our Girls (Utah)

Iowa Women Against the ERA

League for the Protection of Women and Children (Missouri)

Minnesota T (Taxpayer) Party

Minnesotans Against the ERA

Montana Citizens to Rescind the ERA

Parents of Minnesota

Parents of New York United

People Leadership (Florida)

Protect Our Women (Wisconsin)

Repeal ERA (Nebraska)

Restore Our American Republic (Ohio)

Revolutionary Union (Wisconsin)

Right to Be a Woman (Illinois)

Right to Life (Minnesota, Kansas)

Scratch Women's Lib (Connecticut, Indiana)

Union Women's Alliance to Gain Equality (California)

United Conservatives of Indiana

Winsome Wives and Homemakers (Wisconsin)

Wisconsin Legislative and Research Committee, Inc.

Women Against the Draft (Florida)

Women for Maintaining the Differences Between the Sexes and Against the ERA (Wyoming)

Women Opposed to ERA (Kansas)

Women United to Defend Existing Rights (New York)

Women's Committee to Rescind the ERA (Kentucky)

Women's Freedom Fund (New York)

Wyoming Women for Privacy and Against the ERA

Young Parents Alert (Minnesota)

Source: Boles (1979); literature from various groups.

B / NATIONAL AND STATE ORGANIZATIONS OPPOSING ABORTION

OLD RIGHT
American Conservative Union
Young Americans for Freedom

PRO-FAMILY RIGHT
American Family Institute
Americans for Family and
    Freedom
Eagle Forum
Family America
Family and Freedom Institution
Intercessors for America
International Federation for
    Family Life Protection
Happiness of Womanhood
Library Court
National Association of Pro
    America
National Pro-Family Coalition
    on the White House Conference
    on Families
Pro Family Forum
Women Exploited

ABORTION SINGLE-ISSUE
Ad Hoc Committee in Defense
    of Life, Inc.
American Citizens Concerned
    for Life
American Life Lobby
Americans Against Abortion
Americans Concerned for Life
Americans for Life
Americans United for Life
Anarchists for Life
Birthright
Crusade for Life
Feminists for Life of America

For Life
Human Life and Natural Family
    Planning Federation
Libertarians for Life
Life Advocates
Life and Equality
Life Amendment Political
    Action Committee
Life-Pac
March for Life
National Committee for a Human
    Life Amendment
National Pro-Life Political
    Election Committee
National Right to Life Committee
National Youth Pro-Life
    Coalition
Pro-Life Nonviolent Action
    Project
Pro-Lifers for Survival
Right to Life Crusade
Socialists for Life
United States Coalition for Life

RELIGIOUS
Baptists for Life
Catholic Church
Catholic League for Religious
    and Civil Rights
Catholic Parents Coalition
Catholics for Christian Political
    Action
Catholics United for the Faith
Christian Action Council
Christian Family Renewal
Christian Voice
Christian Voters' Victory Fund
Christian Women's National
    Concerns

Council for National Righteous-
ness
Moral Majority
National Alliance for Family
Life Through Christian
Family Renewal
Pax Center for Christian Non-
violence
Religious Roundtable

SECULAR NEW RIGHT
American Legislative Exchange
Council
Committee for the Survival of a
Free Congress
Conservative Caucus
National Conservative Political
Action Committee

OTHER
Coalition for Human Justice
Couple to Couple League
PEACE (People Expressing a
Concern for Everyone)
Operation Avalanche
Republican Party

STATE GROUPS
FLAG (Arkansas)
Illinois Citizens for Life
Minnesota Citizens Concerned
for Life
Parents of Minnesota
People Concerned for the Un-
born Child (Pennsylvania)
Right to Life Party (New York)
Tennessee Volunteers for Life

Source: Literature from various groups.

C / MEASURES EMPLOYED IN CHAPTER FIVE

I. MEASURES OF MEANING
    A. Cognitive Variables:
        1. Sex Roles:
            Beliefs about sex roles were measured in terms of
            four questions (#186a, b, c, and d) adopted from the
            General Social Surveys, 1972-78 Codebook, compiled
            by the NORC at the University of Chicago, pp. 153-154.
            Responses were summed across the four questions to
            form a scale ranging from 4 to 20 (very "traditional"
            to very "liberated") and having a reliability (coefficient
            alpha) of .88.
        2. Women's Status:
            Beliefs about women's status in society were measured
            in terms of four questions (variable numbers 3802,
            3811, 3813, and 3809) adopted from the American
            National Elections Studies Codebook: 1972, 1974, and
            1976 Vol. 1, compiled by the Center for Political
            Studies. Responses were summed to form a scale
            ranging from 4 to 12 ("traditional" to "liberated" per-
            spectives) and having a reliability of .78.
        3. Morality:
            Respondents were asked whether they approved or dis-
            approved of (1) sex education in the schools; (2) the
            distribution of birth control information; (3) pre-marital
            sex; (4) homosexual sex; (5) the distribution of por-
            nography; and (6) the liberalization of divorce laws.
            For each of these policy measures which they approved
            of, respondents were given a point. These points were
            then summed to form a scale ranging from 0 to 6 ("tra-
            ditional" to "liberated") morality and having a reliabil-
            ity of .91.
    B. Evaluative (Symbolic) Variables:
        Respondents were read the standard CPS feeling thermome-
        ter question for the list of groups mentioned in Chapter 5.

II. BASES OF SUPPORT
    A. Political Variables:
        1. Party Identification: Standard CPS format. Responses
            to the questions form a seven-point scale ranging from
            "strong Republicans" to "strong Democrats."

216

2. Liberal-Conservative Identification:
   Respondents were asked:
   "To change the subject, we hear a lot of talk these days about liberals and conservatives. Here is a seven-point scale on which the political views that people might hold are arranged from extremely liberal to extremely conservative. Where would you place yourself on the scale or haven't you thought about it?"

3. Patriotism:
   This measure was based on responses to four questions (#22, 23, 30, and 34) adopted from Lutzker's (1960) Internationalism scale. Individual scores on all four questions were combined to form a scale ranging from 4 to 20 and having a reliability of .81. High scores on the scale indicate high patriotism.

B. Religion Variables:
   1. Religious preference—Respondents were asked if they had a religious preference, and if they responded "yes" what that preference was. For the purposes of this analysis, Catholics and fundamentalist Protestants were coded "1." (Fundamentalist Protestants included Southern Baptists, Church of God, Free Methodists, Church of Christ, Free Will Baptist, and other denominations of that type.) The remaining religious preferences were coded "0" for the purpose of this analysis.

   2. Church Attendance—Respondents were asked "would you say you go to church/synagogue every week, almost every week, once or twice a month, a few times a year, or almost never." Responses were coded so as to range from low attendance to high attendance.

C. Status Variables:
   1. Occupation: The respondent's occupation was ascertained in an open-ended question. The answers to this question were then coded into one of eight categories which range roughly from those occupations having relatively high prestige to those occupations having lower prestige. Specifically, the categories are as follows: (1) Professional—law, medicine, etc.; (2) College professors; (3) Professional social welfare workers; (4) Public school teachers; (5) Members of the clergy;

(6) Self-employed workers; (7) Clerical and sales workers; (8) Manual workers (skilled and unskilled); (9) Unemployed (includes students, housewives, and retired persons).

2. Income: Based on a close-ended question, the respondent's income was coded into one of four categories: (1) Under $10,000; (2) Between $10,000 and $20,000; (3) Between $20,000 and $30,000; and (4) Over $30,000.

3. Education: Respondents were asked "what was the last grade of school you completed?" Responses were coded into one of the following categories: (1) 0-8 years—grade school; (2) 9-11 years—some high school; (3) 12 years—high school graduate; (4) 13-15 years—technical school; (5) 13-15 years—some college; (6) 16 years—college graduate; (7) 17 or more—some graduate training such as M.A.s and other incomplete degrees; (8) 17 or more—professional degree, i.e., Ph.D., LLB, M.D., D.D.

D / MEASURES EMPLOYED IN CHAPTER SIX

Because of the large number of variables involved in this analysis, exact question wordings will not be presented here. Instead, we provide the variable numbers of the questions used. Interested readers can find the exact question wording in the appropriate codebook.

Data from the 1972, 1976, 1980 National Election Studies (Center for Political Studies, University of Michigan), released by the Inter-university Consortium for Political and Social Research.

I. Dependent Variables
   A. Abortion attitudes:
      1. 1972: V238   2) 1976: V3796   3) 1980: V1024
   B. ERA attitudes:
      1. 1976: V3799   2) 1980: V1014

II. Measure of Meaning
   A. Cognitive Variables:
      1. Sex roles (i.e., should women have equal roles)
         a) 1972: V232   b) 1976: V3738   c) 1980: V982
      2. Women's status
         a) 1972: 3-item additive scale based on V246, V244, V860. Reliability (coefficient alpha) = .64. Range = 3 to 15.
         b) 1976: 3-item additive scale based on V3802, V3811, and V3813. Reliability = .61. Range = 3 to 15.
         c) 1980: 2-item additive scale based on V1026 and V1028. Reliability = .65. Range = 3 to 10.
   B. Evaluative (symbolic) variables:
      1. 1972: Feeling thermometers—V707, V709, V713, V714, V717, V721, V724, V725, V726, V727, V729
      2. 1976: Feeling thermometers—V3821, V3823, V3827, V3828, V3831, V3835, V3838, V3839, V3840, V3841, V3843, V3849
      3. 1980: Feeling thermometer—V747, V749, V752, V755, V757, V761, V763, V765, V766, V768, V773, V775

III. Bases of Support
   A. Political Variables
      1. Party Identification
         a) 1972: V140   b) 1976: V3174   c) 1980: V663

2. Liberal–Conservative Identification:
   a) 1972: V652   b) 1976: V3286   c) 1980: V267

B. Religion Variables
   1. Preference:
      a) 1972: V422   b) 1976: V3510   c) 1980: V581
   2. Attendance:
      a) 1972: V423   b) 1976: V3511   c) 1980: V582
   3. Evangelical membership, 1980: an additive scale based on responses to V1061, V1063, V1064. Range = 0 to 3.

C. Status Variables
   1. Education:
      a) 1972: V3955   b) 1976: V3389   c) 1980: V436
   2. Income:
      a) 1972: V3598   b) 1976: V3507   c) 1980: V574
   3. Subjective Social Class:
      a) 1972: V400   b) 1976: V3486   c) 1980: V579

IV. Data from NORC
   A. Dependent Variables
      1. Abortion attitudes, 1972, 1976, 1980: An additive scale based on the sum of "yes" responses to the following questions and ranging from 0 to 6: ABDEFECT, ABNOMORE, ABHLTH, ABPOOR, ABRAPE, ABSINGLE
      2. ERA attitudes 1977: ERA
   B. Measures of morality:
      1. 1972: The item PREMARSX. Range = 1 to 3.
      2. 1976: Additive scale based on HOMOSEX, PORNMORL, XMARSEX, PORNLAW. Reliability = .69. Range = 4 to 20.
      3. 1977: Additive scale based on PREMARSX, HOMOSEX, XMARSEX. Reliability = .65. Range = 3 to 15.
      4. 1980: Additive scale based on XMARSEX, HOMOSEX, PORNMORL, PORNLAW. Reliability = .66. Range = 4 to 20.

E / MEASURES EMPLOYED IN CHAPTER SEVEN

METROPOLITAN POPULATION CHANGE:
U.S., Department of Agriculture. 1981. "Rural and Small Town
Population Change, 1970-80." Washington, D.C.: Government
Printing Office, p. 3.

1976 PERCENT OF WOMEN IN LABOR FORCE:
U.S., Department of Labor. 1977. Geographic Profile of Employment and Unemployment, 1976. Washington, D.C.: Government Printing Office, pp. 10-21.

1979 PERCENT OF WOMEN IN LABOR FORCE:
U.S., Department of Labor. 1980. Geographic Profile of Employment and Unemployment, 1979. Washington, D.C.: Government Printing Office, p. 3.

PERCENT OF CHURCH MEMBERS:
Johnson, Douglas W., Paul R. Picard, and Bernard Quinn.
1974. Churches and Church Membership in the United States.
Washington, D.C.: Glenmary Research Center, pp. 3-14.
Denominations were classified according to statements in Mead,
Frank S. 1975. Handbook of Denominations in the United States,
6th ed. Nashville: Abington Press, 1975; and statements on
abortion in Religious Coalition for Abortion Rights. 1979. "We
Affirm." Washington, D.C.: Religious Coalition for Abortion
Rights.

1979 ABORTION RESTRICTIONS:
Alan Guttmacher Institute. 1979. Abortion: Need, Services and
Policies: Minnesota. New York: Alan Guttmacher Institute, pp.
24-28. Scored according to Johnson and Bond system in which a
state is given a score of 2 if it enacted an abortion law. If there
are exceptions in the law that make it less restrictive, the state's
score equals 1 or if provisions make it more restrictive, the
score is 3.

STATES WHICH HAVE CALLED FOR CONSTITUTIONAL CONVEN-
TION TO OUTLAW ABORTION:
Abortion Law Reporter, May 1980, p. 6.4; also interview with
Minnesota Citizens Concerned for Life, July 2, 1981, by Glen

Halva-Neubauer. Call directly for the HLA or asked Congress to call is coded 1; done neither is coded 0.

1980 ABORTION RATE:
"Abortion Services in the United States, 1979 and 1980." Family Planning Perspective, 14: p. 8.

1974 ABORTION RATE:
Alan Guttmacher Institute. 1979. Need and Services in the United States, Each State and Metropolitan Area. New York: Alan Guttmacher Institute, p. 37.

ERA RATIFICATION:
Private communications from ERAmerica, February 1981, and May 1981. Failure to ratify is coded 2; rescission is coded 1; ratification is coded 0.

1979 DIVORCE RATE:
U.S., Department of Commerce. 1979. Advance Report of Final Divorce Statistics, 1979. Washington, D.C.: Government Printing Office, p. 3.

1970 AND 1975 DIVORCE RATE:
U.S., Department of Commerce. 1979. U.S. Statistical Abstract, 1979. Washington, D.C.: Government Printing Office, p. 84.

EARLY FEMINIST GROUPS:
Gager, Nancy, ed. 1974. Women's Rights Almanac 1974. Bethesda, Md.: Elizabeth Cady Stanton.

POLITICAL CULTURE:
Elazar, Daniel J. 1972. American Federalism: A View from the States, second edition. New York: Harper and Row, p. 117. Moralistic culture is 2; individualistic is 1; traditionalistic is 0.

ABORTION LAW REFORM:
Tatalovich, Raymond, and Byron W. Daynes. 1981. The Politics of Abortion, p. 24. New York: Praeger. Repeal is 2; reform is 1; no reform is 0.

SIMULATED ABORTION OPINION:

Uslaner, Eric M., and Ronald E. Weber. 1980. "Public Support for Pro-Choice Abortion Policies in the Nation and States: Changes and Stability after the Roe and Doe Decisions." In The Law and Politics of Abortion, edited by Carl E. Schneider and Maris A. Vinovskis, pp. 217-218. Lexington, Mass.: Lexington Books.

REFERENCES

Adams, Carolyn, and Kathryn Teich Winston. 1980. Mothers at Work. New York: Longman.

Akey, Denise, ed. 1981. Encyclopedia of Associations. Vol. 1. Detroit: Gale Research.

American Life Lobby. 1980. "Planned Parenthood." Washington, D.C.: Mimeographed.

Arrington, Theodore, and Patricia A. Kyle. 1978. "Equal Rights Amendment Activists in North Carolina." Signs 3: 666-680.

Atkinson, Ti Grace. 1974. Amazon Odyssey. New York: Links.

Baker, Ross K., Laurily K. Epstein, and Rodney D. Forth. 1981. "Matters of Life and Death: Social, Political and Religious Correlates of Attitudes on Abortion." American Politics Quarterly 9: 89-102.

Barnett, Sharon N., and Richard J. Harris. 1982. "Recent Changes in Predictors of Abortion Attitudes." Sociology and Social Research 66: 320-334.

Bell, Charles G. Undated. "The Equal Rights Amendment: A Case Study in the Diffusion of an Innovation." Working Papers on the Future #3, California State University, Fullerton.

Bennett, W. Lance. 1980. Public Opinion in American Politics. New York: Harcourt Brace Jovanovich.

Berry, Jeffrey M. 1977. Lobbying for the People. Princeton, N.J.: Princeton University Press.

Blake, Judith. 1971. "Abortion and Public Opinion: The 1960-1970 Decade." Science 71: 540-549.

Blake, Judith, and Jorge H. Del Pinal. 1980. "Predicting Polar Attitudes Toward Abortion in the United States." In Abortion Parley, edited by James T. Burtchaell, pp. 27-56. Kansas City, Kansas: Andrews and McMeel.

Bokowski, Debrah, and Aage R. Clausen. 1979. "Federalism, Representation, and the Equal Rights Amendment." A Paper prepared for delivery at the Annual Meeting of the Midwest Political Science Association, April 1979, at Chicago, Illinois.

Boles, Janet. 1979. The Politics of the Equal Rights Amendment: Conflict and the Decision Process. New York: Longman.

Brady, David W., and Kent L. Tedin. 1976. "Ladies in Pink: Religion and Political Ideology in the Anti-ERA Movement." Social Science Quarterly 56: 564-575.

Breton, A., and R. Breton. 1969. "An Economic Theory of Social Movements." American Economic Review, Papers and Proceedings 59: 198-205.

Brody, Richard A., and Benjamin L. Page. 1972. "Comment: The Assessment of Policy Voting." American Political Science Review 66: 450-458.

CBS/New York Times. 1980. "September 1980 News Release." CBS/New York Times Poll September, pp. 12-14.

Carden, Maren Lockwood. 1974. The New Feminist Movement. New York: Russell Sage Foundation.

Chafe, William Henry. 1977. The American Woman: Her Changing Social, Economic, and Political Roles, 1920-1970. New York: Oxford University Press.

Chesler, Mark, and Richard Schmuck. 1969. "Social Psychological Characteristics of Super-Patriots." In The American Right Wing, edited by Robert A. Schoenberger, pp. 139-164. New York: Holt, Rinehart and Winston.

Christian Action Council. Undated. "Abortion on Demand?" Washington, D.C.: Mimeographed.

Clark, Peter B., and James Q. Wilson. 1961. "Incentive Systems: A Theory of Organizations." Administrative Science Quarterly 6: 129-166.

Clayton, Richard R., and William L. Tolone. 1973. "Religiosity and Attitudes Toward Induced Abortion: An Elaboration of the Relationship." Sociological Analysis 34: 26-39.

Cobb, Roger W., and Charles D. Elder. 1972a. "Individual Orientations in the Study of Political Symbolism." Social Science Quarterly 53: 79-90.

_____. 1972b. Participation in American Politics: The Politics of Agenda-Building. Baltimore: Johns Hopkins University Press.

_____. 1973. "The Political Uses of Symbolism." American Political Quarterly 3: 305-338.

Cohen, Richard. 1980. "Reagan's Code Words." Minneapolis Tribune, August 3, 16A.

Comparative State Politics Newsletter. 1982. "State Polls." 3: 16. University of Kentucky, Lexington.

Congressional Quarterly. 1981. "'Pro-Life' Interest Groups Try a New Tactic in Effort to Crack Down on Abortion." Congressional Quarterly Weekly Report, February 28, pp. 383-387.

_____. 1980a. "Candidates Differ on Federal Role in Setting Social Policies." Congressional Quarterly Weekly Report, October 25, pp. 3197-3200.

_____. 1980b. "Evangelical Conservatives Move from Pews to Polls, But Can They Sway Congress?" Congressional Quarterly Weekly Report, September 6, pp. 2627-2634.

_____. 1980c. "GOP Wins Senate Control for First Time in 28 Years." Congressional Quarterly Weekly Report, November 8, pp. 3300-3302.

_____. 1980d. "'New Right' Wants Credit for Democrats' November 4 Losses But GOP, Others Don't Agree." Congressional Quarterly Weekly Report, November 15, pp. 3372-3373.

_____. 1980e. "With Only Two Years to Go, ERA Still Faces an Uphill Fight and Murky Legal Questions." Congressional Quarterly Weekly Report, June 28, pp. 1813-1815.

Conover, Pamela Johnston, and Stanley Feldman. 1981. "The Origins and Meaning of Liberal/Conservative Self-Identifications." American Journal of Political Science 24: 617-645.

Conservative Digest. 1980a. "Pro-Life PAC Eyes 1980 Races." Conservative Digest 6: 12-14.

_____. 1980b. "The Pro-Family Movement." Conservative Digest 6: 14-24.

_____. 1980c. "Library Court: The Washington Hub." Conservative Digest 6: 26-27.

Costain, Anne N. 1981a. "Representing Women: The Transition from Social Movement to Interest Group." Western Political Quarterly 34: 100-113.

_____. 1981b. "The Struggle for a National Women's Lobby: Organizing a Diffuse Interest." Western Political Quarterly 34: 476-491.

Crawford, Alan. 1980. Thunder on the Right. New York: Pantheon Books.

Curtis, Russell L., Jr., and Louis A. Zurcher, Jr. 1974. "Social Movements: An Analytical Exploration of Organizational Forms." Social Problems 21: 356-369.

_____. 1973. "Stable Resources of Protest Movements: The Multiorganizational Field." Social Forces 52: 53-61.

Daniels, Mark R., and R. Darcy. 1982. "ERA: A Case of Arrested Diffusion." Paper presented at the Annual Meeting of the Midwest Political Science Association, April 1982, at Milwaukee, Wisconsin.

Degler, Carl. 1980. At Odds. New York: Oxford University Press.

Dodson, Debra L. 1982. "The Impact of Institutional Factors upon the Ratification of the Equal Rights Amendment." Paper presented at the Annual Meeting of the Midwest Political Science Association, April 1982, at Milwaukee, Wisconsin.

Downs, Anthony. 1972. "Up and Down with Ecology—the Issue-Attention Cycle." Public Interest 28: 38-50.

Eagle Forum. No date a. "Eagle Forum: Leading the Pro-Family Movement Since 1972." Mimeographed.

_____. No date b. "The Blank Check Called 'ERA.'" Mimeographed.

Edelman, Murray. 1964. The Symbolic Uses of Politics. Urbana, Ill.: University of Illinois Press.

Editorial Research Reports. 1978. The Rights Revolution. Washington, D.C.: Congressional Quarterly.

Elazar, Daniel J. 1972. American Federalism: A View from the States. Second Edition. New York: Harper and Row.

Elms, Alan C. 1969. "Psychological Factors in Right-Wing Extremism." In The American Right Wing, edited by Robert A. Schoenberger, pp. 143-163. New York: Holt, Rinehart and Winston.

Epstein, Lee. 1981. "The Impact of the ACLU Reproductive Freedom Project." Paper presented at the Annual Meeting of the Midwest Political Science Association, April 1981, at Cincinnati, Ohio.

Ervin, Sam J., Jr. 1977. "Why the Equal Rights Amendment Should Be Rejected." The Phyllis Schlafly Report 10: 2-5.

Etzioni, A. 1968. The Active Society. New York: Free Press.

Evans, Sara. 1979. Personal Politics. New York: Alfred A. Knopf.

Fairbanks, James David. 1981. "The Evangelical Right: Beginnings of Another Symbolic Crusade?" Paper presented at the Annual Meeting of the American Political Science Association, September 1981, at New York City.

Falwell, Jerry. 1980. Listen America! Garden City, N.Y.: Doubleday.

Felsenthal, Carol. 1981. The Sweetheart of the Silent Majority. Garden City, N.Y.: Doubleday.

Finner, Stephen L., and Jerome D. Gamache. 1969. "The Relation Between Religious Commitment and Attitudes Toward Induced Abortion." Sociological Analysis 30: 1-12.

Fireman, Bruce, and William A. Gamson. 1979. "Utilitarian Logic in the Resource Mobilization Perspective." In The Dynamics of Social Movements, edited by Mayer N. Zald and John D. McCarthy, pp. 8-44. Cambridge, Mass.: Winthrop.

Firestone, Shulamith. 1970. The Dialectic of Sex. New York: David McKay.

Fitzgerald, Frances. 1981a. "A Reporter at Large: A Disciplined, Charging Army." New Yorker, May 18, pp. 53-141.

_____. 1981b. "The Triumphs of the New Right." The New York Review of Books 28: 19-26.

Flexner, Eleanor. 1972. Century of Struggle: The Woman's Rights Movement in the United States. New York: Atheneum.

Freeman, Jo. 1975. The Politics of Women's Liberation. New York: David McKay.

_____. 1979. "Resource Mobilization and Strategy: A Model for Analyzing Social Movement Organization Actions." In The Dynamics of Social Movements, edited by Mayer N. Zald and John D. McCarthy, pp. 167-189. Cambridge, Mass.: Winthrop.

Friedan, Betty. 1982. "Are Women Different?" Public Opinion 5: 20, 41.

_____. 1981. _The Second Stage_. New York: Summit Books.

Frolich, Norman, Joe Oppenheimer, and Oran Young. 1971.
Political Leadership and Collective Goods. Princeton, N.J.:
Princeton University Press.

Gager, Nancy, ed. 1974. _Women's Rights Almanac 1974_. Bethesda,
Md.: Elizabeth Cady Stanton.

Gallup, George. 1980. "Religious Influence in Politics Opposed."
Minneapolis _Tribune_, November 1, p. 1C.

Gallup Report. 1981a. "Participation in Interest Groups High."
Gallup Report, August, pp. 45-56.

_____. 1981b. "Public Evenly Divided on 1973 Decision." _Gallup
Report_, July, pp. 18-22.

_____. 1981c. "Public Support for ERA Reaches New High."
Gallup Report, July, pp. 23-25.

_____. 1980. "Attitudes Toward Abortion Have Changed Little
Since Mid-70s." _Gallup Report_, June, pp. 6-7.

Gamson, William A. 1975. _The Strategy of Social Protest_. Home-
wood, Ill.: The Dorsey Press.

Gasper, Jo Ann. 1981. "The Dichotomy—Pro-Family/Anti-Family."
The Right Woman 5: 57-64.

Gelb, Joyce, and Marian Lief Palley. 1982. _Women and Public
Policies_. Princeton, N.J.: Princeton University Press.

_____. 1981. "Women Divided Among Themselves: 'The Right to
Life' versus 'Free Choice.'" Paper presented at the Annual Meet-
ing of the Midwest Political Science Association, April 1981, at
Cincinnati, Ohio.

Gilder, George. 1981. _Wealth and Poverty_. New York: Basic
Books.

Godwin, Kenneth, and Robert Cameron Mitchell. 1982. "Rational Models, Collective Goods and Non-electoral Political Behavior." Western Political Quarterly 35: 160-181.

Granberg, Donald. 1981. "The Abortion Activists." Family Planning Perspective 13: 157-163.

_____. 1977/1978. "Pro-Life or Reflection of Conservative Ideology? An Analysis of Opposition to Legalized Abortion." Sociology and Social Research 62: 414-429.

Granberg, Donald, and Beth Wellman Granberg. 1980. "Abortion Attitudes, 1965-1980: Trends and Determinants." Family Planning Perspective 12: 250-261.

Gurr, Ted R. 1970. Why Men Rebel. Princeton, N.J.: Princeton University Press.

Gusfield, Joseph R. 1963. Symbolic Crusade: Status Politics and the American Temperance Movement. Urbana, Ill.: University of Illinois Press.

Guth, James L. 1981. "The Politics of the 'Evangelical Right.'" Paper presented at the Annual Meeting of the American Political Science Association, September 1981, at New York City.

Hacker, Andrew. 1980. "ERA—RIP." Harper's. September, pp. 10-14.

Hansen, Susan. 1980. "State Implementation of Supreme Court Decisions: Abortion Rates Since Roe v. Wade." Journal of Politics 42: 372-395.

Hershey, Marjorie Randon. 1977. "A Social-Learning Theory of Innovation and Change in Political Campaigning." Paper presented at the Annual Meeting of the American Political Science Association, September 1977, at Washington, D.C.

Hershey, Marjorie Randon, and Darrell M. West. 1981. "Single-Issue Groups and Political Campaigns: Six Senatorial Races and the Pro-Life Challenge in 1980." Paper prepared for delivery at the Annual Meeting of the Midwest Political Science Association, April 1981, at Cincinnati, Ohio.

Higgins, George G. 1980. "The Pro-Life Movement and the New Right." America, September 13, pp. 103-110.

Hinckley, Barbara. 1981. Coalitions and Politics. New York: Harcourt Brace Jovanovich.

Hirshman, Albert O. 1970. Exit, Voice and Loyalty. Cambridge, Mass.: Harvard University Press.

Hofstadter, Richard. 1964. "The Pseudo-Conservative Revolt." In The Radical Right, edited by Daniel Bell, pp. 75-96. New York: Criterion Books.

_____. 1965. The Paranoid Style in American Politics. Chicago: University of Chicago Press.

Hole, Judith, and Ellen Levine. 1971. Rebirth of Feminism. New York: Quadrangle Books.

Huber, Joan, Cynthia Rexroat, and Glenna Spitze. 1978. "A Crucible of Opinion on Women's Status: ERA in Illinois." Social Forces 57: 549-565.

Intercessors For America. Undated. "Intercessors For America: A Call for Christians to Unite in Prayer and Fasting for America." Mimeographed.

Jacob, Charles E. 1981. "The Congressional Elections." In The Election of 1980. Reports and Interpretations, edited by Gerald Pomper et al., pp. 119-141. Chatham, N.J.: Chatham House.

Jaffe, Frederick S., Barbara L. Lindheim, and Philip R. Lee. 1981. Abortion Politics: Private Morality and Public Policy. New York: McGraw-Hill.

Jelen, Ted G. 1982. "Religion, Sex-Role Stereotypes, and Opposition to the Equal Rights Amendment." Paper prepared for delivery at the Annual Meeting of the Midwest Political Science Association, April 1982, at Milwaukee, Wisconsin.

Johnson, Charles A., and Jon R. Bond. 1980. "Coercive and Non-coercive Abortion Deterrence Policies: A Comparative State Analysis." Law and Policy Quarterly 2: 106-128.

Johnson, Douglas W., Paul R. Picard, and Bernard Quinn. 1974. Churches and Church Membership in the United States. Washington, D.C.: Glenmary Research Center.

Killian, Lewis M. 1973. "Social Movements: A Review of the Field." In Social Movements: A Reader and Sourcebook, edited by Robert Evans, pp. 9-53. Chicago: Rand McNally.

Kinder, Donald R., and Robert P. Abelson. 1981. "Appraising Presidential Candidates: Personality and Affect in the 1980 Campaign." Paper delivered at the Annual Meeting of the American Political Science Association, September 1981, at New York City.

Kinder, Donald R., and David O. Sears. 1981. "Prejudice and Politics: Symbolic Racism Versus Racial Threats to the Good Life." Journal of Personality and Social Psychology 40: 414-431.

Klecka, William R. 1980. Discriminant Analysis. Beverly Hills, Calif.: Sage.

Kornhauser, William K. 1959. The Politics of Mass Society. New York: The Free Press.

Kowalewski, David. 1980. "The Protest Uses of Symbolic Politics: The Mobilization Functions of Protester Symbolic Resources." Social Science Quarterly 61: 95-111.

Ladd, Everett, Jr. 1978. "The New Lines Are Drawn . . . Class and Ideology in America." Public Opinion 1: 48-53.

Lader, Lawrence. 1973. Abortion II: Making the Revolution. Boston: Beacon Press.

Lake, Celinda C. 1982. "Guns, Butter, and Equality: The Women's Vote in 1980." Paper prepared for delivery at the Annual Meeting of the Political Science Association, April 1982, at Milwaukee, Wisconsin.

234

Laver, Michael. 1981. The Politics of Private Desires. The Guide to the Politics of Rational Choice. Middlesex, England: Penguin Books.

Leites, Nathan, and Charles Wolf. 1970. Rebellion and Authority. An Analytic Essay on Insurgent Conflicts. Chicago: Markham.

Lipset, Seymour Martin. 1955. "The Sources of the 'Radical Right.'" In The New American Right, edited by Daniel Bell, pp. 166-233. New York: Criterion Books.

Lipset, Seymour Martin, and Earl Rabb. 1970. The Politics of Unreason. Chicago: University of Chicago Press.

_____. 1981. "The Election and the Evangelicals." Commentary, March, pp. 25-31.

Lipsky, Michael. 1970. Protest in City Politics: Rent Strikes, Housing and the Power of the Poor. Chicago: Rand McNally.

_____. 1968. "Protest as a Political Resource." American Political Science Review 62: 1144-1158.

Lorentzen, Louise J. 1980. "Evangelical Life Style Concerns Expressed in Political Action." Sociological Analysis 41: 144-154.

Lowi, Theodore J. 1971. The Politics of Disorder. New York: Basic Books.

Lutzkers, Daniel R. 1960. "Internationalism as a Predictor of Cooperative Behavior." Journal of Conflict Resolution 4: 426-430.

Margolis, Michael, and Kevin Neary. 1980. "Pressure Politics Revisited: The Anti-Abortion Campaign." Policy Studies Journal 8: 698-717.

Marsh, David. 1976. "On Joining Interest Groups: An Empirical Consideration of the Work of Mancur Olson Jr." British Journal of Political Science 6: 257-271.

Marshner, Connaught. 1980. Washington, D.C.: Personal communication (letter).

Marwell, Gerald, and Ruth E. Ames. 1980. "Experiments on the Provision of Collective Goods. II. Provision Points, Stakes, Experience, and the Free-Rider Problem." American Journal of Sociology 85: 926-937.

_____. 1979. "Experiments on the Provision of Public Goods. I. Resources, Interest, Group Size, and the Free-Rider Problem." American Journal of Sociology 84: 1335-1360.

Marx, Gary T. 1979. "External Efforts to Damage or Facilitate Social Movements: Some Patterns, Explanations, Outcomes, and Complications." In The Dynamics of Social Movements, edited by Mayer N. Zald and John D. McCarthy, pp. 94-125. Cambridge, Mass.: Winthrop.

Marx, Gary T., and James L. Wood. 1975. "Strands of Theory and Research in Collective Behavior." Annual Review of Sociology 1: 363-428.

McCarthy, John D., and Mayer N. Zald. 1977. "Resource Mobilization and Social Movements: A Partial Theory." American Journal of Sociology 82: 1212-1241.

McEvoy, James, III. 1971. Radicals or Conservatives? The Contemporary American Right. Chicago: Rand McNally.

McGlen, Nancy E. 1981. "The Theoretical Foundations of Countermovements." Paper presented at the Annual Meeting of the Midwest Political Science Association, April 1981, at Cincinnati, Ohio.

McGuigan, Patrick. 1981. "Pro-Family FLAG Group Is Fighting for Traditional Values in Arkansas." Conservative Digest 7: 36-38.

McIntyre, Thomas J., with John C. Obert. 1979. The Fear Brokers. Peddling the Hate Politics of the New Right. Boston: Beacon Press.

Mead, Frank S. 1975. Handbook of Denominations in the United States, 6th ed. Nashville: Abington Press.

Miami Herald. 1980. "State to Probe Mormon Contributions." Miami Herald, April 22, pp. 1, 33A.

Miller, Arthur H., and Martin P. Wattenberg. 1981. "Policy and Performance Voting in the 1980 Election." Paper prepared for delivery at the Annual Meeting of the American Political Science Association, September 1981, at New York City.

Miller, Margaret O., and Helene Linker. 1974. "Equal Rights Amendment Campaigns in California and Utah: State Politics and Public Interests." Society 11: 243-254.

Miller, Warren E., and J. Merrill Shanks. 1981. "Policy Directions and Presidential Leadership: Alternative Interpretations of the 1980 Presidential Election." Paper prepared for delivery at the Annual Meeting of the American Political Science Association, September 1981, at New York City.

Minneapolis Tribune. 1978. "Catholic Church Closely Tied to State Pro-Life Group." Minneapolis Tribune, July 16, pp. 1, 8A.

_____. 1982. "Foes Celebrate, Supporters Plot Return as ERA Deadline Passes." Minneapolis Tribune, July 1, pp. 1A, 5A.

Minnesota Citizens Concerned for Life. Undated. "The Right to Life." Minneapolis, Minnesota: Mimeographed.

Mitchell, Robert Cameron. 1979. "National Environmental Lobbies and the Apparent Illogic of Collective Action." In Collective Decision-Making: Applications from Public Choice Theory, edited by Clifford S. Russell, pp. 87-121. Baltimore, Md.: Johns Hopkins University Press.

Moe, Terry M. 1981. "Toward a Broader View of Interest Groups." Journal of Politics 43: 531-543.

_____. 1980. The Organization of Interests. Chicago, Ill.: The University of Chicago Press.

Mohr, James C. 1978. Abortion in America. New York: Oxford University Press.

Molotch, Harvey. 1979. "Media and Movements." In The Dynamics of Social Movements, edited by Mayer N. Zald and John D. McCarthy, pp. 71-93. Cambridge, Mass.: Winthrop.

Moral Majority. Undated. "The Moral Majority, Inc.: Fighting for a Moral America in This Decade of Destiny." Washington, D.C.: Mimeographed.

Morris, William D., and Jeffrey W. Stempel. 1978. "Abortion: Politics and Problems." Paper presented at the Annual Meeting of the Midwest Political Science Association, April 1978, at Chicago, Illinois.

Morrison, Denton E. 1979. "Uphill and Downhill Battles and Contributions to Collective Action." In Collective Decision-Making: Applications from Public Choice Theory, edited by Clifford S. Russell, pp. 130-133. Baltimore, Md.: Johns Hopkins University Press.

Mottl, Tahl L. 1980. "The Analysis of Countermovements." Social Problems 27: 620-635.

National Abortion Rights Action League. Undated a. "NARAL Report: Violence Against the Right to Choose." Washington, D.C.: Mimeographed.

_____. Undated b. Washington, D.C.: Personal communication (letter).

National Organization for Women. 1982. Washington, D.C.: Personal communication (letter).

Newsweek. 1978. "Single-Issue Politics." Newsweek, November 6, pp. 48-60.

Oberschall, Anthony. 1978. "Theories of Social Conflict." In Annual Review of Sociology, edited by Ralph Turner, James Coleman, and Renee C. Fox, pp. 291-315. Palo Alto: Annual Review.

_____. 1973. Social Conflict and Social Movements. Englewood Cliffs, N.J.: Prentice-Hall.

O'Connor, Karen. 1980. Women's Organizations' Use of the Courts. Lexington, Mass.: Lexington Books.

Okin, Susan. 1979. Women in Western Political Thought. Princeton, N.J.: Princeton University Press.

Olson, Mancur. 1971. The Logic of Collective Action. Cambridge, Mass.: Harvard University Press.

Opinion Outlook. 1982a. "Equal Rights Amendment." Opinion Outlook, June 7, pp. 1-2.

_____. 1982b. "Single Issue Politics." Opinion Outlook, March 29, pp. 1-2.

_____. 1981. "Abortion as a Voting Issue. Strategy for a Candidate." Opinion Outlook, December 14, p. 7.

Page, Ann L., and Donald A. Clelland. 1978. "The Kanawha County Textbook Controversy: A Study of the Politics of Life Style Concern." Social Forces 57: 265-281.

Page, Benjamin I. 1978. Choices and Echoes in Presidential Elections: Rational Man and Electoral Democracy. Chicago: University of Chicago Press.

Parents of Minnesota. Undated. "Equality." St. Paul Park, Minnesota: Mimeographed.

Patel, Kant, Denny Pilant, and Gary Rose. 1982. "Born-Again Christians in the Bible Belt: A Study in Religion, Politics, and Ideology." American Politics Quarterly 10: 255-272.

Penfield, H. Irvin, and Natalie M. Davis. 1981. "The Moral Majority and Politics: Religious Attitudes as Correlates of Voting Behavior." Paper presented at the Annual Meeting of the Midwest Political Science Association, April 1981, at Cincinnati, Ohio.

Petchesky, Rosalind Pollack. 1981. "Introduction." Feminist Studies 7: 207-246.

_____. 1980. "Reproductive Freedom: Beyond 'A Woman's Right to Choose.'" Signs 5: 661-685.

Peterson, Larry R., and Armand L. Mauss. 1976. "Religion and the 'Right to Life'—Correlates of Opposition to Abortion." Sociological Analysis 37: 243-254.

Petrocik, John R. et al. 1981. "Choosing the Choice and Not the Echo: A Funny Thing Happened to the Changing American Voter on the Way to the 1980 Election." Paper prepared for delivery at the Annual Meeting of the American Political Science Association, September 1981, at New York City.

Phillips, Kevin. 1982. Post-Conservative America. New York: Random House.

Planned Parenthood. Undated. New York: Personal communication (letter).

Plotkin, Henry A. 1981. "Issues in the Presidential Campaign." In The Election of 1980. Reports and Interpretations, edited by Gerald Pomper et al., pp. 38-64. Chatham, N.J.: Chatham House.

Pomper, Gerald. 1981. "The Presidential Election." In The Election of 1980. Reports and Interpretations, edited by Gerald Pomper et al., pp. 65-96. Chatham, N.J.: Chatham House.

Public Opinion. 1982. "Opinion Roundup: A New Era in Men's and Women's Attitudes." Public Opinion 5: 27-32.

Reichley, A. James. 1981. Conservatives in an Age of Change. Washington, D.C.: The Brookings Institution.

Riker, William H., and Peter C. Ordeshook. 1973. An Introduction to Positive Political Theory. Englewood Cliffs, N.J.: Prentice-Hall.

Robinson, Gertrude Joch. 1978. "Women, Media Access and Social Control." In Women and the News, edited by Laurily Keir Epstein, pp. 87–108. New York: Hastings House.

Rosenberg, Tina. 1982. "How the Media Made the Moral Majority." Washington Monthly 14: 26–34.

Salisbury, Robert H. 1969. "An Exchange Theory of Interest Groups." Midwest Journal of Political Science 13: 1–32.

Schlafly, Phyllis. 1977. The Power of the Positive Woman. New Rochelle, N.Y.: Arlington House.

Schuman, Howard, and Stanley Presser. 1981. Questions and Answers. New York: Academic Press.

Schuman, Howard, Stanley Presser, and Jacob Ludwig. 1981. "Context Effects on Survey Responses to Questions About Abortion." Public Opinion Quarterly 45: 216–223.

Sears, David O., and Jack Citrin. 1982. Tax Revolt: Something for Nothing in California. Cambridge, Mass.: Harvard University Press.

Sears, David O., Carl P. Hensler, and Leslie K. Speer. 1979. "Whites' Opposition to 'Busing': Self-Interest or Symbolic Politics." American Political Science Review 73: 369–384.

Sears, David O., Richard R. Lau, Tom R. Tyler, and Harris M. Allen, Jr. 1980. "Self-Interest versus Symbolic Politics in Policy Attitudes and Presidential Voting." American Political Science Review 74: 670–684.

Sigelman, Lee. 1981. "Lexington Iranian Hostage Survey #2." Lexington: University of Kentucky.

Singh, B. Krishna, and Peter J. Leahy. 1978. "Contextual and Ideological Dimensions of Attitudes Toward Discretionary Abortion." Demography 15: 381–388.

241

Skerry, Peter. 1978. "The Class Conflict Over Abortion." The Public Interest 52: 69-84.

Smelser, N. J. 1963. Theory of Collective Behavior. New York: Free Press of Glencoe.

Smith, Vernon. 1980. "Experiments with a Decentralized Mechanism for Public Good Decisions." American Economic Review 70: 584-599.

Snow, David A., Louis A. Zurcher, Jr., and Sheldon Ekland-Olson. 1980. "Social Networks and Social Movements: A Microstructural Approach to Differential Recruitment." American Sociological Review 45: 787-801.

Snyder, David, and William R. Kelly. 1979. "Strategies for Investigating Violence and Social Change: Illustrations from Analyses of Racial Disorders and Implications for Mobilization Research." In The Dynamics of Social Movements, edited by Mayer N. Zald and John O. McCarthy, pp. 212-237. Cambridge, Mass.: Winthrop.

Sobran, Joseph. 1981. "Why Conservatives Should Care About Abortion." Conservative Digest 7: 14-16.

Spokeswoman. 1975. December 15, p. 2.

Steiner, Gilbert. 1980. The Futility of Family Policy. Washington, D.C.: The Brookings Institution.

Steinhoff, Patricia G., and Milton Diamond. 1977. Abortion Politics: The Hawaii Experience. Honolulu: University Press of Hawaii.

Strickland, D. A., and R. E. Johnston. 1970. "Issue Elasticity in Political Systems." Journal of Political Economy 78: 1069-1092.

Tatalovich, Raymond, and Byron W. Daynes. 1981. The Politics of Abortion. New York: Praeger.

Tedin, Kent L. 1980. "If the Equal Rights Amendment Becomes Law: Perceptions of Consequences Among Female Activists and Masses." Paper presented at the Annual Meeting of the Midwest Political Science Association, April 1980, at Chicago, Illinois.

_____. 1978. "Religious Preference and Pro/Anti Activism on the Equal Rights Amendment Issue." Pacific Sociological Review 21: 55-66.

Tedin, Kent L., David W. Brady, Mary E. Buxton, Barbara M. Gorman, and Judy L. Thompson. 1977. "Social Background and Political Differences Between Pro- and Anti-ERA Activists." American Politics Quarterly 5: 395-408.

Tedrow, Lucky M., and E. R. Mahoney. 1979. "Trends in Attitudes Toward Abortion: 1972-1976." Public Opinion Quarterly 43: 181-189.

Thomson, Rosemary. 1981. Withstanding Humanism's Challenge to Families. Morton, Ill.: Traditional Publications.

Tillock, Harriet, and Denton E. Morrison. 1979. "Group Size and Contributions to Collective Action: An Examination of Olson's Theory Using Data from Zero Population Growth." Research in Social Movements 2: 131-149.

Tilly, Charles. 1978. From Mobilization to Revolution. Reading, Mass.: Addison-Wesley.

_____. 1975. "Revolutions and Collective Violence." In Handbook of Political Science, edited by Fred Greenstein and Nelson Polsby, Vol. 3, pp. 483-556. New York: Addison-Wesley.

Tolchin, Susan, and Martin Tolchin. 1974. Clout: Womanpower and Politics. New York: Coward, McCann and Geoghegan.

Traugott, M. W., and M. A. Vinovskis. 1980. "Abortion and the 1978 Congressional Elections." Family Planning Perspectives 12: 238-249.

Useem, Bert. 1980. "Solidarity Model, Breakdown Model, and the Boston Anti-Busing Movement." American Sociological Review 45: 357-369.

Uslaner, Eric M., and Ronald E. Weber. 1980. "Public Support for Pro-Choice Abortion Policies in the Nation and States: Changes and Stability after the Roe and Doe Decisions." In The Law and Politics of Abortion, edited by Carl E. Schneider and Maris A. Vinovskis, pp. 206-223. Lexington, Mass.: Lexington Books.

Viguerie, Richard A. 1981. The New Right: We're Ready to Lead. Falls Church, Va.: The Viguerie Company.

Volgy, Thomas J. 1979. "Dimensions of Support for Women's Issues: The Salience of Sex Roles." Paper prepared for delivery at the Annual Meeting of the American Political Science Association, August 1979, at Washington, D.C.

Washington Post. 1982. "Led by Conservative Groups, PACs Net Over $109 Million." Washington Post, July 1, A4.

Weber, Max. 1946. From Max Weber: Essays in Sociology. (Eds. and Trans.) H. H. Gerth and C. Wright Mills. New York: Oxford University Press.

Weber, Ronald E., and Eric M. Uslaner. 1981. "Cognitive Consistency and the Politicization of the Abortion Issue Among the Mass Public." Paper prepared for the Annual Meeting of the Midwest Political Science Association, April 1981, at Cincinnati, Ohio.

Welch, Susan. 1975. "Support Among Women for the Issues of the Women's Movement." Sociological Quarterly 16: 216-227.

Westoff, Leslie A., and C. F. Westoff. 1971. From Now to Zero: Fertility, Contraception, and Abortion in America. Boston: Little, Brown and Co.

White, L. 1976. "Rational Theories of Participation." Journal of Conflict Resolution 20: 255-277.

Wilson, James Q. 1973. Political Organizations. New York: Basic Books.

Wilson, John. 1973. Introduction to Social Movements. New York: Basic Books.

Wilson, Kenneth L., and Anthony M. Orum. 1976. "Mobilizing People for Collective Political Action." Journal of Political and Military Sociology 4: 187–202.

Wohlenberg, Ernest H. 1980. "Correlates of Equal Rights Amendment Ratification." Social Science Quarterly 60: 676–684.

Wolfinger, Raymond E., Barbara Kaye Wolfinger, Kenneth Prewitt, and Sheilah Rosenhack. 1969. "America's Radical Right: Politics and Ideology." In The American Right Wing, edited by Robert A. Schoenberger, pp. 9–47. New York: Holt, Rinehart and Winston.

Woodward, Bob, and Scott Armstrong. 1979. The Brethren: Inside the Supreme Court. New York: Avon Books.

Zald, Mayer N., and Roberta Ash. 1965–66. "Social Movement Organizations: Growth, Decay and Change." Social Forces 44: 327–341.

Zellman, Gail L., and David O. Sears. 1971. "Childhood Origins of Tolerance for Dissent." Journal of Social Issues 27: 109–136.

Zurcher, Louis A., Jr., R. George Kirkpatrick, Robert G. Cushing, and Charles K. Bowman. 1971. "The Anti-Pornography Campaign: A Symbolic Crusade." Social Problems 19: 217–237.

Zurcher, Louis A., and Russell L. Curtis, Jr. 1973. "A Comparative Analysis of Propositions Describing Social Movement Organizations." Sociology Quarterly 14: 175–188.

Zwier, Robert. 1981. "The Moral Majority in the 1980 Elections: The Cases of Iowa and South Dakota." Paper presented at the Annual Meeting of the American Political Science Association, September 1981, at New York City.

Zygmunt, Joseph F. 1972. "Movements and Motives: Some Unresolved Issues in the Psychology of Social Movements." Human Relations 25: 449–467.

INDEX

ABOUT THE AUTHORS

PAMELA JOHNSTON CONOVER is an Assistant Professor of Political Science at the University of Kentucky in Lexington. She is also the Director of the University of Kentucky Survey Research Center's Biannual Poll.

Professor Conover's recent research has been in several different areas. Articles dealing with the nature of mass belief systems and the process of political perception have appeared in the American Journal of Political Science, Western Political Quarterly, and American Politics Quarterly. In addition, work on public opinion, presidential influence, and the Iranian Hostage crisis has been published in Public Opinion Quarterly, Social Science Quarterly, Political Behavior, Polity, Co-Existence, and Journal of Peace Research.

Professor Conover received her B.A. from Emory University in Atlanta in 1973 and her Ph.D. in Political Science from the University of Minnesota in 1979.

VIRGINIA GRAY is an Associate Professor of Political Science at the University of Minnesota. She is also Director of Graduate Studies.

Professor Gray's published research has been in the areas of public policy, women and politics, methodology, and state politics. It has appeared in the American Political Science Review, American Journal of Political Science, Polity, Journal of Politics, Journal of American History, Policy Studies Journal, Policy Studies Review, American Behavioral Scientist, and a number of edited books. In addition, she has coauthored or coedited several books: Political Issues in U.S. Population Policy, The Determinants of Public Policy, The Organizational Politics of Criminal Justice, and Politics in the American States (4th edition).

Dr. Gray holds a B.A. with honors from Hendrix College and an M.A. and Ph.D. from Washington University. She has held appointments at the University of Kentucky and at the Brookings Institution as a Guest Scholar, and has served as a consultant to the Minnesota Department of Agriculture, the Governor's Commission on Crime Prevention and Control (Minnesota), and NBC News.